D0069541

THE FRUGAL LIBRARIAN

ALA Editions purchases fund advocacy, awareness, and
accreditation programs for library professionals worldwide.

THE FRUGAL LIBRARIAN
Thriving in Tough Economic Times

Edited by Carol Smallwood

AMERICAN LIBRARY ASSOCIATION
CHICAGO   2011

© 2011 by the American Library Association. Any claim of copyright is subject to applicable limitations and exceptions, such as rights of fair use and library copying pursuant to Sections 107 and 108 of the U.S. Copyright Act. No copyright is claimed in content that is in the public domain, such as works of the U.S. government.

Printed in the United States of America
15 14 13 12 11   5 4 3 2 1

While extensive effort has gone into ensuring the reliability of the information in this book, the publisher makes no warranty, express or implied, with respect to the material contained herein.

ISBN: 978-0-8389-1075-7

Library of Congress Cataloging-in-Publication Data
The frugal librarian : thriving in tough economic times / edited by Carol Smallwood.
    p. cm.
  Includes bibliographical references and index.
  ISBN 978-0-8389-1075-7 (alk. paper)
  1. Library finance--United States. 2. Libraries--United States--Cost control.
3. Libraries--Economic aspects--United States. 4. Library science--Economic aspects--United States. 5. Libraries and community--United States. 6. Libraries--United States--Case studies. I. Smallwood, Carol, 1939-
  Z683.2.U6F73 2011
  025.1'10973--dc22

                                                                    2010034317

Book design in Charis SIL and Avenir by Casey Bayer.

∞ This paper meets the requirements of ANSI/NISO Z39.48-1992 (Permanence of Paper).

ALA Editions also publishes its books in a variety of electronic formats. For more information, visit the ALA Store at www.alastore.ala.org and select eEditions.

CONTENTS

PART VIII: STAFFING

PART IX: PROFESSIONAL DEVELOPMENT

FOREWORD

THE THIRTY-FOUR CHAPTERS of *The Frugal Librarian* present insight-ful—and often personal—responses and recommendations on how to not only survive but also thrive in tough economic times. Some chapters focus on what librarians naturally do best as they serve as the public's key trusted source for information. Thus, the first section in the book provides advice for serving patrons and their job-seeking needs. Marwin Britto describes how librarians can help faculty advance their technology skills. Many chapters provide descriptions of useful resources including social networking sites such as LinkedIn.com, business information websites, and sources of grants. Patron-centered concerns also underlie the chapters on public programming, which describe such successful events as a Rooftop Poetry Club and a "Green Talk" series of workshops. James Lund, Wayne Finley, and Joanna Kluever take the glass-half-full view, advocating taking advantage of the economic crisis by calling on librarians to expand their loyal patron base and create programs that are based on community needs.

Job loss is the greatest concern during economic shifts. J. James Mancuso writes more closely from the heart, as he learned to "turn the box sideways," to create new part-time employment after he lost his position as a theological librarian. Margaret Lincoln took on new responsibilities in anticipation of a change in her job as a school librarian. Kacy Vega and Kim Becnel consider how to continue to add a service, in this case outreach, when staff positions are eliminated.

In the early days of the development of librarianship as a profession, the focus was on library economy. Librarians are rediscovering efficiencies in efforts to reduce costs. This volume's contributors present various approaches to better cost efficiency—through bidding service contracts, streamlining digitization, selling gifts and weeded items, using green features, and relying more on data in making decisions.

For alternatives to face-to-face continuing education, Colleen S. Harris describes other opportunities to stretch oneself and learn, including writing for publication. For those who attend library conferences, Regina Koury shares her strategies for limiting the usual expenses. In tough times, librarians turn to making new connections and partnerships. The five chapters in part V, Sharing, cover such collaborations as joint-use facilities, the advantages of multitype regional libraries, and partnering in technical services through communal acquisitions decisions, shared catalogs, and open-source products.

Though all library staff are involved in identifying and implementing creative means to reduce expenses while continuing—or even expanding—services, it is natural that staff turn to management (part VI) for vision, advice, and coordinated decision making. The chapters on staffing (part VIII) offer ideas to meet and satisfy the largest budget category—personnel.

When all is said and done, the contributors to this volume illustrate that libraries serve as vital and central human services centers. The library public has responded, with library borrower's cards and visits at an all-time national high. Although faced with the necessity of reducing expenses, and even reducing staff, libraries and librarians demonstrate once again their versatility and their ability to adjust to and be creative in the face of economic challenges.

Dr. Loriene Roy
Professor, School of Information
University of Texas at Austin

PREFACE

LIBRARIANS ACROSS THE United States are experiencing rises in prices while cutbacks shrink their resources as they struggle to keep up with information technology and patron needs. Economics, as in other professions, is affecting all types of libraries, but librarians are meeting the challenge with creativity and dedication.

To prepare this volume I sought chapters from practicing public, school, academic, and special librarians from different areas in the country to help colleagues manage their libraries. I asked contributors to share 2,100–2,300 words written by one librarian or coauthored by two and to use sidebars and headings to guide the reader.

Contributors were chosen for the relevance of their topics as well as their ability to convey information clearly after being given Gustave Flaubert's advice: "Whenever you can shorten a sentence, do. And one always can. The best sentence? The shortest." Their contributions have not been published elsewhere.

It was a pleasure working with these professionals willing to share their experiences with colleagues. Their innovation and dedication are evident in this timely anthology.

Carol Smallwood

PART I

Helping Patrons Job Search

KNOWLEDGE-BASED JOB HUNTING AND INTERVIEW PREPARATION

Michael A. Germano

CURRENT STATISTICS ON joblessness tell a story unlike any other in the history of labor in the United States: specifically, unemployment that hovers near 10 percent and almost doubles when one factors in the under-employed, those working part-time who prefer full-time employment, and the discouraged job seekers who have given up altogether (Dugan 2009). The competition for jobs is fierce, with an astounding six applicants for every opening (Evans and Blumberg 2009). More people are chasing fewer jobs than during any previous recession, at numbers that in some ways rival those of the Great Depression. Virtually all industries, even relatively safe havens like education, have been subject to furloughs, cutbacks, layoffs, and reorganizations (Mattioli 2009). With such a drastically changed unemploy-ment landscape, it follows that job hunting has changed as well. It has become more unpredictable, more competitive, and more frustrating than ever, with all indications that the changes are here to stay, maybe even irrevocably. Welcome to Job Hunting 2.1, the Great Recession version.

Although the job market may have changed dramatically in the past two years, the tactics used to find a job have not. For many it is business as usual, with an outdated approach to job hunting based on using a host of competing websites to send out as many applications as possible, despite the fact that the number of posted jobs has fallen (Dresang 2009). As librarians we are in a unique position to advocate a whole new way to look for a job: the use of research, intelligence gathering, and knowledge management to produce a more thoughtful, strategic job hunt that is premised on actionable knowledge that results in targeting industries and companies instead of the random, scattershot approach that highlights today's online job searches. In short, it is time for librarians and information professionals to take a leadership role in the job search process by doing what we do best and most naturally—advocating the use of credible, evaluated information to facilitate problem solving.

KNOWLEDGE-BASED JOB HUNTING

Although nothing can substitute for qualifications, experience, and credentials packaged in a compelling resume and conveyed during a persuasive interview, a gap in research and knowledge goes into the creation of these critical narratives that leaves many job seekers stuck in place as they send resume after resume with no results. Job seekers falling into this category could benefit from a new knowledge-driven job search strategy that uses business research skills and information sources for refining the job search process. The goal is a more strategically planned job search that is based on and informed by current, reliable business intelligence directed at uncovering the best opportunities. As librarians who are primarily concerned with acquiring, evaluating, and applying information in order to answer questions or solve problems, we can guide job searchers through a process premised on using business information sources to produce a more knowledge-based job hunt that looks something like this:

- Uncover broad economic indicators to understand their impact on career choices and job searching.
- Examine industry surveys for target companies as well as new products and markets.
- Create and maintain a file on targeted companies including profiles and recent Securities and Exchange Commission (SEC) filings.
- Polish resume and create a list of keywords relevant to industries, companies, and positions that can be used to tailor cover letters and resumes.
- Constantly review company profiles, industry surveys, and SEC filings as a means of presenting a compelling application, resume, and interview presence informed by business solutions.
- Update online profiles for professional social networking sites complete with reviews of people who have worked with you and references.

- Execute interview process with confidence based on strong knowledge of company and industry in which it operates.
- Engage in timely follow-up that reaffirms value to employee and solicits feedback on interview performance.
- Use newfound information and knowledge to attend career fairs, trade shows, and chamber of commerce meetings to network more effectively, armed with meaningful knowledge and compelling ideas to share.
- Constantly reassess cover letters, resume language, and interview positioning of skills in order to learn continually from job-hunting failures and successes.
- Maintain a knowledge-based job-hunting journal that documents applications, interviews, and follow-up communication by industry and company in order to identify trends or patterns behind failures and successes.
- Negotiate offers by researching data on working conditions and salary.
- Continue to use research and analytical skills to convey value to new employer and securing promotions.

Directing job hunters more effectively through a process that involves the steps listed above may require some brushing up on business information sources for many librarians. The bibliography and materials may appear complicated or nuanced, but their application to job hunting and interview preparation is easily understood. The applicable business resources can be divided into three broad categories: economic trends and statistics, company information, and industry data.

SOCIAL NETWORKING SITES

Social networking sites can play a vital supporting role for job hunters who target companies and industries and not necessarily specific jobs (Elmore 2009). Facebook is increasingly relevant to job searchers as a way to connect with companies and recruiters, made possible by recently relaxed rules regarding company pages (Dutta and Fraser 2009). The most useful site, however, is LinkedIn.com. Corporate recruiters use LinkedIn as a means of identifying talent, confirming job history, and getting references. Establishing a current LinkedIn profile is a great first step. Follow up by inviting former colleagues and supervisors to write reviews of your performance. The most valuable reviews from the recruiters' perspective are those that speak to specific competencies, skills, or successes.

ECONOMIC TRENDS AND STATISTICS

Economic indicators can provide important information for job seekers. Some, like the percentage of unemployed by state and region, are obvious. Others, such as factory orders, can be the factual basis for assessing growth or retraction in an industry or region. Use such data to consider future growth potential or hiring on a broad scale, and don't get discouraged.

Without doubt, the best one-stop shop for economic statistics directly related to knowledge-based job seeking is the U.S. Bureau of Labor Statistics website (www.bls.gov). It is full of relevant hiring statistics and projections for specific careers, industries, and geographic regions. Also worth noting is the bureau's job satisfaction, compensation, and benefits tracking data, since these are critical components in negotiating an offer.

COMPANY INFORMATION

Many employment seekers already use information about companies in their job searches. As information professionals, it becomes incumbent

BEST BUSINESS INFORMATION WEBSITES

Standard & Poor's Net Advantage: Premium site most notable for its industry surveys.

LexisNexis: One specific application of note for job hunters: Company Dossier's "Create Company List" feature can be used by job hunters to create a customized prospect list of companies.

Mergent: Premier company and industry intelligence research tool.

Yahoo! Finance: Free business information site, particularly useful for tracking stock prices, evaluating solvency, and retrieving current SEC filings.

Company websites: An individual company's website can be an excellent information source for understanding corporate culture, identifying critical keywords, and getting a window on management's perspective of performance and upcoming challenges. Look for the section titled "Investor Relations." The most useful data can be found in annual reports for shareholders as well as investor webinars and conference calls.

on us to ensure that the use of such information is reaching its full potential. Many job hunters who research companies take a shallow approach, neglecting critical resources that can make the difference as they try to present themselves through applications, cover letters, resumes, thank-you notes, and interviews in a way that conveys deep knowledge of the prospective employer and demonstrates a fit between applicant and company.

Company information is either quantitative or qualitative. Quantitative information includes financials such as the income statement and balance sheet, which can tell a story regarding solvency and future viability (Bensoussan and Fleisher 2008). Qualitative information, normally found in company profiles from a variety of databases or the company's own website, is mostly related to markets, products, or management strategy. For knowledge-based job seekers the ideal scenario is a public company, since these companies answer to shareholders and as a result must file a wide range of disclosures that can provide insight into the company's culture, challenges, and growth potential. Such intelligence can be used to tighten up keywords on resumes, demonstrate laser focus on cover letters, and provide a strong basis for informed and intelligent interviewing—all of which are especially important at the screening level, when mere minutes can be the determining factor between gaining a full-fledged interview and falling off the candidate slate altogether.

SEC FILINGS

SEC filings are easy to use once you know what to look for. For knowledge-based job hunters, information professionals should direct researchers to three specific filings—the most recent 10-K, 10-Q, and 8-K. Older information is too stale to be used for cover letters, resumes, or interview preparation. The 10-K is the annual filing, similar to the annual shareholders' report but with more detailed disclosures on risk and challenges in the sections titled "Risk Factors" and "Management's Discussion and Analysis . . ." The 10-Q is the quarterly report and has the same type of information as the annual but for the most recent quarter. The 8-K is an irregular interim filing that discloses any material event related to the business environment about which shareholders should know, such as recent sales performance, changes in strategic partnerships, or management defections (Stanko and Zeller 2003).

Most company profiles include succinct business descriptions, products, brands offered, locations, top-line revenue analysis, and analyst opinion of the company's potential. Datamonitor, one of the leading publishers of company profiles, packages this useful information in a SWOT (strengths, weaknesses, opportunities, and threats) analysis. Job seekers can use this kind of analysis to demonstrate their ability to add value by concretely tying those corporate-wide potentials and problems to skills and competencies, regardless of the level of the position applied for. For example, if a company's SWOT analysis mentions a specific threat like "inability to manage costs associated with rising prices from suppliers," the savvy knowledge-based job hunter can use that nugget of intelligence to demonstrate experience and past proficiency in working with or managing cost controls. The result is much more compelling than a cover letter that responds only to a more generic competency like "familiarity working with budgets." Using company profiles and SWOT analyses can make an applicant stand out from the pack, since it demonstrates a keener understanding of the business in question while providing a framework to demonstrate value. If Datamonitor is unavailable, the same information can be extracted from SEC filings.

INDUSTRY INFORMATION

Industry information is also quantitative or qualitative. Such data as overall sales for an industry as well as specific sales for the leading companies in that industry are great examples of the more quantitative side of the information landscape for industries. This kind of information can be used to identify and target leading companies for openings. The qualitative data and analyses, however, are the more useful for knowledge-based job hunters. The best resources for this type of research are industry surveys from publishers such as Standard & Poor's or Mergent. Industry surveys are a critical information source for knowledge-based job hunting; they put companies in context, especially with regard to competition and broader economic conditions that may represent enormous challenges or opportunities to which one can anchor specific skills or competencies and make them relevant to an employer.

Similar to company information, industry-wide analysis can be used at the application stage up through interviewing and negotiating an offer. It is worth noting that some of the most critical data points for knowledge-based job hunters come from analyses of the industry's growth potential in the coming quarters or years as well as the potential for growth in narrower subindustries. Such information can be used to target companies that may be engaged in future hiring, since the trends outlined in industry surveys are virtual treasure troves when it comes to future growth, expansion, and viability.

CONCLUSION

As information professionals we are in a frontline position to help those suffering the most during the Great Recession—the jobless. Librarians have traditionally provided guidance and assistance to the jobless. There is nothing new in this. What is new is the current job market, which has dramatically and irrevocably changed in the past few years. Sharing our knowledge and skills relevant to researching companies and industries could provide a valuable edge to job seekers who may be stuck in a process they don't fully understand or feel they have little or no control over. We can play a vital role by arming job hunters with the knowledge to amp up their employment search by using business information to target companies and industries. Instead of merely helping job seekers find information about where jobs are posted, librarians should encourage the unemployed to rethink their search by digging deeper through traditional business information resources to uncover potential openings by company and industry. Additionally, we can encourage them to use that knowledge to make a stronger impression during the application process and interview stage. This guidance could provide the critical edge required to get someone hired in this competitively challenging and altogether unprecedented job market. In the best case, it can result in not just a new job but a job with a new skill set that allows employees to continually reassess their value and contributions.

WORKS CITED

Bensoussan, Babette E., and Craig S. Fleisher. 2008. *Analysis without Paralysis.* Upper Saddle River, NJ: FT Press.

Dresang, Joel. 2009. "Online Want Ads Down Again." *McClatchy-Tribune Business News,* September 29, D1.

Dugan, Ianthe Jeanne. 2009. "After the Boom: Working Two Jobs and Still Underemployed." *Wall Street Journal,* December 1, D2.

Dutta, Soumitra, and Matthew Fraser. 2009. "When Job Seekers Invade Facebook." *McKinsey Quarterly,* no. 3: 16–17.

Elmore, B. 2009. "Social Networking Strategies." *Baylor Business Review* 28 (1): 25.

Evans, Kelly, and Deborah Lynn Blumberg. 2009. "Work Openings, New Hires Decrease." *Wall Street Journal* (Eastern ed.), December 6, A2.

Mattioli, Dana. 2009. "A Hard Lesson for Teachers." *Wall Street Journal* (Eastern ed.), August 11, D1–D4.

Stanko, Brian, and Thomas L. Zeller. 2003. *Understanding Corporate Annual Reports: A User's Guide.* New York: Wiley.

START YOUR JOB SEARCH HERE

Jason Kuhl

LIKE MOST PUBLIC libraries, the Arlington Heights (Illinois) Memorial Library has felt the impact of the recession through greater numbers of patrons visiting our facility, increased circulation, and an influx of patrons needing assistance finding jobs and filling out employment applications. We knew that if we wanted to provide the high-quality service our patrons had come to expect, help for job seekers needed to be one of our top priorities. We quickly mobilized and began a library-wide campaign called "Start Your Job Search Here."

DETERMINING WHAT TO ADDRESS

In *Surviving a Layoff,* Epstein (2009, 23) likens the loss of a job to that of a family member or friend. The loss of identity that comes with job loss can be "just as devastating, if not more personally devastating, as losing a loved one."

We librarians are not accustomed to working with so many patrons struggling with so many conflicting emotions. True, we occasionally find ourselves in emotionally charged situations, but the economic crisis has brought an all but unprecedented number of people facing trying circumstances through our doors. An initial reaction may be haphazardly to offer all the help we can, but it is beneficial to step back and take a more systematic approach to determining what help is needed. Through our analysis, we determined that our job searchers needed help in these areas:

- Knowing where to begin
- Locating job openings and networking
- Putting together a resume and cover letter
- Conducting an effective job interview
- Increasing computer skills
- Dealing with the emotional impact of losing a job
- Managing finances while out of work

IDENTIFYING *YOUR* PATRONS' NEEDS

The needs you identify at your library may be different from ours. Is much of the unemployment in your community because the area's major employer closed? Do you have a high percentage of single parents who are out of work or a significant immigrant population facing language barriers? Before you can address your community's unique needs, you need to identify them.

WHO SHOULD ADDRESS EACH NEED?

As librarians, we are not expert in all things. Though it is tempting to try to serve every need with in-house staff, we do a disservice to our patrons by attempting to instruct them in areas outside our expertise. Keep in mind our role in helping patrons with legal or medical needs: we are expert in sifting through information to find resources, both inside and outside of the library, but we do not have the expertise to interpret that information or make recommendations based on it. Nevertheless, providing a comprehensive campaign was important to us. That meant finding outside experts to fill in the gaps.

Interviewing users to determine their needs and sorting through resources to address them are the foundations of our profession; our library staff focused on job search activities revolving around those principles. We have become a source for help with basic computer skills, so we are qualified to address that niche. We left anything requiring an in-depth knowledge of a subject area to experts in the appropriate field.

We could meet these needs with library staff:

Knowing where to begin

Submitting resumes and cover letters

Locating job openings

Increasing computer skills

We needed outside help to address these areas:

Resume content

Dealing with the emotional aspects of losing a job

Managing finances while out of work

HOW TO ADDRESS EACH NEED

After identifying the areas we were qualified to address, we set out to determine how to meet each need. We sought out qualified individuals or organizations to focus on the areas we could not address ourselves. Ultimately, our campaign combined public service points and one-on-one instruction with printed materials and a series of classes and seminars.

Job Search Desk

Like most libraries, one of our challenges is making the public aware of the services we provide; often even frequent visitors to the library do not know all that we do. We understood the importance of the "Start Your Job Search Here" campaign and wanted to make it a focal point of our service. For the first three months, we set up a temporary desk in the highest-traffic area of our building and each weekday afternoon staffed it with reference librarians trained to answer questions about job searches.

> ### IDENTIFYING *YOUR* LIBRARY'S STRENGTHS
>
> Every library can handle different needs with internal staff. We have a business librarian in our reference department, so we can address some needs that other libraries cannot. Some libraries have computer training departments and can provide more in-depth computer training than we can. Do you know your library's strengths and weaknesses?

The impact was immediate. We helped eighty-four patrons the first week and averaged over sixty job searchers per week over the course of thirteen weeks. Many of the sessions were orientations to the services we offer and guidance on where to begin; others were more in-depth, specialized searches. Often these focused on activities like locating networking groups or companies in a particular industry; other times they centered on finding alternate careers or even starting a business. Follow-up appointments were scheduled for very complex needs.

We knew many of the patrons we helped at the desk would be emotional, but we were unprepared for the volume of heartrending stories we encountered. One of the librarians who worked the desk remembers speaking with a patron who could not take her children to the dentist after both she and her husband lost their jobs. Another remembers her first shift on the desk; she encountered a tearful young woman who had just lost the job it took her two years to find and was in imminent danger of losing her condominium. Sadly, we never found out how either of those stories ended.

Printed Materials

We did not want to overwhelm already frustrated job searchers, so we avoided a large number of printed brochures and lists. We did, however, produce these two important pieces:

Start Your Job Search Here Checklist. We wanted to find a way to let new job searchers know where to begin without contributing to the information overload they already faced. We produced a professionally printed, trifold "Job Search Checklist" that clearly and concisely set out the first six steps a new job searcher should take.

Job Networking and Support Groups Directory. Networking groups are important tools for the job searcher, but locating them can be difficult. We compiled a directory to give the overwhelmed job searcher a place to easily find all of the networking and support groups that meet in the northwest Chicago suburbs.

STAFF SUPPORT

Working closely with so many people in desperate circumstances is emotionally draining for staff. Make staff support a priority. Here are some suggestions. Is there anything else you can do?

- Can you spread around job functions? If all of the frequent contact with job searchers falls to just one or two people, the burden may become too great.
- Does your benefits package include an employee assistance plan? Encourage staff to use it or, better yet, schedule a counselor from the plan to give group or individual sessions at the library.
- What about program presenters? We scheduled a counselor to give a program on dealing with the emotional aspects of job loss. She also put together a presentation for staff.

YOUR COLLECTION

Is your collection adequate? In *The Resume Writer's Workbook*, Stanley Krantman (2008, xiii) discusses the many ways job searching has changed in recent years. If you have older books that do not reflect these changes, you are doing a disservice to your patrons. Weed out old titles and replace them with new ones. Do you have enough to meet demand?

POLICIES

Do you know your library board's position on promoting commercial organizations? An employment agency, for example, may agree to review resumes provided they can also promote their services. Know your library's policy before the situation arises.

Resume Reviews

The most requested service from job seekers is to have their resume reviewed. As librarians, this is not our area of expertise. We felt strongly about addressing this need and located career counselors and human resources professionals to conduct free resume review appointments. This has been our most popular job search service; over three hundred reviews were conducted in the course of nine months.

Most of our resume reviewers came to us through ties already established by our outreach efforts. Several of the reviewers are out of work themselves; volunteering allows them to keep busy, stay involved with their field, and bolster their own resumes. Even if you have not already established relationships with likely reviewers, there are places you can look:

Local government employment offices

Temporary employment agencies

Networking groups

The local chamber of commerce

Your library's human resources department

Job Search Skills Classes

For the first three months of the campaign, librarians who staffed the jobs desk taught these classes each week:

Finding a Job—Where to Begin: Focuses on the first steps of a job search and how the library can help.

Beyond Monster.com—Online Job Search Tools: Focuses on how to use the library's online database to locate job prospects and research companies.

Computer Skills Classes

Use of our Internet computers has increased dramatically during the recession. Among the most frequent uses is to submit job applications—a frustrating endeavor for someone who does not have computer skills or an e-mail address. To tackle this need, computer help staff taught two short sessions—"E-mail for Job Seekers" and "Online Forms for Job Seekers"— several times a week.

Presentations by Outside Speakers

To address areas outside of our expertise, we knew we needed to find speakers to give presentations on some topics. Many waived or reduced their fees, and we received a grant from the vocational committee of the Arlington Heights Rotary Club to fund a speakers series for job seekers. These are some of the topics covered:

- Managing your finances during a job search
- Effective techniques for a job interview
- Coping with job loss
- Job searching after fifty
- Using LinkedIn and other social networking tools for your job search
- Developing alternative career paths

BE FLEXIBLE

Are your policies appropriate? Given the severity of the economic crisis, you may wish to consider modifying some of your library's policies or procedures. We relaxed our usual procedure of opening instructional classes only to residents by allowing nonresidents to attend job search classes if space was available.

LOCATION, LOCATION, LOCATION!

Can you hold classes in unusual locations? Whenever possible, we presented job search classes in public areas of the library instead of tucking them away in meeting rooms. This put the class closer to the resources being discussed, drew attention to our services, and allowed patrons to stop in to listen.

LESSONS LEARNED

The "Start Your Job Search Here" campaign taught us about our community and the challenges our residents face. One librarian put it best: "Before I started working on the jobs desk, I assumed that most of the people in

COMMUNITY INVOLVEMENT

What relationships have you formed in your community? We were able to mobilize our campaign so quickly because our business librarian has maintained a presence in our business community. We had a list of contacts in place, many of whom provided support for free or a reduced fee because of our relationship with them. If your library does not already have a presence with the chamber of commerce, Rotary Club, or other community organizations, what steps do you need to take to become involved?

upper-middle class Arlington Heights were not greatly affected by the recession. One afternoon on the jobs desk certainly put that assumption to rest! It was a real eye-opener to learn that people with good degrees and impressive resumes were having trouble getting jobs." We learned how to mobilize library staff to put together a major campaign in very little time; the first elements of the campaign were put into place in just a few weeks. It is important to keep these lessons in mind:

Define your needs before jumping in.

Do not try to address every need with library staff; know your strengths and find ways to address the other needs.

Involve staff from all areas of the library; when the library is facing a crisis, staff may need to step outside their normal job functions.

Take advantage of the relationships you have already established in your community; you may be able to find help in unexpected places.

Keep it simple; do not overwhelm already frustrated job searchers with too much information.

Plan programs and services to focus on one need at a time; the topic is too big to address in one program.

Do not let the idea of "perfect" lure you into inaction; you can make adjustments as you go.

CONCLUSION

Libraries face many challenges as they deal with the recession; the choices they make help define their values and the role they play in their communities. The "Start Your Job Search Here" campaign is among the most gratifying experiences we have had as librarians. There is nothing so rewarding as having a patron credit your help as the reason she found a job. Rarely do we have the opportunity to have such a profound impact on our patrons' lives; we should be ready to accept the challenge.

WORKS CITED

Epstein, Lita. 2009. *Surviving a Layoff: A Week-by-Week Guide to Getting Your Life Back Together.* Avon, MA: Adams Media.

Krantman, Stanley. 2008. *The Resume Writer's Workbook: Marketing Yourself throughout the Job Search Process.* 3rd ed. Clifton Park, NY: Thompson/Delmar Learning.

HIDDEN BARRIERS

Consider hidden barriers to providing good service to job seekers. Can you ensure you have adequate work space for patrons spending hours each day at your library? What about job seekers who must come with children? Do you have enough parking for the increased use? We leased a portion of a neighboring church's parking lot for staff to use, thus freeing up spaces in the library's lot for patrons.

PART II

Librarian Survival

ENTREPRENEURS IN THE LIBRARY

How an Entrepreneurial Spirit Expanded the Patron
Base and Elevated Its Political Standing

James Lund

AT THE HEIGHT of the current economic crisis, President Obama's chief of staff Rahm Emanuel expressed an entrepreneurial mind-set that propelled the incoming administration's opportunistic economic agenda: "Things that we had postponed for too long, that were long term, are now immediate and must be dealt with. This crisis provides the opportunity for us to do things that you could not do before. . . . You never want a serious crisis to go to waste." When originally hearing this statement, I was not in an "opportunistic" frame of mind. In truth, my outlook had become dour by the prospect of inevitable budget cuts. Yet Mr. Emanuel's ambitiousness revitalized my determination to orchestrate change. Before us was an opportunity to create lifelong library users and remake the library landscape after fifteen years of declining use if we persevered in the face of looming budget cuts. I was determined to press on.

In this chapter I argue that by implementing an exceptional service model a library can create an entrepreneurial spirit—a spirit that encourages risks, alters existing relationships, and allows for failure. This entrepreneurial sprit is the catalyst to dynamic continuous improvement that will result in a larger, more satisfied patron base and greater political standing. As we examine this service model, I first provide a brief overview and how it was implemented. Then I discuss how this service model became the foundation for creating an entrepreneurial spirit. Finally, I present some of the service changes and how their implementation expanded our patron base and elevated our political standing.

IMPLEMENTING AN EXCEPTIONAL SERVICE MODEL

When you think of careers that lure risk takers into the fold, librarianship may be the last one that comes to mind. Our staff, like most, are risk averse. So how do you reset the cultural ethos? Drawing from my experience in high-end retail, I began by implementing a service model tailored to libraries that incorporates the values from the best in retail. After much research, I found kinship with the Starbucks service model, for two reasons: the repeat-customer parallel, and the personalization of service or commitment to develop deeper human relationships that establishes brand loyalty. Our new service model also had to create a buzz and offer service unlike the impersonal big-box store service experience. We needed to create an experience beyond the transaction.

To develop a curriculum with which to teach my staff, I partnered with the local technical college's continuing education department. With the assistance of a customer service consultant, we constructed a course based on Starbucks' principles of service as developed in *The Starbucks Experience: 5 Principles for Turning Ordinary into Extraordinary,* by Joseph A. Michelle. Let us look briefly at each of the five principles:

Make it your own. This principle seeks genuine engagement on a personal level. Remembering patron names and using them visit to visit is a good way to start.

Everything matters. This principle considers every detail—such as cleanliness, layout, and clutter—and the emotive reaction to the total experience.

Surprise and delight. Stand curbside some inclement morning and accept returns. In your patrons' expression of appreciation, you will see the power of this principle.

Embrace resistance. Taking extraordinary steps to satisfy patrons creates lifelong users.

Leave your mark. Public library service is not a trite community amenity. Speak up with passion and make a cogent case for the library's importance.

I decided to use a consultant to introduce the service model to staff because a consultant would possess broader expertise and authority than I and would have an independent voice that could increase the dynamic impact of the message. On many levels, I staked the success of my directorship on the implementation of this service model. I was attempting to orchestrate a paradigm shift; such shifts are risky and demand a dynamic break from the past to take hold. Thus, I needed to ensure the greatest possibility for success.

After our day of full staff training, the library's management team met with the consultant to devise a plan for daily implementation. We agreed on a simple supervisory philosophy: set the standard, model it, and expect it. So, the following day we put our new service model into practice. Wow, did people notice. Staff bagged books, offered curbside pickup, and engaged patrons personally at a level not before experienced.

An unanticipated and welcomed outcome of this service model was the dramatic improvement in staff morale. Altering long-standing relationships by actively seeking personal engagements with patrons makes staff vulnerable to disappointing if not awkward moments. This is a risky prospect for most people. Yet we quickly realized that our patrons longed for a deeper human connection, and the risk was rewarded by overwhelmingly positive reciprocation. The immediate positive human feedback itself improved morale, but more enduring was the ethical transformation. Intentionally using your energy for an altruistic purpose—serving others—is liberating. Casting aside personal concerns and replacing them with actions that improve the lives of others (patrons and colleagues) was a corporately transformative event. Fundamentally, our work as librarians is not about serving ourselves—it is about serving others.

> **EFFECTIVE MANAGEMENT**
>
> Looking for a simple, effective management philosophy? If you are willing to lead by example, this is a powerful method: 1: Set the standard. 2: Model it. 3: Expect it. And you as the library administrator need to take the lead out on the service floor.

CREATING AN ENTREPRENEURIAL SPIRIT

How, you may ask, did this new service model create an entrepreneurial spirit? Fundamentally, the five principles of exceptional customer service are entrepreneurial. Each principle seeks new and dynamic ways to deliver services according to its sphere of influence. Frontline staff are confronted daily with situations that challenge the status quo, and the principles drive them to suggest new ways to deliver services—a challenge, for sure, to their supervisors. Altering familiar relationships and breaking down barriers to access is risky. It may fail. But true entrepreneurs use failure as an opportunity to seed success.

SERVICE IMPROVEMENTS

At this point, a few examples of the improvements and why we made them may be helpful to illustrate our thesis.

Everything matters. We set out to improve an exterior that was unidentifiable and uninviting. The exterior signage had long since been removed from one side of the building and was unnoticeable on the other. Two new architecturally suitable signs were positioned strategically so as to be visible from the highway two hundred yards away. Now identifiable, we wished to improve the building's attractiveness as an anchor to the downtown business district. Three distinct landscape vignettes were created: one features drought-tolerant plantings; the second is a memorial patio garden; the third incorporates prairie plantings, relaxed seating, and a water feature. Our work was included on the community's Garden Tour, but more important was the increased foot traffic around the library and, consequently, around downtown businesses. How your building looks and feels on the outside matters. By making these improvements, we strengthened our standing as an essential economic anchor of the downtown district.

Inside the library, we turned our attention to the traffic flow and the relationship between the collections and their users. We desired a "wow" factor near the entrances—something that would create a feeling entirely different from the expected; in other words, *surprise and delight.* To accomplish this, we installed two oversized wedding cake display tables to accommodate large displays of new materials and Spanish-language materials for the growing Latino population.

> ### MEASURING YOUR SERVICE
>
> How do you measure the impact of customer service? Many retailers use secret shoppers to accomplish this. Our consultant used local, anonymous citizens as secret shoppers to evaluate our customer service. How would I evaluate their success in judging our service? Simply put, I'll never use surveys again.

Next, we tackled the "boxed-in" feeling near the entrances. By flaring all the shelving adjacent to the wedding cake display tables outward, we encouraged exploration of the entire library. The layout is modeled after the increasingly popular roundabout traffic intersections. Finally, we acted on the long-standing request to associate juvenile nonfiction with the children's section. Although well intentioned, mixing juvenile and adult materials made them nearly inaccessible by creating an intimidating environment for kids and discouraging localized family use of the entire juvenile collection. It needed to change.

We also identified barriers to access in our policies and in our social environment. Circulation service is the last opportunity to *leave your mark*. What is our patron's final impression? We started by evaluating the complexity of our circulation policies. Was that one-page enumeration of multiple loan periods, fine amounts, and renewal policies user friendly? The Rule of Two— "two-week checkouts, two renewals, twenty-cent fines on overdues"—became our simplified loan policy. The policy is easy to explain, brandable, and as a mnemonic device quite memorable. My point is not so much to advocate a two-week loan period (although shorter loan periods encourage regular library visits and create an urgency to use the materials, thus forging the habit of literacy) as to create policies with the user's experience in mind.

We looked at circulation policies that imposed unnecessary inconvenience. For patrons who made the effort to come to the library but forgot their library card, we had once turned them away empty-handed. What mark did that leave? Now we have a method in place for these patrons to check out materials. We also reassessed policies that invite unnecessary confrontation. Claimed returns were a point of contention. Instead of taking a patron at his word, we had been offering tips on how to hunt more thoroughly for those items our patrons had "surely misplaced." In fact, over half of the claimed returns we would find on our shelves. This was mostly our problem, and it was not worth casting suspicion or arguing with a patron over a few lost items. So we decided to take patrons at their word and assume the burden of finding or replacing lost material. What a great use of a little fine money.

There are more examples, but these few illustrate our philosophy concerning materials and the patrons who borrow them. We are interested in placing materials into the patron's care where they can be used to develop the habit of literacy. The public owns the library. We owe them much liberty to exercise responsibility over *their* materials until they are proved irresponsible.

Another barrier to access is the social environment. Every weekday afternoon our library experienced a sudden shift in its social environment—from one that encouraged contemplation, respectful interaction, and democratic access to one that was likened to a cage match at Wrestlemania. The teen intrusion left the library virtually vacant but for a few patrons wishing a quick transaction. My predecessors tried nearly everything to encourage respectful coexistence without success. I acted more decisively, removing the disruption, and the patrons returned. This move was risky and could have easily failed. My tactic may not be the preferred approach, but no matter the method the imperative is to create and enforce a social environment based on respect to the inclusion of all who will adhere. Subsequently, the disruptive teens have been reinstated and are coexisting respectfully. Still, the problem of space for teens has not been solved and is currently under study through a grant recently awarded to the library.

EXPANDED PATRON BASE AND POLITICAL STANDING

How, then, did this service model and resulting service changes expand our patron base and elevate our political standing? As is well documented, most libraries are visited more frequently in economic recessions. Historically, our library seemed to be the exception. During the previous two recessions, usage declined and continued to decline through 2006. Yet in a few short years we not only recovered fifteen years of losses but expanded usage to record highs in 2009. More than a recession boost was clearly at play. What became evident from the unsolicited and overwhelming feedback was that our patrons longed for change. They were ready for something dramatically new, and our assessment of what needed changing was right on target. Our best marketing tactic is an overwhelmingly positive service experience. Patrons experienced it, embraced it, and spread the word about it.

> ### BARRIERS TO ACCESS
>
> How often as librarians do we find ourselves uttering the phrase, "We need to educate them"? Make a list of all things that "need educating" and you will have a starter list of barriers that need fixing.

But how did increased usage translate into an elevated political standing? Increased usage led to more satisfied taxpayer touches of our service. Sometimes hard work comes with a little luck, and the city's decision to evaluate fifty-one services via a citizen survey was the instrument we needed. Eighty-one percent of citizens supported maintaining or increasing library hours in the midst of the city's financial crisis—the most support for a service not related to public safety. Since arriving, I had championed the public library as an essential service on par with public safety and public works. Now the people had confirmed that message. Although we did not escape a reduction in funding for 2010, our victory came in the form of minimal cuts in kind with those expected from traditional "essential services." Being identified with the upper tier of services will only help our cause to expand library services when better times arrive.

CONCLUSION

In this chapter I argue for expanding the library's patron base and elevating its political standing by creating an entrepreneurial spirit through implementing an exceptional service model. The ensuing entrepreneurial spirit compels the creation of new and dynamic ways to deliver service, a deeper connection between people, and the drive for continuous improvement. The resulting dramatic increases in usage and patron satisfaction at our library became political capital to elevate our political standing to essential service status. When better times arrive, our strong position will garner support for public library service in the future.

WORK CITED

Michelle, Joseph A. 2006. *The Starbucks Experience: 5 Principles for Turning Ordinary into Extraordinary*. New York: McGraw-Hill.

4

LAID OFF? HERE'S ONE WAY TO LAND ON YOUR FEET

J. James Mancuso

WHEN MY WIFE asked how my day had gone, I responded that we could talk about it after dinner. With her uncanny intuition, she knew instantly—"You lost your job." Well, technically yes. I had been notified that morning by the seminary where I had worked as the theological librarian for the past nine years that my contract, which would expire in five months, could not be renewed this year due to the seminary's severe financial situation. By whatever term you call it, the downturn in the economy that began in the fall of 2008 had hit our household as well, and I was about to find myself in the 7 percent of America that is employed, but not full-time (*BusinessWeek* 2009, 13).

We took a few days just to discuss the situation among our family members, including our three nearly grown children. We approached the need to replace my income in a calm, logical, and comprehensive way.

Our first decision was to treat this job loss in its full context: as a family matter and not just a career change for me. We had lived in the area for more than twenty-five years. Two of the children were in college locally, one in high school. Our roots were deep: the local area holds our circle of close friends, hundreds of professional and church-related acquaintances, and thousands of memories. In viewing the entire situation, this consideration held a lot of weight. None of us wanted to move from the area, or even consider leaving our home.

Our second decision was that we would pursue every means possible to replace my income without moving. Since my job as a theological librarian, including being an adjunct professor of English, was unique in our region, I knew that a similar job within driving distance did not exist. A thorough examination of job listings in the newspapers, library job websites, and other sources did not turn up a single opening for a full-time position that matched my needs, experience, and qualifications. Thus, a dilemma of two unsatisfactory choices presented itself: stay in an area where I could not find a full-time job, or move from the area where all five of us wanted to live.

Most Americans have heard this maxim popularized in the 1980s and 1990s: "Think outside the box." Thinking outside the box involves finding solutions to problems that lie outside self-imposed limitations once one realizes that it is permissible to go outside the lines to find a solution.

TURNING THE BOX SIDEWAYS

As I wrestled with this dilemma, I began to realize that I still needed to think inside the box, but in a different way. It reminded me of the time I was looking through a book of house designs from the 1920s (Gordon-Van Tine Co. 1992, 55). I had found a picture of a house whose designer had dubbed a "bungalow," using a familiar term of his day. He had actually designed the first suburban ranch house plan. How had he done that? He had taken the bungalow floor layout and turned it sideways. From this fresh perspective in the eye of one maverick house designer have now sprung the designs of countless ranch-style houses.

From this observation I coined the phrase "turning the box sideways." The time had come for me to see my job loss situation from a new perspective: I had to turn *my* box sideways. Our family needed the sum total of my income, which had always come from a full-time job, but in turning our box sideways I realized that the income could just as easily come from several part-time jobs.

In other words, the box still remained. Inside that box were our home, friends, church, and all the rest, and thinking *inside* the box precluded moving to a new area geographically. But inside the box were also my expertise, specific talents and skills, and thirty-plus years of experience in the library field, along with the experience and relationships from my work in professional organizations. Why not keep thinking inside the box, valuing its contents as well as its limits as nonnegotiable, but turn it sideways to see my need for a job as a need for a certain amount of income? The sum of several incomes earned from a multiplicity of related jobs in the field of library science can equal the income from a single job.

Our third decision had been made: I would not put my limited time and energy into finding a full-time position; rather, I would secure several part-time jobs, the income from which would equal one full-time job. Limiting the job search gave us the freedom and peace of mind to pursue this course of action without the constant confusion, anxiety, and uncertainty that come from indecisiveness. We knew it might not work. We all knew that we might end up having to move. But this plan held a reasonably good chance of succeeding, and I was willing to try it.

TAKING ACTION

With these fundamental decisions behind us, I plotted out a course of action:

Relearn the art of job hunting.

Spread the news.

Network with colleagues.

Recast my resume entirely.

Brush up on interviewing skills.

With a plan in place and a specific objective in mind, I began.

The Art of Job Hunting

Looking for a new job is tough. Looking for three new jobs can be three times as hard, or one-third as hard. It's all in how you look at it. Looking for just one perfect-fitting, complete, full-time job in a tough economy can be frustrating, daunting, and may take longer than five months. But finding part-time jobs is much different. Employers eager to shed costly full-time employees from their shrinking budgets are far more likely in today's market to be looking to get the work done with a cadre of part-timers. Okay, maybe this is not one's cup of tea forever, but for now it can work.

An added emotional bonus comes with the securing of each part-time job. As each part of the income fell into place, I was encouraged to push forward, knowing that at least some percentage of the income had been replaced.

Job fairs, employment seminars, online classes, and webinars abound. I took advantage of them. Local job fairs probably are irrelevant for finding a professional library job, but often an attendee can take advantage of free classes on the art of job hunting, including resume-writing workshops, honing interview skills, and finding the hidden job market. They are even useful for simply interacting with others who are in the same boat; you can give each other tips and encouragement.

Spreading the News

Possibly the single most important aspect of the experience is just simply getting the word out that you are looking for part-time work. E-mail proved to be an essential tool for me. Through e-mail messages and phone calls I was able to inform dozens of colleagues that I was in the part-time job market.

Networking with Colleagues

Networking with colleagues began seventeen years ago when I became active in local, state, and national professional library associations. It was natural and easy to contact them and ask if there were part-time openings. All three new sources of employment came as a direct result of contacting librarian friends, explaining the situation of the downsizing, and asking if they knew of part-time work.

A New Look for an Old Resume

In fact, several new looks for an old resume. Having been at a full-time job that was extremely satisfying professionally, I had not spent much time keeping up my resume over the past nine years. I had to pull together all the relevant information for the updated resume, which meant using the old information on hand, finding records of recent events and continuing education, and then designing a whole new, fresh look. Having most of the information already in electronic format in WordPerfect surely simplified that process. I found sound advice and effective layouts in some basic books from the public library. I ended up creating one large master resume containing all the information, from which I then created briefer, tighter, more focused resumes to use in specific applications. Thus, each time I applied for a position, I tailored my resume to suit it.

Interviewing Skills

Books on interviewing helped. So did a close friend of mine, a retired human resources manager who really took an interest and gave me some great advice and tips. It is important to note that when someone is interviewing for a part-time job, the stakes are much lower. Both the employer doing the interview and the applicant are much more at ease. This can translate into a much less stressful process of applying and interviewing for a job.

REPLACING THE INCOME

Over the next five months I secured four sources of income. Since I was the only person actually giving library service in the seminary library on a daily basis, the seminary was eager to retain my services, even if they could afford to pay for only ten hours per week. They also immediately agreed to have me continue teaching my courses. With 30 percent of the income replaced, I was off to a good start. The seminary students, faculty, and I were all delighted that I could remain in my office.

News of my need for a part-time position traveled quickly among my colleagues, professional contacts, and seminary friends. Through one of them I heard of a totally online seminary in need of a theological librarian to manage its electronic resources. I interviewed and got the position—a twenty-hour-a-week job that I could do from my home or wherever I and my laptop computer happened to be.

A library consortium whose staff knew me well pulled me in as a ten-hour-a-week consultant, doing the same sort of work I had done in a previous position ten years before. An old friend of mine hired me to do substitute work at the reference desk of a local public library. Though as a source of income it turned out to be minimal, it nonetheless has kept me in touch with public services and the broader library community.

So, when my full-time position came to an end, I had retained my job (at a reduced schedule) and added three additional employers, all in the library field, and replaced all of my income.

IT ALL WORKS

How does it all work? It requires constant flexibility and a great deal of organizational skill to juggle the constantly changing needs of four employers.

On the downside:

- My family cannot easily keep track of my schedule or whereabouts.
- I lack all the benefits of full-time employment, like retirement account contributions, paid holidays, and medical coverage (which we secured through my wife's employer). When the swine flu hit, I had no paid sick leave.
- Having multiple offices, briefcases, business cards, and job titles can be disconcerting. Each morning I have to think out my varying needs and pack accordingly.
- Juggling schedules is a constant exercise in organization and flexibility.

- Working at home sometimes does not work well; it requires a lot of discipline.
- Each job requires its own expertise.
- No two days are alike.

On the upside:

- I can name my own hours, take time off if I need to, and work odd hours.
- I can do my online work at a coffee shop, library, or bookstore, and I do. Truthfully, it is far more productive than working at home, which can be distracting.
- I meet new people, make new friends, learn new things.
- Because we stayed in our home, I and my family members avoided the stress, loss of friends, complexity, and upset involved in pulling up stakes and moving across the country.
- No two days are alike. (Yes, it can be a plus too.)

UNEXPECTED BENEFIT

One aspect of this whole experience of dividing my work week among four employers has become an unanticipated benefit to me and the employers: what I do at each workplace informs what I do at the others. From my work in building an online seminary library, I am now much more in tune with electronic resources that I can utilize at the other, more print-based seminary library. Outside my office door are print resources that can be used to fill interlibrary loan requests for students of the online seminary. At the library consortium office I learn of discounted services and products that I can use to answer questions at the public library reference desk. Because I am still on the front lines of library service, I bring a lively perspective to my consultant role at the library consortium setting, which is quite removed from traditional library settings. Everyone benefits.

EVENTUALLY SPEAKING

I have enjoyed this chapter in my work life. I am learning all I can from it. I have embraced it as a necessary, but probably temporary, phase—a transition time. I do not want to waste this opportunity to expand horizons and learn new things, but I do indeed look forward to having a full-time job again.

WORKS CITED

BusinessWeek. 2009. "Jobless Rate Jumps to 9.7% in August." *BusinessWeek Online,* September 7. www.businessweek.com/investor/content/sep2009/pi2009094_098102.htm (accessed January 14, 2009).

Gordon-Van Tine Co. 1992. *117 House Designs of the Twenties.* Mineola, NY: Dover.

5

LOW- AND NO-COST DEVELOPMENT OPPORTUNITIES FOR LIBRARIANS

Colleen S. Harris

FOR MOST LIBRARIANS, professional development is essential to keeping their skills honed and up to date. For some librarians, professional development is required by their tenure standards. The financial burden of association membership dues, conference registration costs, travel, and lodging can become overwhelming quickly, particularly when development and travel budgets are cut. Luckily, there are low- and no-cost development opportunities available for nearly everyone.

THE BEST THINGS IN LIFE ARE FREE

There are a variety of free services that help you stay informed and build your reputation as a librarian:

Blogging. Many librarians blog to explore pertinent topics, engage in debate about current trends and issues, or simply reflect on their experiences. This is a great opportunity to practice writing well-thought-out mini-articles.

Social networks. One of the easiest things you can do to position yourself well for your future in the profession is to engage in social networking. Twitter, Friendfeed, and Facebook provide a fast and easy way to plug into the active library community and enter the conversation.

Small things count. Other, smaller things do count in the profession. Your participation on professional e-mail lists (such as NEWLIB-L and LIBREF-L) fills in the gaps for folks you may not interact with formally on a regular basis. Professionalism, kindness, helpfulness, and courtesy go a long way and are remembered and associated with your name.

A STRONG FOUNDATION: SKILL BUILDING ON THE CHEAP

Free for-credit classes. Many librarians find that they are eligible for some sort of tuition reimbursement or waiver. You can always brush up on useful skills in educational technology or technical communication or take some of those library science electives you missed, but taking classes is also a great way to keep your brain limber and accustomed to learning (as well as pushing your student loans into deferment status).

Free workshops and training. Librarians often have the opportunities to build their skills through workshops offered through their information technology and human resources departments. Some universities, like the University of Kentucky, offer management classes free through their training and development office. Other places may offer them at a cost lower than that for privately sponsored or conference workshops.

Grassroots skill building. Round-robin workshops involving colleagues at your place of work are a great way to learn—and teach—for not much more than the cost of baking a batch of brownies (optional, but appreciated by the audience). Why not pitch a local workshop series to librarians in your immediate area? Cities with more than one college or university and public libraries are a great environment for this sort of project. Such gatherings give you the opportunity

NO-COST WORKSHOP

At the University of Tennessee at Chattanooga, every librarian is a subject liaison to one or more academic departments. To keep their skills sharp, librarians take turns providing workshops showcasing new database features and best practices for reference in their liaison subjects. Virginia Cairns, head of reference and instruction, says this of the series: "Planning and leading a workshop for your peers offers a rich set of opportunities to hone your skills in front of an audience, try out new teaching methods, and improve the overall service level across your library by making everyone who works a service desk more comfortable with your subject-specific resources and tools."

to present and get feedback, and you are likely to expand your professional network at near-zero cost.

Get creative. There are always the things you can test on your own. You don't need a license to get into Second Life, and you can find books to teach yourself programming languages with the resources at your local library.

The payoff to these skill-building endeavors goes far beyond learning more, meeting new folks online, and demonstrating your capabilities to your colleagues. Depending on the topics you choose to specialize and present in, you build the expertise, the presentation experience, and the stage comfort to move you into a good position to develop presentation proposals for larger venues.

SPEAKING AND PRESENTING

Conference attendance is probably the most expensive type of professional development, but there are ways to ease the burden on your wallet.

Estimate the bang for your buck. Do

LEVERAGING ONLINE NETWORKS

Laura Carscaddon, Kenley Neufeld, Courtney Stephens, Jezmynne Westcott, and Colleen Harris met online via Twitter and decided to pitch a preconference workshop for the Internet Librarian 2008 conference. They presented "Dance, Dance Library Evolution" and worked collaboratively online, not meeting in person until the day of the presentation. Their registration fees were waived, and some of them roomed together to save money. During the conference, the group met Josh Hadro of *Library Journal,* who invited them to write an article on social networking, which appeared later as "Working the Social: Twitter and Friendfeed," by Carscaddon and Harris. How can you leverage your online networks and collaborate with those who share your interests?

a quick cost-benefit analysis. Is a poster session at a large conference better than a speaking presentation at your state library conference? Does a speaking engagement trump an invitation to run a preconference workshop? Weigh the benefits of the speaking experience against the cost of attendance, and factor in whether your place of work weighs speaking engagements based on their local, state, or national level. Also consider whether is it worth presenting at a conference where none of the other presentations are relevant to your work.

Leverage your reputation. Some conferences waive or reduce the registration fee for presenters; others require full registration payment. Others allow you to speak for free but not attend other conference sessions unless you pay the registration fee. The best advice is always, "It can't hurt to ask."

Work the Net. Some conferences now invite virtual presentations. The 2009 ACRL/LLAMA conference invited virtual posters, the 2008 ALA annual conference had a live feed of the top tech trends, and Computers in Libraries 2010 will offer virtual walk-throughs of various web services. Consider these presentation credits with the added bonus of displaying your up-to-date technology skills.

Tag-team the conference. If you are active in the social network and library-land discussion sphere, you have likely made some friends and located librarians with research interests related to your own. Leverage those relationships into copresenting, carpooling, or rooming together, effectively reducing conference costs.

PUBLISHING

Publishing your work is, aside from the time and effort spent, the least-cost mode of professional development. If you are interested in publishing, the first thing to do is read. Read trade publications, magazines, journals, and books in your area of interest to know which publications your work is best suited for and to review their submission guidelines (usually offered on the publisher's website, under such headings as "For Authors," "Submissions," or "Writers' Guidelines").

Consider these popular sources where editors post calls for willing writers:

- A Library Writer's Blog: http://librarywriting.blogspot.com
- University of Pennsylvania, Department of English, Calls for Papers: http://call-for-papers.sas.upenn.edu
- Submission guidelines for various journals, magazines, and newsletters (including *Library Journal, Chronicle of Higher Education,* and more) on their websites
- E-mail lists such as those for RUSA, ACRL, LIBREF, NEWLIB, JESSE (The Open Lib/Info Sci Education Forum), and more.

BE PROACTIVE

Your personal budget need not be a major consideration when you consider paths to professional development, given the various options the Internet and local resources provide. In fact, by accepting the challenge and managing to maintain a healthy professional development portfolio during difficult budget times, you demonstrate your dedication and creativity, traits that any prospective employer will appreciate.

6

ONLINE RESOURCES IN MICHIGAN

A School Librarian Survives Hard Times

Margaret Lincoln

THE STATE OF Michigan has suffered gravely in the current financial crisis (Michigan State Senate 2009). According to the Bureau of Labor Statistics (2009), unemployment has remained above 15 percent since July, the highest among all states. Michigan public schools have been severely impacted by a shortfall in adequate funding (Washtenaw Intermediate School District 2009). An executive order issued by Governor Granholm threatened to undermine services provided by the Library of Michigan but was amended so as to lessen the full extent of cutbacks (Michigan Library Association 2009).

Amid this bleak economic picture, Michigan school libraries are considered inessential to the core curriculum and easy to eliminate. Media specialists risk being pink-slipped or put back into the classroom. After a thirty-seven-year career in school libraries in the Lakeview School District in Battle Creek, beginning in January 2010 I was scheduled to teach a daily ninety-minute block of second-year French while continuing to serve as media specialist. As it turned out, the proposed move did not take place, and I was returned to a full-time library position. Nonetheless, I was prepared to take on this major reassignment. Despite some initial trepidation, I was confident that the classroom experience would be rewarding for students and for me.

Taking a pragmatic and realistic view, however, I have begun to think about other career options in the library field. Over the past ten years, several out-of school library projects have helped to sharpen my job-related skills, provided supplemental income, and fostered professional contacts. In this chapter I focus on how work undertaken for Michigan Teacher Network, for Michigan eLibrary, and for Michigan Online Resources for Educators has eased my ability to weather the present economic situation. Internet resources have let one school librarian survive a recession.

GETTING STARTED AS A MICHIGAN TEACHER NETWORK LIBRARIAN

The year 2000 seems long ago in terms of the World Wide Web historical time line. A quick snapshot obtained through Internet World Stats reveals approximately 361 million Internet users worldwide in 2000 compared to over 1,734 million users in September 2009 (Miniwatts Marketing Group 2009). With the Y2K scare behind us, public schools were to see more instructional rooms with Internet access in 2000 (77 percent), up from 3 percent in 1994 (NCES 2006). Still, educators then as now faced the challenge of effective technology integration. How could the growing number of rich and varied online resources be used to promote meaningful teaching and learning? The opportunity to begin work in 2000 as a digital librarian for Michigan Teacher Network (MTN) allowed me to take part in an exemplary project that addressed this challenge. MTN eventually provided an extensive collection of 7,500 recommended and reviewed education resources. I look back on my MTN work as a rewarding experience that continues to have a bearing on my professional practice.

Having earned an AMLS in 1973, I was considered a veteran school library media specialist. My computer training had been gained on the job and through graduate technology certification courses at Michigan State University. But thanks to a familiarity with cataloging and classification procedures practiced for many years in the pre-online world, I was able to transition to the work of an MTN digital librarian. Each time a new record was added to the MTN database, exact guidelines were followed. It was necessary to input information into specific fields such as title, author, browsing category, resource type, accessibility, commercial content, URL, description, keywords or ERIC descriptors, technology requirements, grade level, and benchmark correlations. The description was the most important field to complete in that this brief, pithy, attention-grabbing write-up of a site's merits would appear on the search results page. Before a record went live in the MTN public database, proofreading and revisions were a must.

Record creation for MTN was not a task that could be done on the fly. Considerable time and effort were required to locate sites that merited inclusion

ABOUT MICHIGAN TEACHER NETWORK

Purpose: MTN provided easy access to PK–12 education web resources chosen for quality, relevance, and effectiveness.

Sponsorship: MTN was a project of Learning Systems at Merit Network, Inc. Support came from a Technology Literacy Challenge Fund Grant and the National Science Foundation.

Audience: MTN users included parents, teachers, school administrators, board trustees, librarians and media specialists, technology coordinators, students, preservice teachers, and college personnel.

Collection: MTN resources supported core content areas of arts education, career skills, English, foreign languages, media center, math, science, social studies, technology, early education, education clearinghouses, educational leadership, special education, Michigan education, events, and job listings.

Best Practices: MTN recommended content/design standards including Dublin Core and GEM standards for metadata and Web Accessibility Initiative standards.

http://web.archive.org/web/20050204091052/mtn.merit.edu/about/

in MTN. There was more to the process than simply Googling "middle school mythology site with lesson plans." After a site was chosen for MTN, it was necessary to navigate, explore, and familiarize oneself with the main page and subpages. Such thorough analysis resulted in a sense of truly knowing a resource and being more likely to recommend it to a teacher colleague.

Working as an MTN librarian entailed a responsibility for collection development. Not only was it important to choose individual resources for MTN, but it was also important to keep in mind the bigger picture. A model job description for a school library media specialist put forth by Riedling (2001) points to the librarian's role in selecting and evaluating materials and technologies that support a school's curriculum and educational philosophy. Because I had a strong subject background in French language and literature from my undergraduate major and secondary teaching endorsement, I was qualified to review MTN resources in this discipline.

During my tenure as an MTN librarian, there were several opportunities for professional development; these experiences helped broaden my knowledge base of web resources and technology integration. Presentations at state conferences provided a means to publicize MTN. I welcomed the chance to give sessions about MTN resources before the Michigan Foreign Language Association (MFLA) in 2001, the Michigan North Central Association in 2002, and the Michigan Association for Media in Education in 2002. Prior to the MFLA conference, I corresponded by e-mail with the creator of a particularly engaging French-language site based in the United Kingdom: bonjour.org.uk (now located at www.linguascope.com). I asked M. Stephane Derone if he might send a short greeting for me to read to conference attendees. To my surprise and pleasure, he responded to my request.

In my home community of Battle Creek, I was able to introduce area teachers to MTN resources as a leader in Project TIME (Technology Integrated into Meaningful Learning Experiences). This U.S. Department of Education Technology Innovation Challenge Grant was funded for 1999–2004 (Ashburn and Floden 2006). Finally, during this period I served as an American Memory Fellow with the Library of Congress and a Mandel Fellow with the United States Holocaust Memorial Museum. These fellowships allowed me to become better versed in the Library of Congress online primary source materials and in the museum's Holocaust instructional resources, which I was then better able to incorporate into my work as an MTN librarian.

BRANCHING OUT AS A MICHIGAN ELIBRARY DATABASE TRAINER

Shortly after my involvement with MTN began, another opportunity arose to branch out and build on my knowledge of instructional web resources. In 2001 I became a database trainer for the Library of Michigan and began teaching classes about Michigan eLibrary (MeL), the statewide resource network available to Michigan residents. MeL classes were organized by the Michigan Library Consortium (MLC) following a "train the trainer" model. In working with school and public librarians, I not only offered database training but also demonstrated how these resources were incorporated into Lakeview High School's instructional program and how our library website (http://remc12.k12.mi.us/lhslib/Electronic.htm) was designed to promote use of MeL. I gave presentations in 2008 highlighting the Best of MeL at the Michigan Association for Computer Users in Learning Conference and at a workshop for a local Teaching American History Grant group. A final result of my affiliation with MeL was my appointment in 2008 to the MLC board as the school library representative.

ABOUT MICHIGAN ELIBRARY

Mission: MeL provides all Michigan residents with free access to online full-text articles, full-text books, digital images, and other valuable research information at any time via the Internet and provides an easy-to-use interlibrary loan system.

Sponsorship: MeL is funded by the federal Library Services and Technology Act via the Institute of Museum and Library Services through the Library of Michigan. The cost of MeL is approximately $5 million per year, with a savings to the state's libraries, schools, colleges, and universities of over $72 million per year.

Components: MeL includes over forty subscription databases, MeLCat (statewide resource sharing network), MeL Michigana (photographs, diaries, oral histories, and local records), MeL Gateways, and Michigan Online Resources for Educators.

History: MeL has grown from the combination of several statewide projects including Michigan Electronic Library (1992), Access-Michigan (1997), ATLAS, the Action Team for Advancement of Libraries Statewide (1999), and the Making of Modern Michigan (2003).

Current Outlook: MeL will continue to promote its services and has contracts in place through 2010.

http://mel.org/

CONTINUING INVOLVEMENT WITH MICHIGAN ONLINE RESOURCES FOR EDUCATORS

MTN is no longer administered by Merit Network. Many of the originally recommended MTN resources, however, have been added to Michigan Online Resources for Educators (MORE), a part of MeL. MORE is identifying thousands of high-quality educational websites tied to the state's curriculum and professional development needs. Because of my prior connection to MTN and my current association with MeL, it seemed logical that I should continue to be involved with MORE. During the summer of 2009, I joined a team of teachers, library media specialists, and library/information science graduate students who were utilized to input supplemental resources into MORE and to align with state standards an additional 55,000 recommended online resources from the Verizon Foundation's Thinkfinity.org site.

MORE is aligned with foundational common beliefs set forth by the American Association of School Librarians' new Standards for the 21st-Century Learner. MORE materials lend backing to the AASL common belief that "inquiry provides a framework for learning" (AASL 2007, 2). Through MORE's portal, a teacher can find exemplary resources to challenge students as well as self-assessment tools and tutorials to foster independent learning.

Technological innovation is altering the educational and library landscapes at a breathtaking speed. A reported 90 percent of today's teens use browsers for cloud computing activities, and 70 percent of teens log on to social networking sites (Rainie 2009). In spite of change, MORE materials will continue to support AASL's common belief that "technology skills are crucial for future employment needs" (AASL 2007, 2). MORE builds on the success of the MTN project, allowing our students to develop information skills that will enable them to use technology as an important tool for learning, now and in the future.

Despite difficult economic circumstances facing schools and libraries in Michigan, our state is fortunate to have access to high-quality materials from MeL, MTN, and its successor, MORE. These valuable online resources are a

ABOUT MICHIGAN ONLINE RESOURCES FOR EDUCATORS

Overview: MORE allows teachers and parents to find lesson plans and curriculum aids searchable by Michigan's Grade Level Content Expectations (GLCEs) and High School Content Expectations (HSCEs) as mandated by the state for Michigan's school curriculum.

Structure: MORE uses the Collection Workflow Integration System (CWIS), an open-source software solution developed at the University of Wisconsin, Madison, with support from the National Science Foundation. The system is customizable, with records backed by Dublin Core metadata standards.

Partners: MORE is a joint project of the Library of Michigan, the Michigan Department of Education, and Wayne State University.

http://more.mel.org

true asset for Michigan residents and have helped one library media specialist to survive in a recession.

WORKS CITED

AASL American Association of School Librarians. 2007. "AASL Standards for the 21st-Century Learner." www.ala.org/ala/mgrps/divs/aasl/ guidelinesandstandards/learningstandards/AASL_LearningStandards.pdf (accessed November 28, 2009).

Ashburn, Elizabeth A., and Robert E. Floden, eds. 2006. *Meaningful Learning Using Technology: What Educators Need to Know and Do.* New York: Teachers College Press.

Bureau of Labor Statistics. 2009. "Regional and State Employment and Unemployment Summary, November 20, 2009." U.S. Department of Labor. www.bls.gov/news.release/laus.nr0.htm (accessed November 28, 2009).

Michigan Library Association. 2009. "Amending Executive Order 2009–36." www.mla.lib.mi.us/files/Amended%20EO.pdf (accessed November 28, 2009).

Michigan State Senate. 2009. "Michigan Economic Indicators, September 2009." www.senate.michigan.gov/sfa/Publications/Econind/MEI_SEP09.PDF (accessed November 28, 2009).

Miniwatts Marketing Group. 2009. "Internet World Stats." www.internet worldstats.com/emarketing.htm (accessed November 29, 2009).

NCES National Center for Education Statistics. 2006. "Internet Access in U.S. Public Schools and Classrooms: 1994–2005." www.nces.ed.gov/ pubs2007/2007020.pdf (accessed November 29, 2009).

Rainie, Lee. 2009. "Teens and the Internet." Pew Internet and American Life Project, January 9. www.pewinternet.org/Presentations/2009/Teens-and -the-internet.aspx (accessed November 29, 2009).

Riedling, Ann Marlow. 2001. "In Search of Who We Are: The School Library Media Specialist in the 21st Century. *Book Report* 20 (3): 28–32.

Washtenaw Intermediate School District. 2009. "Facing Michigan's School Funding Crisis." www.wash.k12.mi.us/movies/misfc3/ (accessed November 28, 2009).

PART III

Grants

7

GRANT PROPOSALS FOR THE WORKING LIBRARIAN

From Idea to Implementation

Lois Stickell and Lisa Nickel

THE RECENT ECONOMIC downturn has affected businesses and organizations in every sector of the economy. Libraries have been hit particularly hard, with budgets slashed, positions eliminated, and hours cut. Fortunately, all the news is not grim. Grants offer a way to help libraries get needed funds to enhance services or collections in a time when libraries are being asked to do more with less. In this chapter we discuss the grant-writing process, from identification of grants to the final reporting, and present our own successful grant proposal as a case study.

IDENTIFYING GRANTS

Patrons often ask librarians for help in identifying grants for funding. Although librarians regularly refer patrons to grant sources, few librarians have gone through the grant process themselves. This is unfortunate since grants specifically for libraries are available. There are two main ways to approach the process. One is to have a good idea what project you need funding to implement and then search for a grant that meets that need. The second is to find available grants and then determine whether your library meets any of their stated goals. Either one can be effective in getting you to a list of possible grantors. "Getting grant money is a matter of matching library needs with the grant focus. The closer the match, the better the chance of receiving money. So the library must look at the library's users' needs relative to the potential funder's goals" (Farmer 1993, 110).

Although grant information is free and easily accessible, a few key strategies can help you organize your search. Be methodical. Pay attention to grant announcements and deadlines. Make a list of potential grant ideas so you are ready if the opportunity presents itself. Use the resources available on the grant websites by creating an RSS feed of websites that announce grants so that you will be the first to know when they are available. If your institution subscribes to grant sourcing databases (e.g., Community of Science), set up an alert so that you are notified when a grant that matches your search is posted.

GRANT SOURCES

Grants.gov: www.grants.gov

Institute of Museum and Library
    Services: www.imls.gov

Community of Science: www.cos.com

In our particular case, we were already aware of the North Carolina State Library's grant cycles and announcements because we had looked at the list of available grants during the previous year. At that time we did not believe we had a strong enough argument for need. In addition, we could not meet the deadline. However, when the grant cycle was announced again, we were ready to apply with a clearly articulated argument and plenty of time to get our application together. *Hint:* If you are going to have to rush to apply for a grant, consider giving it a pass. The process is competitive enough that you don't want your application to appear to have been done in a last-minute rush.

WRITING A SUCCESSFUL GRANT

Writing a successful grant is basically making a good argument for your need. Although there is quite a bit of grant money available to libraries, grant-funding agencies can be particular in deciding where to award money. Making a strong argument for why your library needs funding is important. Statistics are key because they back up your claims with numbers. The grant-awarding agency is more likely to be swayed by the specifics of statistics than by a vague "a lot of patrons would use this." In our case, we used university enrollment growth numbers as well as local and regional census data to strengthen our request for grant money. We also used facts about the number of students enrolled in the respiratory therapy program for which we were awarded the grant.

Funding agencies like to support "winners," so it is to your advantage to showcase your library's successes and plans, not simply point out your lack of money. Put your grant request in a positive light, explaining how the money would help your library be more successful in doing what it already does well. Be specific. How will your project help your library be more successful? How will it meet the goals of the grant agency?

START SMALL

Look for local grant opportunities in your town or on your campus. Many colleges and universities offer personal grants for research or travel, and municipalities often offer small local grants to agencies. Going through the grant-writing process the first time, even if it is for a relatively small grant, prepares you for the organizational steps you will need to follow to obtain larger grants in the future. "Getting one's feet wet, with even a relatively small form of support, is a good way to get the experience needed to begin to hone your skills and develop a successful track record" (Herther 2009, 26). Funding agencies look for a successful track record, and having one grant under your belt can help you get larger grants in the future. "Receiving a grant opens doors. Receiving a grant implies confidence, a good track record, legitimacy—which leads to getting other grants. Successful grantees receive positive publicity for the library and are also more apt to get additional grants" (Farmer 1993, 109).

On a more personal note, receiving a grant feels a little like winning the lottery. It's exciting and morale boosting to receive a letter or phone call announcing that your grant proposal was selected for funding. Your library administration will be pleased as well.

ASK FOR HELP

Some grant agencies make available copies of successful grant applications as guidelines for applicants. These can be helpful. In addition, ask colleagues to share their successful grant applications with you to gain insight into what grant agencies are looking for. We were lucky enough to have colleagues at a local community college who had won the same grant the previous year. They were eager to share their experience and offer suggestions. The final product of our applications was very different, but the opportunity to look over their application helped us tremendously.

We were fortunate enough to know someone who had applied for a grant similar to ours. If you are not in that position, still consider contacting previous recipients of a grant and ask if they would be willing to give you some tips or answer specific questions.

CASE STUDY

In 2008 the University of North Carolina, Charlotte campus, was preparing to offer a new program within the College of Health and Human Services in respiratory therapy. The problem was that the university library, Atkins Library, had very few books to support this program, and the economy made it impossible to purchase the necessary books. Lisa Nickel, the library liaison to the College of Health and Human Services, and Lois Stickell, chair of the liaison advisory team, decided to seek a grant for books in respiratory therapy. The funds purchased much-needed research materials for the new program, getting it off to a strong start. It also allowed us to collaborate with another department on campus, thus strengthening our relationships with that department.

CHECKLIST

Is there a strong need for something—a program, service, or collection—that your library cannot provide without help?

Can you quickly identify a grant that will help pay for this program, service, or collection?

Do you have support from your library administration?

Do you have the time to devote to writing a grant proposal and to tracking the grant's progress if you receive it? (*Hint:* Budget 10 percent of your work time for the grant at the beginning and end of the grant.)

Can you partner with someone in your library who can help share the responsibility and time needed for the grant?

Are you enthusiastic about this project? If the answer is no, don't do it.

If you decide to submit a proposal, fill out the forms honestly and completely.

If you are awarded the grant, congratulations! If you are not awarded the grant, remember—they can be competitive, so try again.

Our Grant

The grant we applied for and received was from the Institute of Museum and Library Services (IMLS), a federal grant-making agency that supports museums and libraries of all types. The agency maintains a search feature on its website that allows libraries to search for grants suitable to their particular institution and situation. Our grant, the "EZ Strengthening Public and Academic Library Collections" grant, was administered through the North Carolina State Library. The award amount for this grant was $10,000 and required a $2,500 match from our library. Guidelines for the grant stated that the money could be used only for the purchase of books—no serials or electronic resources, and no salaries. We could, however, pay for shipping, taxes, and processing with the funds.

Strategy

Once we determined that the respiratory therapy collection was seriously deficient, we did a quick scan of books in WorldCat and consulted several book vendors on prices. This allowed us to estimate how many books we could reasonably hope to purchase with the funding offered. Our major concern was about the matching funds. Because of the poor economy, library funds were already stretched thin, and we did not know whether the university librarian would be willing or able to provide the matching funds. However, we believed strongly that the library needed the books, so we met with the library director and requested the matching funds. Fortunately, she agreed with us about the necessity for these books and made the match available. If she had not been willing to do so, we could not have proceeded further with the application.

Staying on Track

The EZ Strengthening Public and Academic Library Collections had a definite time line for ordering, submitting receipts and invoices, writing a brief report, and explaining how and when the grant was publicized. Each grant comes with its own set of deadlines. For example, our grant was announced in December, had an application deadline in February with winners announced in June, and final reporting was due the following June. One important lesson we learned was that, although our grants office on campus assisted us with reporting, we were responsible for making certain all deadlines were followed. We recommend going through the time line and putting every event of significance into an online calendar (such as Outlook) or starting a paper calendar with key dates highlighted so that you don't miss any submission or reporting deadline.

Documentation

Applying for and receiving grants is a way to add books, bring in programs and speakers, and improve your library creatively. However, all grants come with stipulations. The money *must* be used as directed by the grant. That means that documentation is critical. Not only must the grant writer keep a careful accounting of funds, he or she must also be able to articulate concisely how the money was spent, if it accomplished the purpose for which it was intended, and if the results merited the expenditure. This statement is not meant to discourage grant seeking but to make potential grant applicants aware of the expectations of the grant provider. In our case, the State Library of North Carolina wanted to know the money it provided was used judiciously and resulted in an improvement in library materials for our patrons. They requested a simple review of the project and provided a form for this review. This made their expectations, our obligation, and the end result clear. Had the goal of providing relevant books for the new degree program been accomplished?

Lessons Learned

One of the lessons we learned is that overseeing a grant can be time consuming. Tracking the money can be particularly challenging if this is not part of your ordinary responsibilities. Frankly, we sometimes struggled to balance the accounts. Setting up a spreadsheet and keeping it updated can make tracking easier. In addition, because there were two of us, we were able to divide the work. If you are considering applying for a grant, you may want to find a coworker who is also interested in working with you on the grant.

GRANTS ARE COMPETITIVE

Because grants are essentially free money, there can be a lot of competition for them. That means that some applications will be rejected. If your grant application is rejected, don't be discouraged. Consider improving your application and trying again. Ways to improve include looking at the winning grants to try to determine what gave them an edge over you. Review your own application or ask a colleague to review it, looking for weaknesses that may have derailed you. Reread the guidelines. Did you meet all of them? If not, how can you improve and retry next year. You may conclude that your particular project was not grant worthy, but you may have another idea that would make a successful grant project.

CONCLUSION

In this chapter we describe our experience with one type of grant, but there are many different types out there that focus on a wide variety of areas in libraries: career enhancement, travel, training, research, technology, digitization, book purchasing—the list goes on and on. We had both been awarded grants for professional travel, again from our state library. Our library had won grants for other projects—for purchasing laptops to outfit the library's instruction classroom, purchasing laptops to circulate for student use, developing and teaching a course on digitization for local teachers, and several more. These examples illustrate the wide variety of opportunities available to libraries and awarded to librarians willing to attempt writing a grant proposal. We encourage you to try.

WORKS CITED

Farmer, Lesley S. J. 1993. *When Your Library Budget Is Almost Zero.* Littleton, CO: Libraries Unlimited.

Herther, N. K. 2009. "21st-Century Fundraising." *Searcher* 17 (8): 24–31.

8

TOOLS FOR GRANT SEARCHING

Victoria Lynn Packard

DURING THIS UNSETTLING time, with funding disappearing from the federal and private sectors, everyone is scrambling for money. We can no longer depend on past sources, and many of those still funding are limiting the amounts they are providing. A new way of looking at funding is to apply to multiple donors instead of a single donor. It takes more time and effort, but it could mean the difference between continuing and discontinuing a program.

In this chapter I discuss how Texas A&M University–Kingsville is providing access to resources and teaching users how to locate funding for the benefit of universities, faculty, individuals, and communities in the South Texas area.

TEXAS A&M UNIVERSITY–KINGSVILLE

Texas A&M University–Kingsville was chartered in 1917 and is the oldest university in South Texas. Many of the current 6,200 students come from South Texas, the remainder from more than thirty-five states and forty-three countries. The school population is 62 percent Hispanic, 27 percent white, 5 percent African American, and 6 percent international.

Texas A&M–Kingsville offers fifty-six bachelor's degrees in fifty-two fields and sixty-one graduate degrees in thirty-nine areas through seven colleges.

Many of these programs are not available at other colleges and universities, such as industrial technology, wildlife sciences, communication science and disorders, and logistics. This is the only university in the United States to offer a master's degree in ranch management.

The Texas A&M University–Kingsville James C. Jernigan Library has been teaching federal government grant research for several years. When we received the opportunity to become a Foundation Center Cooperating Collection for the South Texas region, we were happy to take advantage of the opportunity. We have expanded our outreach to community members to include information on nonprofit donors to the federal and state grant resources with growing results. We are now providing workshops in collaboration with the Office of Research and Sponsored Programs on campus and creating working relationships with nonprofits from other Texas regions.

Each month we offer the two-hour workshop "Getting Started with Foundation Center Databases" as well as Foundation Center specialty workshops and federal and Texas state grant workshops. The workshops include hands-on time so attendees are able to learn how to maneuver around websites. Searchers may repeatedly attend workshops and come to the Jernigan Library to search on their own. There are trained librarians able to help with questions on grant searches.

FOUNDATION CENTER ONLINE COOPERATING COLLECTION

To explain the benefits of nonprofit grants, let's take a tour of the Foundation Center Online Cooperating Collection. To access the Foundation Center you must be in the James C. Jernigan Library using computers in the reference area. This is a Foundation Center requirement to make sure the databases are being used properly to their best advantage by the greatest number of users.

The home page (figure 8.1) provides a FAQ link, search tutorials, guided tours, newsletters, a blog, current headlines about new or changing grants, and RFPs (requests for proposals). A new feature for the Foundation Center is the Power Search, which allows the user to do basic searching of nine databases.

In the Newsletters page (figure 8.2), users can subscribe to newsletters and digests electronically. Subscribers receive e-mail weekly or biweekly. Users are advised to subscribe to only one or two newsletters to learn how much information is sent each week. Otherwise, a mailbox could be overrun with newsletters in a short time.

On the far right of the page are subject-specific newsletters and alerts, which include items for artists, students, health, education, and so forth.

Searching Grantmakers and Companies

If the user knows the exact name of the grantmaker (figure 8.3), she can click on View Index and the company name. The Foundation Center database does not allow for name variances or incorrect spelling, so it is easier to use the index. Searchers can choose to search by state, county, city, metro area, or congressional district. Remember, most grants are accepted and dispensed through the parent company location.

Fields of Interest and Types of Support are two special search categories. There are specific terms used in the databases that may not follow discipline

FIGURE 8.1
FOUNDATION CENTER ONLINE HOME PAGE

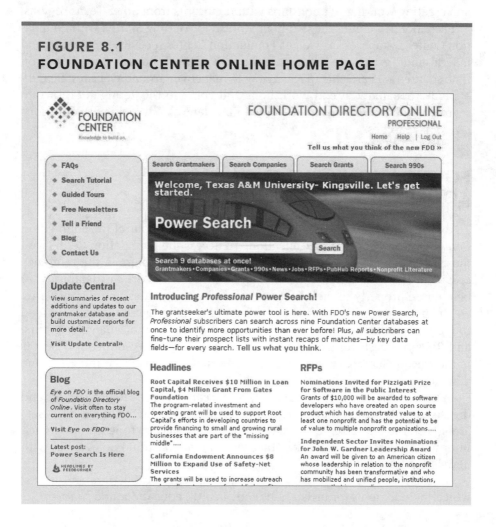

jargon. For example, if a searcher uses "start-up costs" as a search term he will not get results, but if he uses "seed money" there are almost 3,000 results.

Geographic Focus is an interesting search. Users searching by state find grants for their state. Searching by geographic focus broadens the search, such as a company residing in Pennsylvania that donates money in Texas. User searching by state only would not find this Pennsylvania grantmaker.

Another area of great benefit is the statement "Grantmakers not accepting applications" at the bottom of the screen. A searcher should mark the box to exclude these grantmakers from the search. On the other hand, a searcher may want to include these grantmakers whenever there are Donor Parties, New College Openings, and Galas. Grantmakers may remember your group and what you are doing if they have extra monies or are changing their donation lists.

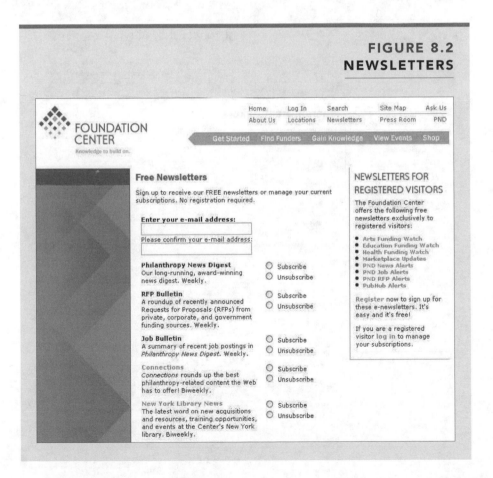

FIGURE 8.2
NEWSLETTERS

Searching Companies is comparable to searching Grantmakers, except here users can search by business type and subsidiary information. This is helpful for searchers who lack complete information about a company (figure 8.4).

Searching Grants and 990s

Grants can be searched by grantmaker name and state, as above, but there are other search capabilities (figure 8.5). For example, someone looking for money to fund a symphony group can search the Recipient Location or Recipi-

FIGURE 8.3
SEARCH GRANTMAKERS

ent Type sections to see if another symphony group in the area is receiving funding.

Another way of searching grants is by congressional district. By typing in a district number, a searcher can see if there are donors not found in regular searches.

The IRS 990 form (figure 8.6) provides a great deal of information about a grantmaker of benefit to searchers. It provides a history of the company's grantmaking, how much that organization gives each year or over several years, and to which sectors it gives money (e.g., education, research). This section also lists how much money the organization has made over a number of years, what percentage of its income is provided for grants, and if it has made changes in its funding policies.

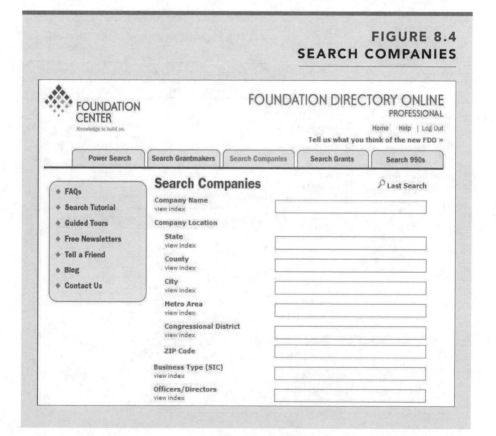

FIGURE 8.4
SEARCH COMPANIES

GRANTS TO INDIVIDUALS

The Grants to Individuals database contains 8,000 to 9,000 donors, compared to the 90,000 donors in the Foundation Directory Online database. The grants in this database (figure 8.7) are for groups such as historical societies and individuals. Individual funding is usually at the graduate level or higher for fellowships and stipends. These grants have specific criteria that must be met. As with the Foundation Online database, there are subscription newsletters and reference guides for individuals and groups. The reference guides include information on proposal writing for individuals, how to start a nonprofit organization, and many other tools and resources.

FIGURE 8.5
SEARCH GRANTS

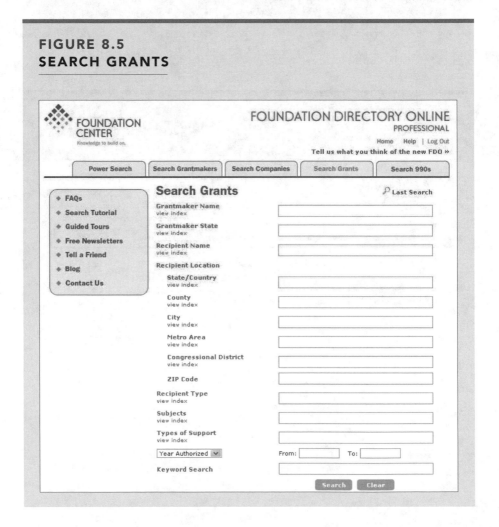

Foundation Grants to Individuals Online (GTIO) can be searched by various ways such as foundation name, state, city, field of interest, types of support, and geographic focus (figure 8.8). When searching the GTIO database, it is important that the search terms be fluid. A searcher would look for "wildlife research support" without success but would find several resources under "animal/wildlife." Some individuals in our classes begin by thinking they will not find anything for themselves, but they are pleasantly surprised. One graduate student was amazed to find funding for a female graduate-level student of Lithuanian descent.

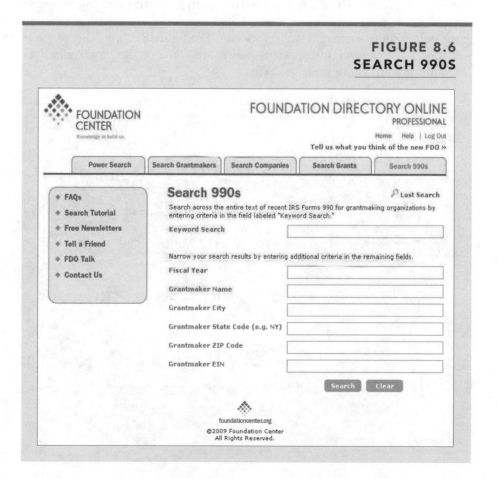

FIGURE 8.6
SEARCH 990S

FOUNDATION CENTER
Knowledge to build on.

FOUNDATION DIRECTORY ONLINE
PROFESSIONAL

Home   Help | Log Out
Tell us what you think of the new FDO »

| Power Search | Search Grantmakers | Search Companies | Search Grants | Search 990s |

◆ FAQs
◆ Search Tutorial
◆ Free Newsletters
◆ Tell a Friend
◆ FDO Talk
◆ Contact Us

Search 990s   🔎 Last Search

Search across the entire text of recent IRS Forms 990 for grantmaking organizations by entering criteria in the field labeled "Keyword Search."

Keyword Search

Narrow your search results by entering additional criteria in the remaining fields.

Fiscal Year

Grantmaker Name

Grantmaker City

Grantmaker State Code (e.g. NY)

Grantmaker ZIP Code

Grantmaker EIN

Search   Clear

foundationcenter.org
©2009 Foundation Center
All Rights Reserved.

BLOGS, RSS FEEDS, AND NONPROFIT PERIODICALS

The *Philanthropy News Digest,* published by the Foundation Center, lists many blogs and RSS feeds. On the Jernigan Library Foundation Center web page (figure 8.9) are listed many of the larger sites that provide another source of information for grant searchers.

The Foundation Center also has a list of nonprofit periodicals available from the main Foundation Center (figure 8.10). It includes annotations for periodicals available through the Jernigan Library databases.

FEDERAL GRANT RESEARCH

The federal government is a rich source of information and funding. You just need to know where to search. Many federal government websites provide grant information, some of it subject specific. See figure 8.11 for a list of grant websites, both general and specific. Below are some of the larger websites with information about their strengths.

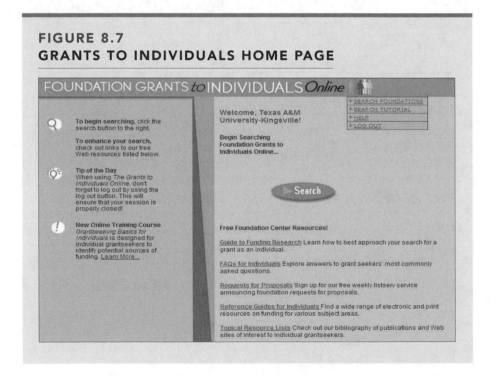

FIGURE 8.7
GRANTS TO INDIVIDUALS HOME PAGE

Grants.gov is a good place to start. It lists many agencies but is not the only place to search for federal funding. It offers general search capabilities. Someone searching by subject-specific jargon may be better off searching individual agencies.

Catalog of Federal Domestic Assistance is one of the largest federal resources—known among some federal documents librarians as the "kitchen sink" resource. This website covers education, health, children, agriculture, business, and much more. In printed format it runs two hundred to three hundred pages. This is a great website to use if you are going back to school or starting a business.

Department of Justice Grants website from the U.S. Department of Justice is not just for legal information. Try this website for developing afterschool or at-risk programs. It is a wonderful resource for statistics.

Environmental Education Grants from the Environmental Protection Agency is good for afterschool programs, wetland protection, and business opportunities.

Institute of Museum and Library Services offers another large website. Do not let the name discourage you. It has funding for many programs for schools, universities, groups, and more.

FIGURE 8.8
SEARCH GRANTS TO INDIVIDUALS

This is just the tip of the iceberg of federal funding and well worth researching.

In teaching federal grant workshops, we find that many people forget about statistics. We cover how to find statistical data in all grant workshops (figure 8.12). It may be adequate if you state that you have a large percentage of a certain ethnic group in your area whose needs would be helped by a certain grant. But you will be more successful by stating, for example, that in your city of 3,000 people, 55 percent are first-generation Italian adults with English-language reading levels of the sixth grade and that this is why you need a literacy program at your public library.

When you are searching for any grant it is important to understand that at nonprofit or federal agencies people are there to make the process easier. Make use of them. Introduce yourself. Ask if you can send your grant application for them to read in advance and provide suggestions. The main idea to remember is that if donors (federal or nonprofit) ask for information (e.g., budget, board members, and statistics), you must supply it to them or be eliminated from consideration.

FIGURE 8.9
BLOGS AND RSS FEEDS

Foundation Center Blog & RSS Feed

Blog URL:
http://literature.foundationcenter.org

RSS Feed for blog:
http://feeds.feedburner.com/nonprofitliterature

Philanthropy Blogs

The GiveWell Blog:	http://blog.givewell.net
Inside Philanthropy	http://philanthropyjournal.blogspot.com
New Voices of Philanthropy	http://www.newvoicesofphilanthropy.org
Nonprofit Literature Blog	http://ocnl-librarian.blogspot.com
The Nonprofiteer	http://nonprofiteer.typepad.com/the_nonprofiteer
Perspectives from the Pipeline	http://fromthepipeline.blogspot.com
PhilanthroMedia	http://www.philanthromedia.org
Philanthropy 2173	http://philanthropy.blogspot.com
PhilanTopic	http://pndblog.typepad.com/pndblog
Social Edge	http://www.socialedge.org/blogs
Stanford Social Innovation Review Opinion Blog	http://www.ssireview.org/opinion

COLLABORATION

As a result of our success in grant research, in the past year Jernigan Library has been collaborating with the Office of Research and Sponsored Programs (ORSP) and hosting many joint presentations. During these presentations the ORSP demonstrates how faculty and staff can access the Sponsored Program Information Network (SPIN) to search for funding resources. The Jernigan Library demonstrates both of the Foundation Center databases, federal grant resources, and statistical research. These presentations include hands-on opportunities for attendees.

OUTREACH

We have created working relationships with the Texas A&M University–Kingsville faculty and staff through workshops using the Foundation Center databases and federal grant workshops. On the community level we have had members from the Kingsville Symphony, the Ricardo Beautification

---

FIGURE 8.10
NONPROFIT PERIODICALS

FOUNDATION CENTER
Knowledge to build on.

Non-Profit Periodicals

The following titles are reviewed by the bibliographic services staff of the Center for articles in the field of philanthropy, and represent a majority of the periodical articles cited in the Catalog of Nonprofit Literature.

Across the Board. Conference Board, Inc., 845 Third Avenue, New York, NY 10022. 10/yr. (212) 339-0345.

Advancing Philanthropy. Association of Fundraising Professionals, 4300 Wilson Boulevard, Suite 300, Arlington, VA 22203. Bimonthly. (703) 684-0410; Fax: (703) 684-0540.

AFP News and Professional Postings. Association of Fundraising Professionals, 4300 Wilson Boulevard, Suite 300, Arlington, VA 22203. Bimonthly. (703) 684-0410; Fax: (703) 684 -0540. (Last issue April 2002.)

AIP Charity Rating Guide & Watchdog Report. American Institute of Philanthropy, 3450 N. Lake Shore Drive, Suite 2802 E., P.O. Box 578460, Chicago, IL 60657. (773) 529-2300.

Alliance. 25 Corsham Street, 1st Floor, London N1 6DR, UK. Quarterly.

American Libraries. American Library Association, 50 E. Huron Street, Chicago, IL 60611. Monthly. (800) 545-2433, ext. 4216; Fax: (312) 440-0901.

Association, and the Kingsville Beautification Association, to list a few groups that attend the workshops. We are currently developing a relationship with the Texas A&M University–San Antonio campus.

GENERAL INFORMATION AND SEARCH TIPS

Be versatile in your searching—think of multiple terms.

Search frequently. Searching once is not enough—especially now. Donors come and go.

Just because there are layoffs now does not mean the funding is not already in place for this year. For example, Ford has had massive layoffs, but grant money from Ford was budgeted and available for 2009.

Introduce yourself to the grantmakers.

Search their website and learn what they do and support.

FIGURE 8.11
RESOURCES FOR GRANT WRITING

Texas A&M University-Kingsville

James C. Jernigan Library

■ Library Home ■ TAMUK Home ■ About Foundation Center ■ Foundation Center Databases
■ Foundation Center Paper Resources ■ Link to Other Internet Grant Resources
■ Foundation Center Reference Guides ■ Non-profit Periodicals ■ Philanthropy Blogs and RSS Feeds

Specialty Grants

Grant Writing Resources

Apply for a Grant	http://www.neh.gov/grants/
Catalog of Federal Domestic Assistance	http://www.cfda.gov
DOJ: Grants Dept. of Justice	http://www.usdoj.gov/10grants/
Environmental Education Grants	http://www.epa.gov/enviroed/grants.html
EPA Business Opportunities: Grants	http://www.epa.gov/epahome/grants.htm
Grants & Contracts - ED.gov	http://www.ed.gov/fund/landing.jhtml?src=rt
Grants.gov	http://www.grants.gov/
Grants Management	http://www.whitehouse.gov/omb/grants/
GrantsNet	http://www.hhs.gov/grantsnet/

Nothing makes a donor angrier than
  misspelling
  missed deadlines
  giving more information than they ask for
  not giving the information they request
  not using *their* forms
  incomplete budgets
  sending blind applications when they do not accept them

You can always ask for help from
  the Foundation Center
  the grants department of your university
  professional grant writers
  books and newsletters
  federal grant agencies
  the grantmakers themselves

When in doubt, *ask someone*. You do not want to miss out on a grant
  because you did not want to "bother" someone.

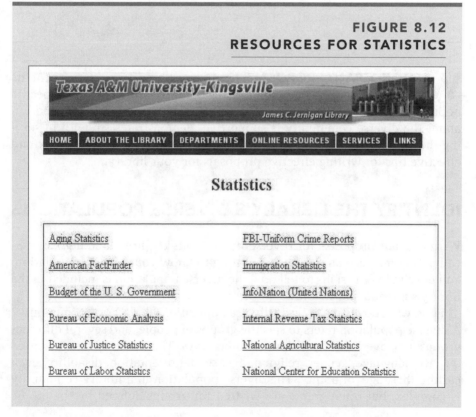

FIGURE 8.12
RESOURCES FOR STATISTICS

9

WRITING GRANT PROPOSALS FOR DIVERSE POPULATIONS

Vandella Brown

WRITING GRANT PROPOSALS for diverse library populations benefits the whole library community. Writing a proposal to target a specific population does not have to be complex or frustrating when information about the diverse community is supportive, demonstrates strength in serving the group, and has sustaining results. This chapter offers some easy and effective tips for writing effective proposals for your library.

IDENTIFY THE LIBRARY'S DIVERSE POPULATIONS

Writing grant proposals for diverse populations requires thinking strategically. That means planning ahead, getting to know your diverse population, and developing the skills to tell how the diverse population is included in the library's mission and vision.

First, what do we mean by a "diverse population" in a library community? A diverse population refers to specific groups of people, and several different groups may overlap in varied and similar ways. The diversity may be based on race, language, gender, religion, age, sexual orientation, disability, even culture, heritage, or ability. The diverse population in a library community is complex, but often grants are written for groups defined by the ethnic diversity—Africans, Asians, Hispanics, Native Americans, and Eastern Europeans, to name a few examples. Another diverse group is often based on age, focusing on seniors, teenagers, or parents/children.

Defining and describing the diverse population is an important point in making a case for a grant that will serve a targeted population. The U.S. Census's demographic data can be supportive as you attempt to identify diverse populations. Go directly to www.census.gov, click on American FactFinder, type in your town or zip code, and you will obtain a great deal of information about your community. There are also several other Internet sites that provide demographic data for cities and communities. Spend some time getting acquainted with that data.

GET TO KNOW THE DIVERSE POPULATION

The library staff spend a lot of time making sure routine users' resources and services are available. The staff know what regular users want and need, often without asking. That's because a community of knowledge has developed over time.

A similar environment has to be developed and communicated from the diverse population. The library, after defining its diverse population, needs to get acquainted with the diverse organizations, churches, social clubs, volunteers, patrons, and diverse businesses in the library's community. Learn where the library's diverse population lives and congregates, what they read, and what radio and television stations they follow. Organize a library advisory

GETTING ACQUAINTED QUESTIONS

Conduct a survey to ask about services, collections, and programs. Ask questions and get answers and ideas for grant writing:

- What problems does the community have?
- Who are the trusted people and local leaders?
- Where do the people go for information, social services, and advice?
- Where do they look for jobs? Where do they work?
- What skills are needed? What would they like to learn?
- Where and what are the programs and events they attend?

group to involve the diverse population. All these things will make it easy to write about the population and to establish a real knowledge to enhance trust between the library and the population.

At its core, writing a diversity grant proposal is not just about low economic levels, race, or minority identity. For libraries, a proposal should be based on a need or service that will inform and enrich the lives of the diverse participants. A grant proposal that uses demographic facts builds a visual description for the granting agency and makes a strong case for funding.

SELECTING APPROPRIATE GRANTS

Once the library has defined and identified its diverse population and a targeted group for a grant, the next step is to look at appropriate grant offerings. It doesn't make sense to apply for every grant when some possibilities are stronger than others. Make it easy. First, search out grant offerings from organizations that have awarded funding to diverse populations similar to yours or for a project like yours. Search for grants that appeal directly to the library's population and others that may not identify a specific group but will extend an existing project. If you are serious enough about a grant application, telephone the grant administrator's office or e-mail to express your idea before writing it. Consider whether the library is eligible. Is the grant open to the diversity project you have in mind? How many branches of the library can apply? Can awarded funds be used for food? Is there a population/income quota or a membership requirement? Everything may not be detailed in the grant description. A conversation with agency staff may provide the clarity needed.

> ### COMPILE A REPORT
>
> Use the census statistics and the information about the diverse community to compile a report that describes demographic data, five to ten organizations or individuals from the diverse population, their contact information, and a list of things the diverse population needs, wants, or deserves.

Get to know something about the granting organization before you apply. Who are the founders? Is it a stimulus project? Is the organization an online entity only? Where does the funding come from? Read the application carefully and outline how you plan to follow the guidelines.

Getting to know your diverse population, the funding organization, and the application will help you select the appropriate grant for the library's diverse population.

WRITING THE GRANT INTRODUCTION

The proposal's introduction focuses on the diverse population and the library's mission and vision of their needs. In the introduction, sell the library's awards, noteworthy programming, qualifications, and services. Even use the library's location if it is supportive in serving the participants' needs. The introduction should reflect the pride the library takes in serving the targeted group. Carefully plan sentences that focus on the importance and values of the diverse population and the unique opportunity the library can perform if the award is granted.

In the introductory statement use the census data blended with a human interest story obtained from patrons or the advisory committee. Demonstrate partnerships with the diverse population by taking a reference from the diversity contact list. Write the proposal in third person ("he/she," "it," "they"), not first person (don't use "we," "us," or "our"). Limit the use of abbreviations—spell out everything. Explain so that the grant reader will know exactly what you are talking about. In other words, don't assume that the funding organization knows about your library or diverse population. Be concise. Use well-structured sentences to detail the scope of the project and close the introductory statement with the expense of the project.

STATING THE PROBLEM

The grant problem statement is used to describe the population, the situation, or dilemma and its solution or resolution. Use the problem statement to lay out the problem, to tell why it exists and what the solution is. Describe how the proposed project will solve the problem.

Many grant application forms posted on the Internet provide little space for introductions and ask the applicant to get to the root of the problem. In designing the problem statement, use comparative and compelling statements. Discuss the uniqueness of the population, use demographic facts to prove key points, and make reference to a newspaper article about the population or the problem. Also refer to individuals who know about the problem. It is invaluable to involve diverse individuals or organizations who can contribute to as well as benefit from the grant.

WRITING A CLEAR PROJECT DESCRIPTION

The project description statement explains the importance of the library roles, partnerships, and the funding organization's assistance in executing the project. Besides giving the project a neat name, make sure the project description provides discrete details of the new product or improved service. Be specific about the persons who will be involved from the diverse population and what the project will provide—speakers, training, equipment, and so forth. Grantees like to see that the library has developed a working relationship with its diverse population. The project description is the place to show that and to justify the budget and objectives. Describe how the project will benefit the targeted group and be an outstanding example for the funding organization. After writing the description, use numbers to highlight what the project will produce.

POWER POINT OBJECTIVES

The diversity grant is driven by objectives—activities that make the project proactive. Objectives tell what will happen. Objectives show solutions to the stated problem. Use as many objectives as you need to describe how the project will meet its goal. In specific statements, write what will happen, giving dates and directing the activities of speakers and targeted participants. Summarize the objectives using bullet points to list the benefits expected for the diverse population.

HIGHLIGHT METHODS

The diversity grant project should measure what will be sustaining after the grant project is over. The methods statement tells how the project will get done. Make it realistic and achievable. It is a description of all the project elements—an action plan, a dateline, and individuals' activities and roles. Tell who the diverse partners are and what or how they will contribute. Describe the job duties of the staff and their qualifications. Justify why professionals, technology, or specialists are needed. It often works well to present this information in table form. A column table may be used if a specific format is not provided in the application.

DESIGN EVALUATION OUTCOMES

The evaluation outcomes statement describes what data the library will collect to evaluate the diversity project. There are many useful tools for evaluating projects: collecting library records, using trained evaluators, interviews, targeted individuals, reports, mechanical measurements, pre/posttesting, group

THE METHODS TABLE

The column headings for a table of methods might include the following:

Time line   Explaining activities by day or month

People   Describing jobs, expertise, and responsibilities

Program   Describing events, activities, and educational value

comparison, online surveys, and questionnaires. Select methods that will help you tell how successful the project will be.

TELL WHY A BUDGET IS NEEDED

The written budget statement must be convincing and realistic in explaining why the funds are needed. State the total budget cost up front. Explain the budget plan by describing all expenses, such as salaries, contracts, equipment, supplies, in short paragraphs. Reassure the donor that all funds will be used solely for the diversity project. Don't forget to check the math twice. End the budget statement by telling the grantor how the money will enhance the services to the diverse population.

SUMMARY AND SUPPORT DOCUMENTS

The summary statement reminds the donor why your library is best qualified to carry out the project and convinces them that your library can do it. Mention other successful grants, programs, or projects that demonstrate the library's leadership with the diverse population. Highlight new challenges and how this grant offers solutions. In closing, thank the grantee for considering the proposal.

COVER LETTER

You may want to write the cover letter last—after you have written the grant application and know what is included there. Use your library's letterhead and a formal letter format, and don't forget your signature. Address your cover letter to the funding organization or the coordinator, acknowledging the library's opportunity to submit a proposal. Give an overview of the diverse population and how this project pro-posal will make a difference.

The cover letter should summarize the list items enclosed according to the grant's guidelines. Many diversity grants do not want additional infor-mation such as photos, appendixes, or more letters of recommendation than the number requested. So don't add them. Use attachments if there is a reference to them in the body of your application and if they enhance understanding.

In the closing statement, provide your (project director) name, e-mail address, and phone number in case more information is needed.

> **A SECOND PAIR OF EYES**
>
> After you have drafted all sections of the grant proposal, ask someone familiar with the diversity community and the library to review it and make suggestions.

CONCLUSION

Libraries that serve diverse racial and ethnic heritages and new immigrants are libraries with much to offer and to receive. There are numerous grants for diverse populations, and learning to apply for them successfully can be easy with planning.

PART IV

Programming

10

CREATING AND SUSTAINING COMMUNITY-FOCUSED PROGRAMS

Wayne Finley and Joanna Kluever

FROM FY 2008/9 to FY 2009/10, the Julia Hull District Library (JHDL) of Stillman Valley, Illinois (pop. 7,900), has experienced an increasingly common juxtaposition for public libraries: growth in patronage and decline in funding. Although various economic threats have challenged the library, they have also inspired library staff to utilize the current recession as an opportunity. Staff have collaborated to create unique, community-focused programming and have marketed these programs for little to no cost. The result has been the library's transition from a traditional library into a community center with continued increases in overall attendance, new user registration, and circulation.

IDENTIFY THE NEEDS OF YOUR COMMUNITY

To create successful programming, it is important to first identify the needs of the library community. This is especially true in economically challenging times, since libraries like JHDL may find themselves cutting costs in nonessential areas like programming before they make cuts to necessities like operations, materials, or staff. Thus, libraries must make the most efficient and effective use of their dollars.

JHDL began assessing its community's needs by examining some general demographics in response to the following questions:

What is the current population of the library district?

What percentage are library cardholders?

Of current library cardholders, what percentage are children, young adults, adults and senior citizens; what percentage are men and women?

What are some of the socioeconomic factors of the community?

What types of library programs has the library run in the past and how well have they been attended?

What types of materials or genres circulate most to library patrons?

CREATE COMMUNITY-CENTERED PROGRAMS ——

It was only after gathering demographic information about its patronage that JHDL was able to focus on its community's *needs*. In assessing its past

GATHERING INFORMATION

In many cases the demographic information needed to determine community needs has already been collected and is readily available. Utilize the following resources to better understand your community's demographics:

Automation system. To find information on your library's current cardholders, use your automated circulation system to run user statistics. Most current systems have features that enable libraries to seek and sort such information. If you are uncertain how to use this feature, contact your system vendor or the technical department at your library consortium.

School district. Public school districts annually report statistical data about their student body, including social makeup, literacy scores, and how many students qualify for free or reduced lunch. Check your community school district's website for this information or contact the local superintendent of schools.

Census. Libraries can utilize U.S. Census information, though it is not updated annually, to determine socioeconomic factors and population information within their community.

programs, JHDL staff learned that library patrons tended to utilize two primary types of library programs: those that taught specific skills and those that provided opportunities for leisure. More specifically, the library previously had high attendance for instructional programs in the areas of computer and technology training, home and gardening, and health sciences as well as more leisurely activities such as arts/crafts, reading groups, and family experiences. Understanding such information enabled JHDL to provide community-focused programming without risking funds on projects patrons had little interest in.

It was, however, equally important that while assessing the *needs* of the community the library simultaneously assessed the *strengths* of its staff, resources, and facilities. The JHDL director knew that to provide good programming at a low cost the library would have to meet most of its programming needs internally.

Use Library Staff to Create Programs

No matter how large or small a library, its staff is certain to include individuals with an array of experiences, education, and talents. At JHDL, one employee had work experience in web page design and blogging, though the library had never offered instructional courses in either of these areas because it presumably was not equipped to do so. Uncovering staff talents thus provided new opportunities for library programming that met identified community needs, saved the library financial resources, and provided staff with opportunities for job growth.

Matching community needs to staff talents was the easy part. In this case, the library was able to provide the community technology skills training (e.g., web design) that could benefit many aspects of patrons' lives. At the same time, offering programs that utilized staff strengths proved economically advantageous to the library.

Another example: To meet the leisure needs and expressed interest of the community, the library wanted to provide yoga instruction. However, hiring an outside instructor would cost the library an estimated $10–$12 per student per hour, plus travel expenses. Further, because of these costs, the library would be able to offer the class only on a onetime basis. Fortunately, the library director had years of yoga experience, so the library could offer yoga instruction for no extra cost to the library or to patrons, and the program could be offered continuously.

Solicit Help from the Community

No matter how talented a library's staff are, they will likely never be able to address all patron needs entirely on their own. Similarly, though some staff may have a talent in a particular area, they may be uncomfortable leading a program individually. Thus, in the interest of saving money, it is essential to solicit volunteer help from the community.

Most solicitation from JHDL comes from the simple idea of relationship building. Library staff use working relationships with patrons, friends, and neighbors who are willing and able to assist with programming. One example of relationship building at JHDL involves a reliable patron who is also a retired science teacher and avid master gardener. After determining a community interest in home and gardening programming, staff approached this particular patron about offering gardening courses uniquely designed to meet the needs of the community. He acknowledged an interest, and as a result the library has developed an ongoing relationship with him. He now provides free plant and gardening instruction year-round.

In areas such as health, it is important that libraries offer authoritative information (e.g., from nurses, doctors, dieticians, psychologists). Still, these specialists need not cost the library. In fact, many hospitals and county health departments offer free community outreach programs.

PROMOTE EXTERNALLY AND INTERNALLY

Once a library has called on the talents of its staff and the members of the community to create and implement effective programming for its patrons, the next and equally critical step is to promote the events. With limited funds, library staff may believe this to be a difficult task. Further, staff may assume that only the most expensive marketing media are effective. Actually, though, focusing on certain elements of the promotional mix can make promoting library events simple, cheap, and effective.

Traditionally, the promotional mix comprises these four activities: advertising, personal selling, publicity, and sales promotions. In the case of JHDL, library staff focused on publicity and personal selling combined with limited sales promotions.

External Promotions

Newspapers. Every library should take advantage of its local newspapers as a free source of publicity. Often, local newspapers dedicate print space to promote events of local schools and nonprofit organizations. Each week, JHDL submits an article to the area's newspapers highlighting the library's upcoming events. The events are described in detail, and often a photograph highlighting one of the previous week's events is displayed.

APPLYING THE PROMOTIONAL MIX

Consider the following components of the promotional mix and how they relate to public libraries (from Sandhusen 2008, 479–480):

Publicity. Free, nonpersonal communication about products and services in print or online. *Library applications:* publishing newspaper articles, press releases, editorials, and so on.

Personal selling. In-person sales presentations given to customers. *Library applications:* informing patrons of programming at the circulation desk; giving presentations to local organizations.

Sales promotions. Incentives for customers that stimulate sales. *Library applications:* offering prize drawings for program attendance; giving a new patron a welcome packet.

Advertising. Paid communications used to promote a product or service. *Library applications:* buying space in a local newspaper or phone directory.

Be aware that your library may be competing with other libraries for attention in the newspaper. With limited space and standard fonts, there is little room for visual creativity. Rather, a library's programming must be set apart through descriptive language. Avoid simply listing program names along with times and dates. Instead, grab readers' attention and sell programs by telling them why they should be excited about the events. For library events that require greater detail, submit a letter to the editor or a press release.

Community collaboration. Soliciting help from community members is not limited to creating library programming. The same people that help create the programming can also promote it. For example, for the past three summers, a local elementary teacher has coordinated the JHDL summer reading program. In 2009 the library used this connection with the public school district to distribute promotional summer reading packets to students at all district elementary schools. As a result, summer reading attendance increased, and new events were thus added to accommodate the influx of registrants.

Promotional materials. JHDL also requested support from local organizations to help fund promotional materials. Through the generous donations of local banks, stores, and city government, the library is able to provide reusable gift bags and other promotional materials that rally community enthusiasm for library activities.

Asking for community support to help promote programs and fund or provide promotional materials works the same way as asking for volunteers to provide programming. Rather than randomly soliciting businesses for contributions, library staff should utilize their relationships within the community. Asking individuals, groups, and organizations with which they have already developed relationships can make the process easier.

Internal Promotion: Personal Selling

One of the most cost-effective, albeit intimidating, aspects of a library's promotional mix is personal selling. It may seem out of place to talk about selling in a library setting, where materials and programming are provided for free. However, when convincing patrons to take advantage of library materials and services, library staff at times function as sales staff, with the circulation desk as the point of sale.

Knowing that there was little money for paid advertising, the JHDL staff began focusing on promoting program attendance by informing patrons at the circulation desk. Before beginning to use sales tactics in practice, the staff attended a workshop on the application of personal selling in a library. To follow up, the library director incorporated role-playing practice into library staff meetings.

Once library staff were comfortable with the idea of personal selling, they were encouraged to use it in their daily interactions with patrons. A specific emphasis was placed on "up-selling" and "cross-selling." In commercial sales, *up-selling* means convincing a customer to buy more of the same type of item, or an item of greater value, such as a car dealer convincing a customer to buy more than one car or upgrade from a standard model to a luxury edition. Similarly, a sales person is *cross-selling* when she convinces a customer to buy different items, such as when a car dealer sells a customer an extended warranty in addition to the car itself (Kamakura 2008, 42). JHDL staff were encouraged to up-sell by informing patrons registered for one program to register for a similar program. Likewise, staff practiced cross-selling by encouraging patrons checking out materials to sign up for programs they were unfamiliar with or unconvinced they had an interest in attending.

At first, some of the library staff were uncomfortable with the process. For encouragement, a friendly competition was implemented to see who could sign up the most patrons. (A small gift certificate and personal pride were the incentives for winning.) Soon, library staff felt more comfortable with the process; as a result, personal selling has become commonplace—educating patrons about opportunities for learning and leisure and increasing program attendance.

CONCLUSION

Assessing a program's success can be as easy as counting numbers. For example, JHDL staff maintain a daily log of how many patrons attend each program offered. And the results are telling: since its commitment to creating community-centered programming and low-cost marketing, the library has shown a dramatic increase in program attendance (up 183 percent from FY 2007/8 to FY 2008/9). But it is equally important to examine the whole picture. As a result of its programmatic boost, the library has also experienced boosts in general attendance, circulation, and user registration.

These figures demonstrate the power of programming in public libraries—how offering community-focused programs can, in fact, improve a library's overall success. Perhaps most important, by following the process of assessing community needs, developing programming from these needs, and implementing low-cost program promotions, libraries can develop and sustain their roles as community centers, even in an economic recession.

WORKS CITED

Kamakura, Wagner A. 2008. "Cross-Selling: Offering the Right Product to the Right Customer at the Right Time." *Journal of Relationship Marketing* 6 (3/4): 41–58.

Sandhusen, Richard L. 2008. *Marketing.* Hauppauge, NY: Barron's Educational Series.

11

NOTHING TO LOSE
Creative Programming for the Frugal Librarian

Lisa A. Forrest

AS ACADEMIC LIBRARIES continue to transform from "the building with all the books" into lively spaces for engaged learners, it is imperative that librarians enact the learning mission of their institution. But how can librarians inspire a lifelong passion for learning and extend their influence past the limitations of "one-shot" instruction classes and the reference desk? Literary clubs, booktalks, and workshop series can allow librarians to go beyond simply providing access to information; dynamic programming such as this can support the professional growth, intellectual exchange, and cultural enrichment of the entire community.

But in today's financially strapped times, librarians can be too quick to dismiss innovative programming ideas in their libraries. Contrary to the assumptions of campus administration, many innovative programs can be initiated and run with little or no expense. At E. H. Butler Library (Buffalo State College, State University of New York), creative programming such as the Rooftop Poetry Club, the Rooftop Reading Club, and the "Green Talk" workshop series successfully utilize the talent and resources already present within the community. And, equally important, they serve to strengthen partnerships across campus and to create new roles for librarians along the way.

Obviously, these sorts of programs are great for all involved, but how do we get from here to there?

- Well, it's easy to arrange readings and events when you want to be involved yourself. What are current topics that you would like to learn more about?
- What events are already happening on campus? (It helps to follow the campus news and events calendar.)
- What are folks talking about in your community?
- What are the student organizations doing on campus?

You don't have to be "the expert" to lead a program or club; you just need to be motivated. Start with a genuine curiosity on the subject and then do what you do best—gathering and presenting relevant materials. Contact university and local authorities on the subject, check out books from your own library, and then take the time to explore and learn from these freely available resources. Most of the time, local organizations are looking for venues to get the word out about their mission and will jump at the opportunity to present to an interested audience. For example, our "Green Team" has hosted talks by local experts on earth-friendly cleaning (leading to the making of cleaning solutions to use in the library), city gardening, campus recycling, and reusing old building materials. Our Rooftop Poetry Club features readings by local poets, workshops run by students and faculty, and community poetry/art projects (past projects have used discarded library materials such as card catalog cards, outdated topographical maps, and unwanted LP record albums). Interested in getting similar ideas off the ground? While you're at it, keep in mind some of the following points to help you along.

YOU ARE MORE THAN A GUIDING LIGHT

Librarians are experts at *guiding* patrons to high-quality information, but our role too often ends at this stage. When librarians create programs that incorporate library resources, new life is given to underused collections and to the library itself. Librarians become more than vessels through which patrons simply obtain information; they become educators who actively transform information into meaningful knowledge. An added bonus of this is that patrons get to know *you* as more than just the person sitting behind the desk. Leading programs can foster valuable relationships (some long lasting) and carry out the library's mission far beyond the confines of the reference desk.

MINE YOUR RESOURCES

The first thing we did when starting the "Green Talk" series was to create an online subject guide on environmental topics. The Rooftop Poetry Club's website features all sorts of links to useful resources about poetry. Don't stop with physical resources—who are the local experts in your library, on your campus, and in your community? Contact these people and draw on their expertise. Very often, folks are more than willing to talk to others about their special interests or skills (and will often volunteer to do so for the library). We have had a variety of grassroots organization leaders as featured speakers for our "Green Talk" series. Many faculty members volunteer to read their poetry or lead workshops for the Rooftop Poetry Club.

RECYCLE AND REUSE

When mining your physical resources, remember to make optimal use of recyclable materials for various projects and displays. For example, the Rooftop Poetry Club utilized outdated topographical maps for a community poetry project and discarded book jackets for a journal-making workshop. The library's Green Team has used shredded paper, unwanted CDs, and other discarded library materials for earth conservation displays. In honor of Earth Day, the team encouraged staff and students to contribute to the "Paper Doesn't Grow on Trees" display located in the library lobby. The paper collected in the display was reused to create scratch pads for students. While contributing to the display, students were encouraged to write down (on discarded catalog cards) a "green resolution" (such as "I promise to use a reusable water bottle" or "I promise to shut down my computer when I leave the house") and decorate the tree branches with "green promises." To complement this display, the Rooftop Poetry Club wrote "Poems to the Earth," which were exhibited alongside vintage curriculum posters from our curriculum lab collection.

RETHINK SPACE

When deciding on meeting places for workshops and other events, consider the underutilized spaces within your library (especially the out-of-sight/out-of-mind spaces near the stacks). For the Rooftop Poetry Club and our "Green Talk" workshop series, that means meeting on the rooftop of the library during warm-weather months. During colder months (we do live in Buffalo!) the poetry club hides away on the third floor of the library, concealed near the literature stacks. You don't need a lot of space to set up a few chairs and a podium. Meeting outside of the traditional conference room allows students to become more familiar with unknown parts of the library (and the resources available beyond the computers). You will be surprised at how often participants leave your event with a newly discovered book in hand. We have also used other obscure areas (a quiet table on a desolate floor) for activity-based workshops, such as journal making and personal essay writing. It only takes a little searching to hear a new student exclaim, "Cool . . . I've never been up here before!"

NETWORK

Your community is bustling with activity, so get outside the walls of the library and connect with those who share your interests. There is always networking to be done, whether at your local literary organization, a talk at the history museum, or a jewelry-making class. Join online social networking groups related to your interests or, better yet, start your own group. Network with other similarly minded organizations in your community to develop meaningful (and economical) partnerships.

PROVIDE OPPORTUNITIES

Student and faculty members of the poetry club have taught everything from reading poetry aloud to writing poems about food. As educators, we know that career planning and preparation sometimes fall through the cracks for many college students. Experience in leading workshops, and the evidence of transferable skills that this represents, is a worthy addition to any professional resume (no matter the career). When students ask me for letters of recommendation for graduate school or employment, it's easy to comment on their enthusiasm and abilities when I have experienced them firsthand myself.

WHAT ARE YOUR INTERESTS AND CURIOSITIES?

When starting a new club or program, it is important that you consider your own interests. For me, poetry was a natural fit. The continued success of the Rooftop Poetry Club, which features readings, talks, and workshops by local and nationally recognized poets, is due in part to my own fascination with and dedication to poetry. We likewise started the "Green Talk" series to educate ourselves and others on environmental issues, which led to other positive green initiatives in the library and across campus (such as double-sided printing and our magazine exchange program). Our Rooftop Reading Club (an offshoot of the Rooftop Poetry Club) was started to support the women's studies program and its sponsorship of a visit by *Pink Think* author Lynn Peril. Whether your interest is local history, organic gardening, or graphic novels, the possibilities are absolutely endless (not to mention affordable).

OUTREACH

Offering programming in the library is also great for library liaison with student clubs and departments on campus. For example, we recently invited the Spanish Club and the classical language department to a booktalk on the Spanish Inquisition (given by retired alumni). I notify creative writing faculty on upcoming writing workshops, and in return they keep the Rooftop Reading Club posted on their department's literary events. The Rooftop Poetry Club was recently invited by the local art museum to write poems to accompany an exhibition featuring the art of Charles Burchfield, leading to a scheduled tour, workshop, and reading at the gallery.

BRING IT ALL TO THE TABLE

When the Rooftop Poetry Club offers talks and workshops (e.g., on journal making or sonnet writing), I gather the library's collection of relevant items for a no-cost display during the meeting. Students usually explore these materials with great enthusiasm and often check them out to take home. We also provide an active catalog link to relevant resources on the event's web page announcement. Consider scheduling viewings of related films as well, but check with your acquisitions department to see if public viewing rights were purchased with the video before you show it to a group. When collecting library materials, don't forget to glean bits from archives, print journals (our collection of *Life* magazines is priceless), special collections, curriculum, music recordings, art, and local resources. Be sure to leave information for participants to contact you after the meeting or event. Trust me, *someone* will track you down to share something new that he discovered, to ask you something related to the program, or to ask you for help with a totally different project.

WHAT'S UNDER YOUR NOSE?

When you are arranging for guest speakers or workshop leaders, it is easy to overlook valuable human resources within your own library. We all have unique talents and skills. My own library is filled with writers, music buffs, animal lovers, knitters, cooks, and baseball fanatics. Library staff have voluntarily presented on topics such as making green gifts for the holidays, songwriting, local gardening, and recycling on campus. This is also a great way to get to know your colleagues.

APPRECIATE . . . AND ARCHIVE

Everybody likes to be acknowledged for their hard work and generosity. It is a good idea to provide featured guests *something* in exchange for their time and energy (even if they are already on board with your cost-cutting spirit).

For all of our Rooftop Poetry events, we archive high-quality photos and podcasts on our website. Featured poets and workshop leaders appreciate the publicity our site provides and often link the archive to their personal web pages. The library benefits from archiving the events, since the record serves as tangible evidence of the library as an active learning space. It's a win-win situation for everybody.

CONCLUSION

See? You don't need a big budget to establish innovative programming in the library. Since 2005 the Rooftop Poetry Club has functioned with just enough funding for refreshments (think tea and cookies). We were lucky enough to find a great meeting space—keep an eye out for similarly wasted spaces—but we also do all of our own marketing, including desktop publishing and the use of Web 2.0 technologies to promote and archive our events. And even with this grass-roots effort, I continue to be amazed at the new connections, both on campus and within the community, that are possible through the club—from establishing solid relationships with faculty members and local agencies to being featured on a national radio program. As librarians, we already have the perfect meeting space (the library) and a *world* of resources at our fingertips. Start small (perhaps one booktalk or invited speaker) and see where you can take it. Remind yourself and those around you, you've got nothing to lose.

PROMOTING AND ARCHIVING YOUR EVENTS

There is no shortage of free web tools that you can use to promote and archive your events. Blogs, social networking sites, and photo- and video-sharing sites can provide creative platforms from which to advertise and share group activities. Our library utilizes WordPress blogging, Flickr photo sharing, YouTube video sharing, Twitter, iTunes (for our podcasts), and Facebook. We are currently exploring Voice Thread technology, which allows the creation of unique visual presentations with social commenting features.

PART V

Sharing

12

INCREASING RESOURCES IN TOUGH TIMES

A New Funding Model for the Purdue University Career Wiki

George Bergstrom and Mary Dugan

THE WORLD ECONOMIC situation has resulted in rising costs and shrinking budgets for universities, and the library is not immune to these realities. We are faced with a need not just to be very careful when spending monograph and serial funds but to be creative in finding ways to make the dollars stretch. When we have a real concern on campus requiring an innovative solution, one aspect of that solution must be a pragmatic awareness of the cost, and perhaps the most creativity must therein be applied. Librarians cannot be shy when it comes to instructing users that library resources are not free but have to be paid for with limited funds and that those who want to share resources could also share in the expenses. This approach has the potential to not only procure more resources for the students but build relationships across campus.

BACKGROUND

The Management and Economics Library (MEL) at Purdue University provides research and curriculum support to undergraduate, graduate, and professional programs in the Krannert School of Management and in agricultural economics, consumer family sciences, and interdisciplinary programs such as homeland security and entrepreneurship. The MEL faculty have an excellent working relationship with the teaching faculty in these programs, and they strive to customize and enhance services whenever the opportunity is presented. Such an opportunity was recognized in 2006 when the dean of Krannert was looking for a solution to a persistent problem underlying the job-seeking activities of graduating seniors. Feedback from some of the companies who visited the campus for job fairs indicated that the students did not have the kind of in-depth knowledge about their company that would impress the recruiters. The dean believed that this was not a reflection of the students' lack of interest, merely a lack of applying their research skills to a real-life need. The head librarian knew that MEL had resources that could alleviate this problem.

In December 2006, staff from the university's libraries and career offices met to discuss resources that would solve this problem, and they discovered overlapping subscriptions. This discovery led to the recognition of a need for better communication. To achieve this improved communication, a wiki was proposed that also became an opportunity to develop a new service for students. Before this meeting, career offices staff had not recognized the libraries' resources as tools for themselves and their constituents. To be successful, it was important that the libraries and career offices all regarded this as both a cooperative partnership and a means of increasing resources that would benefit all.

Prior to the collaboration, the MEL faculty were involved with career search assistance for third-year management students. A required course in the Krannert School of Management for these students is focused on preparing for job searches and internships. During the course, MEL librarians present a lecture to the class with general information about the library and, most important, highlight the company information databases. The emphasis during these lectures is that these databases can help students prepare for interviewing by learning about the companies for which they want to work. In addition to this very specific class, MEL librarians have participated in workshops sponsored by the career offices. However, none of these incidental interactions resulted in those offices sustaining an awareness of all the services and resources offered by the library. Neither did any of the career offices seem to have a reciprocal awareness of each other's goals, services, and resources.

WHERE TO START

To start building a base for cooperation, MEL librarians contacted the directors of the three major campus career offices. At the first roundtable meeting, everyone reported on the electronic and hard copy resources they purchased and furnished a wish list for future purchases. It was apparent that efforts and resources were being duplicated among these offices and the libraries and that pooling resources would be an advantage to all. It was also recognized that any combined effort would be most effective if a central online career web space could be set up to function as a portal for all online career resources and to be a gateway to the participating career offices. To accomplish this, the business reference librarian headed up the establishment of the Purdue University Career Wiki. The basic wiki was created in early 2008 with a soft rollout during the spring 2008 semester and the official launch in August. Use of a wiki allowed representatives from all units involved to contribute content.

FUNDING

The resource development librarian concentrated on the goal of identifying partnership opportunities for funding, with each unit contributing to the

FIRST PARTNERS: MAJOR CAREER OFFICES

Center for Career Opportunities: The center provides career development support and job search services, engaging students and alumni in exploring career options and developing effective job search skills. It also facilitates activities that connect students and alumni with employers and develops partnerships with Purdue colleges, schools, and other stakeholders.

Krannert Graduate Career Services: This unit is focused on students in the professional master's degree programs. Its directive is to help all students in these programs secure one or more job offers.

Krannert Undergraduate Career Services: This unit is devoted exclusively to the school's undergraduate students, providing on-campus recruiting, resume assessment, presentations on interviewing skills, and instruction in business etiquette. The staff teaches a course emphasizing academic planning, career exploration, and job search strategies, including video-recorded mock interviews.

purchase of electronic resources jointly agreed on by the group. This type of financial alliance was a well-established practice by which MEL was regularly able to purchase databases and data sets with contributions from academic units such as the school of management. This would be the first time, though, that this type of fiscal cooperation would be attempted among the libraries and nonacademic units.

Through informal conversations, e-mail, and phone calls, the representatives of the career offices and the librarians discussed several databases that they believed would be most useful and have the necessary wide appeal among their colleagues. Several staff expressed a preference for a database that offered information about internships; others favored guides for finding a job outside the United States. Specific features were also singled out: CareerBeam was preferred by at least one director because it did not include a cookie-cutter resume template but instead listed the features that a good resume should include. This component was also favored by the librarians, since it would enhance the objective of increasing student information literacy.

By May 2007, Vault Online, CareerBeam, Plunkett Research, WetFeet Online, and CareerSearch were identified as the databases of most interest. The career offices were willing to defer management of the database acquisitions to the resource development librarian because of her previous experience in managing cooperative purchases. Vendor database demonstrations were a high priority for the group, so the acquisition process had to include them. Clearly the efforts of the librarian would save career staff time and minimize their individual efforts. The resource development librarian contacted the vendors chosen by the group to obtain the basic information that the four units (MEL, Center for Career Opportunities, Krannert Graduate Career Services, and Krannert Undergraduate Career Services) required in order to begin the database selection process. The primary information they needed to make decisions about scheduling demonstrations and possible purchase included cost, mode of access, number of simultaneous users, the mode of campuswide access, training, promotional assistance, and access for alumni. The first vendor demonstration was recognized by all in attendance as an important cooperation for the group.

When one database, CareerBeam, emerged as having the greatest appeal to all of the units involved, the head librarian of MEL provided the top-level leadership needed to gather funds. She approached the associate dean for administration and planning at Krannert, who agreed to contribute funds along with the career offices. According to the agreement between the associate dean and the head librarian, Krannert's contribution to the resource was dependent on contributions of the other career offices. The Center for Career Opportunities contributed 40 percent, Graduate Career Services gave

10 percent, Krannert's executive master's program gave 10 percent, MEL contributed 20 percent, and the dean's office gave the final 20 percent. This cooperative pay plan has subsequently been used several times throughout this project, with the percentages changing according to each unit's budget and need for the resource. Collaborative purchases thus far have been for CareerBeam, Uniworld, Career Spots, and Big Guide.

THE GROUP GROWS

The business reference librarian has identified thirty-five offices on campus that offer some level of career services, from a task informally assigned to an administrative assistant to departmental career professionals. He has contacted these groups through e-mail, delineating the details of the project and extending an invitation to join. Responses were moderate, but by the end of summer 2008 five new career units were on board. As conversations began with these additional units, it became clear that we needed to develop tiers of involvement in order to minimize perceived impediments to participation. Thus, the three newest groups are at the minimal level of link exchange wherein the career wiki includes a link to these offices and they link back to the wiki.

Since the formation of the career wiki collaborative group, the savings derived from the elimination of the duplicate licenses of three databases have allowed the addition of four databases. Of the ten offices represented in this collaborative effort, six have currently provided funds to assist in the purchase of one or more of these additional resources. This has made up 44 percent of the cost of the seven career-related databases provided since the beginning of the effort. Everyone involved considers alumni part of their constituency, and the next target is to begin to allow alumni access to these resources.

LESSONS LEARNED

The wiki group has learned several lessons: how to bring on new partners, how to review potential resources, and, most important, how to collaborate in the purchase of these new resources. In spring semester 2010, we held a meeting to discuss a new funding model, currently dubbed "pay-to-play." We shared information about the resources purchased by the libraries to support the academic mission of the university as well as all the resources that are primarily for career-related services. For the first year, when a new resource was chosen the resource development librarian spent significant time collecting the contributions from as many partners as possible to distribute the costs. Although this has worked to date, disadvantages include the amount of library staff time involved, the constant appearance that the library is asking for money, and the need to go back to these groups every time a resource contract needs to be renewed. The new model will allow the partners to contribute a dollar amount to the career wiki group once each fiscal year based on their ability and budget, to be used to fund cooperative purchases. The libraries will then use that pool to facilitate the purchase of these resources. Although it is agreed that all students must benefit from the resources and the opinions of all career offices will be solicited, the groups that contribute funds will have the final say in the use of those funds.

The group has also discussed assessment and decided that usage data will be monitored, both usage of the resources available on the wiki and data on click-through traffic (hits on the groups' websites that come from the wiki). Librarians recognize that an assessment of potential downsides must also be addressed. For example, other departments may not have funds recurring for the annual renewal of jointly purchased databases. If a career office withdraws financial support for a database, we need a contingency plan. Additionally, efforts are under way to enhance marketing of the wiki and staff training.

CONCLUSIONS

This collaboration has not been a quick fix or temporary patch but a solution that is sustainable. As a group we have increased efficiencies in the procurement of resources, awareness of the services offered by the partner units, and cooperative efforts in training and preparation of our students for all aspects of the career search process. We have created a one-stop-shop web portal for our group that is available to all university constituents. We have begun streamlining the procurement process that will create a single libraries' fund to which the career offices will contribute for the joint purchase of established and proposed resources. The group has begun discussing inclusion of Purdue University's four regional campuses and the possibility of adding alumni access to the contract of these career databases.

The group will need to continue assessment of the new funding model with attention paid to the workloads of staff in all units and the reliance of the career offices on library resources. Although we hope eventually to get all units contributing to this fund, we need to insulate the fund from the possibility of one or more units targeting it for budgetary cuts. This collaborative effort between library, academic units, and nonacademic units on the Purdue University campus adds an adaptable tool in our financial arsenal and promises to yield more benefits for the library, the career offices, and, most important, our students.

INNOVATING AND SAVING WITH JOINT-USE LIBRARIES

Emily Dill

IT IS NO secret that library budgets are shrinking. Library administrators and other stakeholders are keener than ever to save in any way feasible. As a corollary to budget crunches, there is an increased call for accountability in how public monies, which support most libraries, are being spent. One possible model for recouping savings is the joint-use library. A quick search of the literature shows that joint-use libraries are often difficult to plan and difficult to manage. Yet they are also an excellent study in cooperation and in the provision of bigger and better services for patrons. Recognizing that the merging of libraries is a particularly situation-specific means of saving resources, in this chapter I provide clues to the success of one particular venture rather than offer blanket recommendations.

UNIVERSITY LIBRARY OF COLUMBUS: BACKGROUND

A 1997 Hudson Institute study commissioned by the Columbus (Indiana) Economic Development Board identified the discontinuity among educational systems in the community as a problem. The Community Education Coalition (CEC) was created to address this and other local educational

A CLOSER LOOK AT LIBRARY SIMILARITIES

The savings that result from a joint-use library venture depend largely on the characteristics of the merging libraries' patron bases. The most successful cases seem to involve libraries that serve similar clientele. An overlap in customers affords libraries savings on resources and services that might not be realized when two dissimilar libraries join forces.

issues. The partners in this coalition were Indiana University–Purdue University Columbus (IUPUC), Purdue University College of Technology, Ivy Tech Community College Columbus, Bartholomew County Consolidated School Corporation, Flat Rock–Hawcreek School Corporation, and the Department of Workforce Development. The overall aim of the CEC is to reinforce lifelong learning and link educational institutions with each other and with work opportunities in the community. Among the CEC's greatest accomplishments is the creation of the Columbus Learning Center, a shared-use facility including classrooms and administrative offices used by IUPUC, Ivy Tech, the Department of Workforce Development, and the Center for Teaching and Learning. The joint-use University Library of Columbus is housed within the Center for Teaching and Learning.

It was during the initial planning process for the Columbus Learning Center that the idea arose to combine the two libraries (the IUPUC/Purdue University College of Technology Library and the Ivy Tech Library) within a new location in the Center for Teaching and Learning. Because one of the main goals of the CEC was to create better bonds among educational institutions in the community, a joint-use library seemed like a perfect fit for the new facility. The space the libraries merged into also houses a computer lab, a faculty lounge, a curriculum resource lab, an innovations classroom, and the Academic Resource Center (shared tutoring services for IUPUC/Purdue University College of Technology and Ivy Tech students). In addition to rethinking the traditional divisions between academic libraries that serve advanced degree–granting institutions and those that serve community colleges, the joint-use library being housed within a Center for Teaching and Learning also breaks down the prevalent divisions between libraries and other campus centers.

PLANNING

For an ultimately successful joint-use library, extensive planning is required. The first planning documents for the University Library of Columbus were created at least six years before the doors opened. One of the first steps to consider when planning a joint-use library is to ensure that all of the players involved (current staff and administrators from the respective libraries as well as all relevant stakeholders) understand the mission, policies, and procedures of the libraries being combined. There will likely be many commonalities, but having a firm understanding of what is important to each of the libraries at the outset helps prevent future problems with the joint-use library's day-to-day operations. It is critical for the satisfaction of patrons to not lose any of the things that the previously distinct libraries did well.

Management of a joint-use library can be a thorny issue. In most cases, one of the libraries assumes primary management of the shared facility, as opposed to an evenly shared management structure. At the University Library of Columbus the managing partner is IUPUC. Ivy Tech contributes staff (a librarian and work study staff who report directly to Ivy Tech) and collection development and services funds (cataloging, acquisitions, etc.) to the library. This can be a delicate balance, both for the managing partner and the partner being managed. It is important for stakeholders involved with the partner being managed to feel assured that the library's interests will be preserved in the new facility.

INCLUSIVE PLANNING

One strategy for making sure each participating library's voice is heard is to use an outside consultant or facilitator to coordinate the planning process. Having a person or team who is not emotionally invested in one of the institutions helps guarantee that the final plan will satisfy both parties.

POTENTIAL SAVINGS

Collection

Before physical spaces were merged, the Ivy Tech Library collection was searched against the IUPUC Library collection using IUPUC's OPAC (since the IUPUC collection was the larger of the two) to identify redundancies. In some cases, the redundant copies were discarded in favor of a more streamlined collection, but in cases of heavily used items duplicates were kept. Because the institutions served by the University Library of Columbus offer several similar academic programs, the collection strength improved for all institutions in many key areas after the merger because of the unique titles added. Thankfully neither of the formerly discrete libraries' materials budgets was cut during the merger. Adding that budget boon to the growth experienced from the integrated materials resulted in the establishment of a collection far better than the libraries could have ever had on their own.

The real savings recouped in the University Library of Columbus's materials budget came after the merger of the collection. There are certain items that every library must have—dictionaries, subscriptions to the most popular newspapers and magazines, classic literature. In a joint-use library, only one copy of many of those standards is usually needed. The two budgets are now used in concert to provide a deeper collection of materials covering the academic programs both schools support (i.e., education, nursing, business) while still strongly supporting each school's unique programs.

Staff

The need for staffing is often not reduced when libraries join forces. There may be only one building to staff rather than two, but there will also be more patrons than either of the previously distinct libraries is used to serving. In fact, many joint-use libraries see an increase in usage above what the combined statistics of the merging libraries might predict. But though there may be no fewer hands on deck, there can be a streamlining of duties, resulting in staff being reallocated to previously underserved library operations. For example, having one interlibrary loan specialist rather than two might allow the library to use the extra staff time to focus on more outreach activities. The combination of two libraries' staffing pools can also result in expanded operating hours for joint-use libraries.

In the case of the University Library of Columbus, both of the merging libraries were able to bring all of their existing staff into the new facility. It is definitely helpful to have a balance of workers from each partner library represented in any joint-use facility. Each library has its own culture and institutional knowledge that cannot be known by those unfamiliar with the institution. The learning curve for all staff is steep in the beginning, so extensive training on any modified procedures is essential for maintaining continuously good patron service in the midst of change.

STAFF FEELINGS

It is only natural that some staff need a little time to get used to a new set of policies and procedures, let alone a new boss and a new parent institution. If from the outset all conversations about workplace changes are based on mutual respect and the ultimate goal to provide the best possible service to all patrons, some of the inevitable uneasiness can be avoided.

Facilities

The complexity of facilities planning for joint-use libraries depends largely on whether one library is "moving in" with the other or if they are both moving into a new space. In the former case, room might be especially tight, since what was originally meant to house one library is now housing the contents of two. In the latter case, significant planning is still needed to ensure that the combined collection, staff, and services have adequate space. This is especially important, for example, when thinking about the number of computer workstations needed. Still, there are many instances when facilities savings can be recouped. For instance, a joint-use library typically needs to purchase fewer supplies (lightbulbs, staplers) than two separate libraries do. In the academic realm, establishing a joint-use library can also free up some space on campus, which is always at a premium.

> ## ENERGIZING THROUGH CHANGE
>
> Being thrown out of their comfort zone by entering into a joint-use library can be a great energy boost for library staff. Doing something a new way can invigorate people who may have become complacent about their work.

Governance

Though somewhat hard to quantify, joint-use libraries can also result in time savings for staff and administrators by streamlining procedures and services. One of the benefits of joint-use libraries is that each partner has fresh perspectives on how to manage library operations. Library staff can certainly learn from reading professional literature or attending conferences, but spending time ironing out procedures collaboratively can really bring personal lessons into play that result in better service for patrons and less needless effort expended by staff. It is easy to get stuck in a rut of doing things a certain way just because they have always been done that way. Deliberately analyzing the motivations behind library policies and procedures during a merger can result in happier patrons with less time cost for staff.

WHAT IS NOT SAVED

In spite of the thrifty nature of joint-use libraries, there are certainly areas that do not realize savings. One is the management of electronic resources. Many prices for electronic resources are based on the size or credentials of the patron base. Entering into a joint-use library will undoubtedly throw off such measures and quite possibly result in higher price tags. Negotiating new contracts for the not easily classifiable merged patron base can result in a frustrating and time-consuming task for libraries that wish to continue to provide the same levels of access to electronic resources that their patrons have been used to.

Another obstacle might be the initial ease of use for patrons. As hard as the merging libraries try to keep policies and procedures seamless, it is inevitable that some patrons will be confused or disappointed in changes. It is important in these instances that library staff remain patient and sympathetic to users' frustrations. Most patrons will weather the changes just fine and eventually come to appreciate the enhancements in the merged library.

ASSESSMENT AND CONCLUSION

Measuring the success of joint-use libraries can be done through many methods, often in the same manner as the libraries did before merging. Comparing figures such as gate counts, circulations, or computer log-ins with those of the formerly discrete libraries can be a good indication of usage levels (assuming the libraries kept statistics in the same way). For example, during the University Library of Columbus's first year of operation, the gate count increased 17 percent over the best figures available for the IUPUC Library and the Ivy Tech Library combined for the previous year. What cannot easily be measured is the boost in goodwill a joint-use library can bring. In times of greater accountability, showing a community that you are thinking about saving while providing services to a larger clientele can result in a very positive image for the library.

Although planning for and implementing a joint-use library can be a time-consuming and delicate operation, it can reap many benefits in the long run for the libraries being merged. In addition to offering patrons bigger and better services, joint-use libraries are prime examples of doing more with less, which is arguably more important now than ever before.

14

MULTITYPE REGIONAL LIBRARY RESPONSES TO THE ECONOMIC CRISIS

Tom Taylor

DURING THE CURRENT economic downturn, many libraries in south-central Kansas have experienced increased usage. Public, academic, school, and special libraries have had to or will have to accommodate increased usage and service demands with stagnant or reduced budgets and a significant reduction of state aid to public libraries. Furthermore, budgetary pressure from state, local, and school officials is likely to affect library funding in the coming years. In response to these challenges, the South Central Kansas Library System (SCKLS) invited members to attend meetings during 2009 that focused on the libraries' responses to these uncertain economic times. Information from these sessions was compiled and shared within the system and throughout the state of Kansas. The project was titled "Libraries in Uncertain Economic Times."

SCKLS (www.sckls.info/) is a regional system of cooperating libraries serving and governed by local libraries in south-central Kansas. Its mission is to assist member libraries to provide excellent service to their communities. SCKLS provides grants, consulting, continuing education, and cost-effective support services to its member libraries. It serves twelve counties and has a service population of approximately 762,000. There are 147 members participating and eligible for system services and programs. Among these are seventy-three public libraries, fifty-five school districts, fourteen academic

libraries, and five special libraries. Membership and participation are volun-
tary, and each member library retains its local self-government and indepen-
dence. SCKLS is funded by a tax on property within the boundaries of the
system that is not taxed for the support of a public library.

THE PROJECT

At meetings in 2009 at four different sites, members got to network with other
librarians, discuss strategies for addressing reduced or maintained funding,
share ways of promoting their libraries as an important economic resource,
and identify resources to assist job seekers. Over thirty different libraries
were represented at these meetings. Paul Hawkins, SCKLS director, and Tom
Taylor, SCKLS continuing education coordinator, facilitated these discussions.

Hawkins and Taylor also identified resources related to library budgets and
job seeking. After the meetings, the results of these discussions and relevant
resources were posted on the SCKLS website and shared at regional and statewide meetings. The following illustrates the kinds of questions asked along
with some of the discussion results.

How Has the Current Economic Climate Affected Your Library Service?

With only one exception, participants indicated increased recent use of the
library in general and, specifically, increased visits by users, circulation
of library materials, use of computers and Internet resources, and interlibrary loans. Participants noted that library users who were self-identified
as unemployed increasingly used library public access computers to file for
unemployment benefits, to complete online job applications, and for personal
education.

What Budget Cuts Have You Already Had and What Cuts Do You Anticipate?

All of the public libraries were affected by a reduction of state aid in 2009.
The state legislature and the State Library of Kansas made further reductions
in state aid for 2010. Municipalities saw reductions in property tax revenue.
School district libraries also faced continued reductions in state support and
in property tax revenue. Many school districts canceled staff continuing education or ceased paying for substitutes that had allowed librarians to attend
trainings. In some cases, professional librarians lost their positions. Private
academic libraries also reduced staff positions through early retirements and

removal of positions. Public academic libraries had their open positions frozen and their collections budgets reduced.

What Are You Doing to Position Your Library during This Economic Downturn? Do You Have Any Suggestions for Addressing the Economic Downturn?

These questions proved to be valuable as participants learned from and shared with each other. The following are direct responses from participating librarians. In some cases, I include explanatory comments:

> We made contact with the local workforce agency and offered them the use of our community room.
> The rotation period for outreach books has been extended [outreach materials are delivered to homebound seniors and residents of nursing homes and assisted living centers].
> Use donations more—including in the book sale.
> Partner with the local community college to offer courses on computers.
> Volunteers do almost everything.
> We are decreasing the length of the summer reading program.
> A class on frugal living—like coupon cutting.
> We are increasing an evening presence in order to make our library accessible to larger numbers of people. We are a bedroom community just outside of Wichita.
> Lease hot titles instead of buying additional copies.
> Use donations of popular titles for multiple copies.
> Focus on the people.
> We are going to provide dollar amounts of the materials that patrons check out during National Library Week. This will call attention to the value of library materials.
> Cut magazine subscriptions.
> Prepare for the minimum wage increase. [In 2009 the minimum wage in Kansas was only $2.65 an hour. In April 2009, then governor Kathleen Sebelius signed a law that aligned Kansas's minimum wage with the federal minimum wage of $7.25 an hour effective January 1, 2010. The small public library in question had been paying its assistants less than the federal minimum wage.]
> Do not overlap large-print titles with regular-print titles.

Get a Friends of the Library group going to help supplement our
library budget.
Be more creative with programming.
Do more partnered programming with local agencies and groups.
Utilize SCKLS services more efficiently.
Dropped our business memberships like SAM's Club.
Dropped ALA membership.
Become choosier on book titles.
Maybe add Saturday hours in order to reach more people.
We could close one hour earlier to save money on labor and utili-
ties.
Our library could decrease our book budget some.
Be careful on supplies.
Not rehire replacement employees.
We hired someone through the SWEP program. [SWEP is the
American Red Cross Senior Work Exchange Program, funded
by the American Red Cross and the U.S. Department of Labor.
SWEP participants are partnered with an agency, in this case
a library, where they work. They are paid by the Red Cross.
This can be an effective way for a library to supplement, but
not replace, its workforce.]
Keep our book buying down.
Board members are helping work library hours.
Coordinate materials purchasing with the school district—alternate
buying certain titles.
Keep the lights off until just before opening.
List the prices of new books and post them in the library.

What Promotions Have You Done or Do You Have Planned?

Promoting library services is an excellent way to illustrate the value and
importance a library brings to its constituents, whether they are students,
teachers, staff, or members of the general public. Participating librarians
shared a variety of promotional ideas:

I am involved with the local chamber of commerce.
Give tours of our library to classes.
Posters both inside of the library and out in the community.
Give circulation numbers to the city managers to keep them
informed.

Go to other fund-raisers in town to see what they are doing.

Spoke to the Lions Club.

Our children's librarian visits the local preschools.

Articles in the local paper.

We pursued movie licensing so we can show movies to the public.

Put a bookmark in interlibrary loan requests that states how much
the service costs. We sometimes get donations that help offset
the cost of postage.

Our library's foundation hosts a golf tournament.

Partner with the Methodist church to pay half of United Methodist Women books.

A local Rotary Club provides bags for the homebound.

Our public library puts publicity information in the school newsletter.

Local TV and newspaper PSAs.

Website.

I have a ready-made collection of promotional material that I take
to philanthropic clubs like Lions and Rotary.

We have a handout about the value of the library.

Have your library board help advocate for you.

Have open and transparent communication with the city.

Work with city government to show how the library can affect
economic development.

Find the active core of your community and elicit their help.

In our bigger community, we cannot just rely on word of mouth.
We have to explain a variety of marketing opportunities.

We are a good partner with the county extension office.

Have a coupon basket in the library.

Promote inexpensive recipes and purchase cookbooks that do the
same.

Newsletter in the city water bill.

We placed an ad on the local pharmacy's bags that lists our hours
and contact information.

Go to businesses that other groups do not always hit up, like law-
yers.

We offer basic computer skills lessons to seniors.

Local cable advertising.

We started a "No-Show Flower Show" where we send a bag of
seeds to encourage people to donate to the library but stay
home. We did this in place of a garden or flower tour. Those
take a lot of time and energy and they met with limited results.
A library could also do a no-show tea party.

Our Friends group sells a "Smart Card." Businesses offer discounts
    to cardholders. The sales of the card benefit the Friends group.
Easter Egg hunt at the library that the local paper will promote.
We have hosted job fairs in the meeting room.
Worked with the humane society.
We bought a Nintendo Wii and formed a game club.
Library book carts in the local parade.
I write a weekly column in the local paper.
Facebook pages that promote your library.
The local computer dealer is offering free instructional classes at
    our library.
We host several Kansas Humanities Council programs.
Use the city marquee and the city TV channel.
Use free local programming opportunities. There are a lot of
    groups and organizations that would like to share with the
    public. We hosted a local mime group.
Use a citywide auction or garage sale to raise money.
Our library offers free computer classes to fill the gap between
    learning on your own and paying for instruction at the local
    college.
We are offering a film class to the general public.
Have a float in the local parade.

CONCLUSION

As has been the case with previous economic struggles, Kansas entered the
recession later than either coast. Indications are that it will also exit the
recession after other areas of the country improve. The libraries of south-
central Kansas face an economic reality of decreased property tax revenue and
decreased state and local support. SCKLS's "Libraries in Uncertain Economic
Times" project gave participating librarians some preparation for this recession. When the project started in early 2009, property tax revenue had just
started to decline in some parts of the region. At the same time, the state of
Kansas entered into a serious economic crisis of its own. It became apparent
that the state had to reduce its expenditures dramatically, cutting state aid
to libraries being just a small part of the picture.

Librarians who participated in the project were able to share ideas. This
sharing actually prompted more thinking about ways to approach the crisis.
The library system was able to compile these brainstorming sessions and
share them on the Web. SCKLS staff also presented this project to librarians

SCKLS ADDRESSES THE RECESSION

Like its members, SCKLS also faced a reduction in state aid and a decrease in property tax revenue. In an effort to not further burden its members with financial reductions, SCKLS continued commitment and support for all 2009 and 2010 budgeted SCKLS grant programs. The system chose to make cuts in other areas. Postage and supplies were reduced. Instead of mailing out notices for all workshops and system events, SCKLS relied on its web page and electronic discussion list for communication. A position was left open. The system also delayed replacing a vehicle. Moreover, all system employees were asked to identify potential reductions in their respective program areas should such cuts become necessary in the future.

both inside and outside of the system at several conferences and meetings across the state.

Besides sharing ideas, participants were able to network with one another. Networking with one's peers proved to be a valuable experience for those involved. Not only did participants develop important professional contacts, but they also gained a sense of camaraderie. In this economic climate, it is of considerable worth knowing that librarians and libraries do not stand alone; rather, libraries and librarians stand together.

Regional library systems or consortiums can undertake similar projects for their members. Facilitating learning and sharing are part of what makes a library system or cooperative successful. Librarians not affiliated with library systems can initiate contact with staff at peer institutions to see what they are doing about this crisis. Asking similar questions or using the responses listed in this chapter as a starting point could be a beneficial way to open a meaningful discussion.

15

MUSEUM PASSES

A Low-Cost, High-Impact Partnership

Rebecca Tuck and Lisa Fraser

PARTNERSHIPS ARE A valuable tool that can help libraries meet the needs of patrons, stretch limited resources, and connect with new users. King County Library System (KCLS) in Washington State has developed partnerships with museums in the local area to provide free passes that are distributed by the library. When organizations are struggling for funding it may seem contradictory to provide free access, but many museums offer periodic free or reduced-entry days as part of their regular outreach. By pairing with the library, the museum demonstrates a commitment to the community, reaches new potential supporters, and gains access to the professional resources of the library. Library patrons enjoy free admission to the museums and interesting programs at the library.

WHERE TO START

As with any partnership, it is important that the museum and library have similar goals for the pass program. Each should make contributions to the partnership that enhance the value of the offering as a whole. The contributions vary depending on the museum and the library; take advantage of your strengths. The library contribution might include books or other resources related to the museum's collection, opportunities for museum staff to present at the library, generic or specialized booklists, or librarian presentations at the museum.

The first museum is the most difficult to approach, since this is a new venture for both organizations. Look for an organization that has a good reputation and is financially stable. Pass programs can take time to attain full use, so your partner should have a history of follow-through and a focus on long-term benefits.

Though it can be tempting to start with the largest, best-known museum in your area, remember that it is likely to be inundated with requests for partnerships. Instead, focus on a museum that may have fewer opportunities to partner. If there is a museum that already has a connection to your library, that may be the ideal starting place. In the absence of a relationship, you can boost your credibility by providing references from organizations with which you have worked.

> ## STARTING THE KCLS MUSEUM PASS PROGRAM
>
> When we started the KCLS museum pass program, we looked for a museum that shared the library's commitment to the community, whose exhibits complemented our collection, and whose staff were open to innovative ideas. Bellevue Arts Museum fit all of those criteria. In addition, the staff at the museum and the library had previously worked together on programs. The initial meeting revealed similar goals: the museum hoped to increase attendance and membership through greater awareness of its programs, and the library wanted to promote collections and programs to a new audience.

THE PARTNERSHIP AGREEMENT

At a minimum, be sure that the individuals entering into the agreement are authorized by their respective organizations to do so, and that the agreement meets the standards of both organizations. In some cases, an informal agreement that is documented in e-mail could be sufficient to ensure that both sides understand the expectations of the partnership. Many organizations prefer a more formal letter of agreement. Whatever the format, have the following information in writing:

- Name and contact information for individuals coordinating the programs at both organizations.
- Information about the passes themselves, including their form, the number available, and any restrictions on their use.

- Criteria to be used to evaluate the program, the evaluation schedule, and the date when the program will be reassessed.
- Method of communicating issues that could affect use of the passes, such as closure dates for the museum or library or the loss of physical passes.
- Process for renegotiating quantity or other restrictions.
- Coordination of publicity, collection of information about users, sharing of contact lists, division of cost/responsibility for printing or other advertising.
- Supplemental activities such as programs or resource lists that will be provided by either organization.

RESOURCES REQUIRED

The main resource used in developing and administering a pass program is staff time. The first program will require the most effort as you learn the issues of your particular organization and area. Though no two agreements are exactly the same, the knowledge gained from each partnership will improve subsequent ones.

It is helpful to have one person at the library serve as the contact for the museum pass program. That person spends time at the beginning of the project exploring the options for administering the passes and then identifying possible partners. Time to meet with internal contacts—administration, cataloging, web services, public relations—as well as with museum representatives is necessary. Once the passes are in circulation, the program contact must maintain the pass mechanisms as well as the relationships with the museums.

It is essential that all library staff are able to speak knowledgably about the museum pass program and understand how to make the passes available to patrons. For a simple program with one museum, an information sheet may provide all the necessary information. If new software is used or there are multiple museums involved, a more comprehensive training program may be needed. It can be helpful to designate one or more staff "experts" who can answer more difficult questions about the passes.

Museum passes provide an opportunity to showcase library collections and programs; these require additional staff time. Library staff may create booklists or subject guides, arrange programming at the library, or conduct outreach. These features enhance the pass program and can be adapted to fit the skills and available time of the staff.

THREE WAYS OF APPROACHING PASSES

Museum passes can be designed in a variety of ways. There are three basic categories of passes, with variations within those categories.

Onetime Pass
- A day pass can be a simple, easy way to provide museum access for your patrons. This approach can be an excellent way to work with museums that are unable to commit to a larger program.
- The museum offers admission to patrons with library cards on a selected day.
- The pass can be a onetime-only arrangement or scheduled yearly, monthly, or quarterly.
- Two-for-one passes are another version of this idea and one that some museums may prefer.

Physical Pass
- For ongoing pass programs, a physical pass may be easiest for small systems and stand-alone libraries to implement.
- Patrons pick up a pass by visiting the library and checking it out.
- The pass can be as simple as a laminated card with the logos of both the library and the museum; a bar code and a small sleeve that accommodates a date due slip should be on the pass.
- Admission to the museum is dependent on the date due slip, which clearly states the date or dates that the pass can be used.
- The date due slip is surrendered at the time of museum admission, which can help reassure museum staff that the passes are not used by more than one person.
- To be accessible, the pass should be visible in the catalog.
- Passes can be reserved in the same way as other library materials, or you can make passes unavailable for holds in order to maximize the amount of time passes are in circulation.
- Details of the pass need to be worked out with your circulation and cataloging departments.

Online Pass
- Online registration is useful for offering larger pass programs involving multiple branches in a library system.
- Online pass software easily tracks how many patrons use the passes and offers ease of use for online patrons.

- Software geared for museum passes is available for purchase and provides an easy option.
- You may also be able to utilize the event software used for programs and storytimes; patrons sign up online and are e-mailed a confirmation that serves as their admission to the museum.
- Patrons without e-mail have the option of calling the library, where a staff member can sign them up and print out a confirmation for mail or pickup.

PROMOTIONS

Museum passes may be just one part of a library's relationship with a museum. Programs, such as ones previewing upcoming exhibits, benefit both organizations. Compiling booklists for a museum offers the library a chance to highlight its collection as well as being useful for the museum. Displays of books related to a current museum exhibit, including flyers about the exhibit, are another way to promote the relationship. Purchasing the museum's exhibit catalogs demonstrates the library's long-term commitment; depending on its budget, the museum may be willing to donate a copy to the library system. All of these ideas offer promotional opportunities for both organizations

DETAILS, DETAILS

When designing your museum passes, be sure to consider these questions:

How many passes will be provided?

Will the pass be valid for one or multiple days?

Will passes be limited to cardholders, or can anyone in the service area use them?

Will there be a limit to how many times a patron can use a pass?

If physical passes are being used, how will unreturned passes be handled?

If online passes are being used, how will you deal with patrons who don't have e-mail?

What statistics will you compile, and how will they be collected?

and provide a chance to showcase both the museum pass program and the ongoing relationship.

Cobranding with a museum can double the number of opportunities for promotion, for the museum will also be eager to get the word out. There are many ways of promoting museum passes:

- Strategic placement on the library's home page.
- Information about the passes on the museum's website.
- Signs and flyers in the library.
- Local media coverage, especially if passes are new in your area.

SNAPSHOT OF THE KCLS PASS PROGRAM

- The museum pass program includes art, history, and children's museums.
- We offer over one hundred passes per week that admit up to 380 people to local museums.
- Although some museums charge libraries for passes, all of our partners provide the passes without cost.
- Patrons reserve passes through our event software; the e-mail confirmation provides entry to the museum.
- Each pass admits two to six people.
- We launch each new program with a soft opening, to ensure that all the details work well before there is any publicity.
- Books about various exhibits are displayed across from the reference desk, giving staff members a chance to promote the program.
- Our pass program was picked up by a local blog and mentioned in its "Bargain of the Week" feature.
- The museums provide exhibit previews and other programming at the library.
- Librarians provide an annotated booklist for selected exhibits at one museum; the museum formats and prints the list.
- KCLS purchases copies of the art museum's exhibit catalogs; the Bellevue Library maintains a run of the museum catalogs in the reference area.
- Although there was an initial outlay of staff time, the ongoing commitment is minimal and is easily outweighed by the benefit to our patrons.

- Book displays related to current museum exhibits, including information about the passes.
- Posting to city or neighborhood blogs.
- Passports that can be stamped on visits to different museums.

MAINTAINING THE RELATIONSHIP

After you have established a great working relationship with a museum, it is important to keep the relationship well oiled. Check back with the museum staff periodically to see how the program is working. Compile and share with museum staff statistics of how many patrons have attended events; be sure to include positive comments from patrons. Reevaluate the program as outlined in the agreement. Attend exhibit openings and express appreciation for the contributions of the museum to the community and to the library.

EVALUATION

Evaluation answers the question, "How well have we done what we set out to do?" Ideally, evaluation is a joint effort between the library and the museum. Using a single method for both organizations is more convenient for the users and acts as a reminder of the agreed-upon goals. One of the challenges in collecting data is to abide by the privacy policies of your library; be sure that you are familiar with them.

Outputs are fairly simple to measure. These include the number of pass registrations or checkouts, the number of times passes are used to enter the museum, or the number of people admitted. Less direct measures include assessing circulation of titles on a booklist or attendance at related events. These methods provide quantitative information and are the least intrusive to users.

Evaluating the experience of patrons who use the passes is more challenging. One of the simplest options is to provide a printed survey to patrons when they enter the museum, with a request that they fill out and return it. If online collection is preferred, patrons can be urged to provide feedback by e-mail or through an online survey. Another alternative, if contact information is being collected by either the library or the museum, is to distribute a follow-up questionnaire.

MAKE THE PROGRAM YOUR OWN ─────────────

Whether you have a wide variety of potential partners or only a few museums from which to choose, there is a strong likelihood that you can develop a pass program that will work within your available resources. In a difficult economy, the library and museum will both benefit from a partnership that draws on the strengths of each organization while providing a valuable service to patrons. Make the program your own by reflecting the goals and values of your library and community.

16

SAVING BY SHARING

Using Open-Source and Shared
Catalogs to Do More with Less

John Helling

THE BLOOMFIELD–EASTERN GREENE County (Indiana) Public Library consists of a main branch in Bloomfield and two branch libraries in Cincinnati (known locally as "Little Cincinnati") and Owensburg. The library district has approximately 14,000 residents, around 2,000 of which live in the town of Bloomfield.

All of Indiana's 239 public library systems are independent library districts funded primarily by property tax. Because of changes to property tax laws, the median Indiana home owner saw a property tax decrease of about 31 percent in 2008. That money came directly out of the budgets of libraries, public schools, and other local tax units (DeBoer 2008).

To counteract this financial loss, the Bloomfield–Eastern Greene County Public Library investigated cooperative solutions. Up to this point, the library was a member of the Shared Catalog of Indiana Online (SCION), which was administered by the Indiana Cooperative Library Services Authority. This shared catalog used SIRSI as its ILS until 2007, when the transition was made to the open-source ILS Koha. Because SIRSI was proprietary, the library was forced to pay a licensing fee for every computer on which SIRSI was installed. Annually, the library spent $14,000 on such fees. It was thought that the transition to Koha would alleviate this expense, but problems with the implementation of Koha forced the consortium to continue to pay fees to LibLime, the implementer of Koha in the United States, for the engineering of solutions.

It was during this time that the library first heard of Evergreen Indiana, which was being developed by the Indiana State Library using Library Services and Technology Act grants. Because the library had a history of cooperating with other libraries in SCION, the nascent Evergreen consortium was an intriguing development. Inspired by the statewide cooperative PINES in Georgia, Evergreen Indiana was envisioned as a consortium of public libraries with the same circulation policies, the same fine levels, a shared catalog, and an open-source ILS.

THE MOVE TO EVERGREEN INDIANA

All Evergreen Indiana libraries agree to adopt the same circulation and fine policies. That way, a patron can go back and forth between Evergreen libraries and know exactly what to expect. A card from any Evergreen Indiana library is valid at any other Evergreen Indiana library. This includes hold privileges, so patrons can place holds in any participating library.

Evergreen was significantly different from the SCION consortium, in which the library did not have to adopt consortium-wide policies and used reciprocal cards. Even though the Evergreen circulation policies and fine structure were considerably different from those already in place (e.g., late fees for books would rise from 10 cents per day to 25 cents), Bloomfield–Eastern Greene County decided that the potential benefits of Evergreen outweighed the drawbacks.

Among these drawbacks was the actual cost of conversion to Evergreen. Though joining Evergreen was free, withdrawal from SCION was not. To have the library's bibliographic and patron data extracted for inclusion into the Evergreen Indiana catalog, the library had to pay for a test extraction, an actual extraction, and the requisite administrative fees. Originally, the SCION administrators requested separate extraction and administrative charges for each Bloomfield–Eastern Greene County location, which would have effectively tripled the cost of extraction. It was later agreed to extract all the data at once and for the cost of a single extraction, but the library board decided that even the inflated extraction

EVERGREEN POLICIES

- Books in Evergreen Indiana libraries check out for three weeks, with one renewal.
- Videos and DVDs check out for one week, with one renewal.
- Fines are 25 cents per item per day for all items.
- Items can be placed on hold and delivered to any Evergreen Indiana library.
- Membership in Evergreen Indiana is free.

price would pay for itself in the long run, when the transition to Evergreen Indiana was complete.

The library also considered the possibility that a move to Evergreen Indiana would not be popular with its patrons, that they might disapprove of materials purchased for their own library being borrowed by other libraries' patrons. The wholesale revision of circulation lengths and fine structures might also cause something of a public relations crisis. To counteract any negative reactions, the library began an information campaign as soon as it decided to switch to Evergreen Indiana. Flyers were placed in the library publicizing the new privileges patrons would enjoy, right alongside the changes in fines and circulation lengths. The director contacted the local newspaper and explained the library's position and thought processes. The Friends of the Library discussed the changes in their newsletter. Thanks to this concerted effort, library patrons were well informed during the entire transition process, and to date the library has received no complaints about the change.

ASSESSMENT: CONCRETE SAVINGS

Evergreen Indiana allows the Bloomfield–Eastern Greene County Public Library to save money in several ways, especially the open-source ILS and cataloging, outsourcing overdue notices, and cooperative collection development.

The primary savings are from the ILS. The library no longer has to pay for a proprietary system, and Evergreen Indiana has thus far avoided the need to pay for extensive outside software solutions. This implementation has allowed the library to save the entire $14,000 that was previously dedicated to paying for its ILS. The library is also no longer restricted to a fixed number of workstations, so Evergreen can be installed on any staff computer that needs it. This has given the librarians greater flexibility in choosing a place to perform non-desk-related duties. A librarian doing collection development, for example, can now take a laptop into the back office instead of using circulation computers to check holdings.

The open catalog structure of Evergreen Indiana has also allowed the library to save significantly. As part of the SCION consortium, if Bloomfield–Eastern Greene County purchased an item that was not already cataloged by another consortium member, it was forced to purchase a MARC record to catalog the item. As more and larger libraries join the Evergreen consortium, Bloomfield–Eastern Greene County will have the opportunity to save money on the purchase of MARC records. In addition to being able to attach items to the records of other Evergreen Indiana libraries, records from the Georgia PINES system (with 275 public libraries), Kansas City Public Library, and the Seattle Public Library are available as well.

The library achieved additional savings through the outsourcing of its overdue notices. It had already been using Unique Management, a collections service, to track down the worst-of-the-worst library offenders; these are patrons that cross a specific fine threshold and are not responsive to the library's usual phone calls and letters requesting payment. Unique was successful in recovering materials from these types of patrons, which the library had written off as a lost cause in the past. Unique also offered a similar service for run-of-the-mill overdues, which the library did not qualify for because it was not big enough. However, Evergreen Indiana partnered with Unique to extend this service to any interested member library. Now Bloomfield–Eastern Greene County outsources the mailing of overdue notices to Unique Management at the cost of 58 cents per notice (by way of comparison, a first-class postage stamp costs 44 cents these days). Also, because Evergreen Indiana can automatically send out e-mail circulation notices to patrons who provide an e-mail address, the need for snail mail circulation notices is further reduced. Allowing Unique to handle overdues saved so much time in terms of actual work performed by library staff that it allowed the library to go without one part-time staff member who retired around the time of the transition.

Joining Evergreen Indiana has also affected how the library makes collection development decisions. Because Evergreen libraries agree to fill holds placed by patrons of other Evergreen libraries, the materials in other member libraries are extremely accessible. This arrangement removes some of the pressure small libraries sometimes feel to have a collection that encompasses all subjects. For example, if a library is considering adding an expensive title to its collection that will be used only marginally, a quick search of the holdings of the rest of Evergreen Indiana may reveal other libraries that have already purchased the title. The library is then spared the expense of purchasing the item while simultaneously knowing it is available for use by its patrons. Although it is obviously preferable to have as many good items on the shelf as possible, the ability to access other collections is a great supplement. Items from other libraries can typically be delivered in about a week. (There are some exclusions, however. DVDs, music CDs, and any items cataloged within the previous six months do not travel to other libraries.)

LESSONS LEARNED

If your library is looking to replicate the savings of the Bloomfield–Eastern Greene County Public Library, the first step is to investigate shared catalog cooperatives in your area. Call your state library and see what libraries in your state are already doing. Shared catalog groups are not always statewide affairs, so there could also be a group specific to your local area. If you cannot find a group that is to your liking, you could consider going open source on your own to unburden your library from costly licensing fees.

Most of the savings realized by Bloomfield–Eastern Greene County are consequences of Evergreen Indiana's cooperative nature. An open-source ILS means that member libraries can run Evergreen on as many workstations as they please without paying a cent in licensing fees. The shared catalog means that the library can scale back its purchasing of MARC records and attach items to the holdings of larger libraries. Shared circulation policies mean that the library's patrons have access to much more than what the library can afford to put on its own shelves. Outsourced overdue notices mean no staff time needs to be devoted to this repetitive and thankless task. Some of these savings are easily quantified, like the absence of a $14,000 software licensing bill, or elimination of a shift from the part-time work schedule. Other savings are more abstract. For example, it would be difficult to put a dollar amount on the library's collection development savings, since the library does not keep a tally of items not purchased because they were on the shelf elsewhere in Evergreen Indiana. Overall, the library estimates its annual savings to be approximately $20,000, which will more than make up for the $16,000 loss in property tax revenue.

OPEN SOURCE INFORMATION

Check out www.koha.org and www.open-ils.org for information on Koha and Evergreen, the two most popular open-source ILS programs. Less known are NewGenLib, PMB, and OpenBiblio.

What's more, Evergreen Indiana allows the Bloomfield–Eastern Greene County Public Library to offer services to its patrons that quite simply did not exist before. Patrons are now able to receive e-mail notification of items checked out to them with upcoming due dates. Patrons can place items on hold from any one of the fifty-three member libraries (as of December 2009) and have them delivered to their home library at no charge. The adoption of Evergreen Indiana's circulation lengths increased the circulation periods for every single item in the library and, with the exception of late fees for books, the adoption of Evergreen Indiana's across-the-board 25-cent per-item per-day late fee resulted in a reduction in late fees across the board. In summation, the transition to Evergreen Indiana has been almost completely positive. It is the very rare initiative that allows a public library to cut costs while increasing services, but Evergreen Indiana has done both.

WORK CITED

DeBoer, Larry. 2008. "The Impact of Property Tax Legislation on Indiana Households." *Indiana Business Review* 83 (1).

PART VI

Management

17

BRINGING THE OUTSIDE BACK IN
Creative and Cost-Effective Outreach Strategies

Kacy Vega and Kim Becnel

WHEN DEEP BUDGET cuts forced the Union County (North Carolina) Public Library to eliminate its outreach department, immediately shutting services to afterschool programs and day cares, we feared we had lost all opportunity to serve the needs of that large majority of the county's children who, for various reasons, never set foot inside our library facilities. As hard times are wont to do, however, these new resource scarcities encouraged us to reexamine and reprioritize our goals for offering these outreach services in the first place and to think creatively about how to achieve those goals.

The reassessment of our outreach activities resulted in the development of two new, essentially in-house programs to meet outreach goals; those programs are the subjects of this chapter. But before describing them, we offer several suggestions for evaluating your outreach program and perhaps, like us, redirecting some of your activities to accomplish similar goals in other ways:

Evaluate your outreach efforts:

- What are your outreach goals? If you haven't already, take the time to write them out. Be as specific as possible.
- Are your current programs meeting these goals?

- What resources is your library currently expending on outreach? Are you putting those resources to the best, maximum use?

Meet your goals in new or more effective ways:

- What other agencies are working toward goals similar or complementary to the ones you've defined? Give them a call and schedule a meeting to see how you might work together.
- Consider working through adults to reach the children you are targeting. What continuing education opportunities can you provide to teachers and childcare workers?

Think about what you have to offer and get patrons to come to you:

- Many grant programs require grantees to partner with other community organizations. If you offer to support a school or other agency's grant project with library programming, your partner may be quite willing to bus children right to your doors. These kinds of partnerships are win-win for everyone involved.
- Investigate the requirements for providing continuing education credits for teachers and childcare workers who participate in your programs. Often, this is easier to arrange than you would think, and it provides a wonderful incentive for participation.

THE OLD MODEL: THE OUTREACH VAN TAKES ITS SHOW ON THE ROAD

For approximately thirty years, the Union County Public Library had reached out to the early childhood community via its outreach department made up of four personnel, an extensive book collection, and two vans. Five days a week, the outreach department traveled in and out of communities in the county, bringing library services to those unable to visit our library locations. Servicing more than seventy-five preschool and day care programs, the department offered storytimes that focused on the development of early literacy skills. Outreach personnel would explain these skills to the childcare providers and model them while conducting storytimes with the children. In addition to working with the early childhood community, the outreach department also extended book-lending and programming services to afterschool centers and homebound adults. When the department was eliminated, homebound services were reassigned to other library staff, but programming at day cares and afterschool facilities simply ceased.

NEW MODELS, PART I: BRINGING CHILDREN TO US

Coincidentally, just when the budget woes were at their worst, our children's department was beginning a partnership with the Union County Public School's 21st Century Community Learning Centers program. 21st Century, a grant-funded program supported by the North Carolina Department of Public Instruction and Title IV federal funds, is designed to help children reach grade-level competency in their major subjects and to provide them with enrichment activities and experiences. Because the library's partnership with 21st Century involved bussing children to their local public library for a series of regular programs, the children's department realized the potential inherent in this new collaborative program to address the gap in services we now faced. We began to think of this venture in terms of a new outreach goal—not simply reaching as many children as possible but actually transforming the children we do reach into regular library users.

For Better or Worse: Old Model versus New

The initial series of programs was very successful. The children enjoyed themselves, learned a lot, and many brought their parents in to get library cards on our special 21st Century Family Literacy Night. The children's staff realized that this new model, which involved having the children bussed to us instead of sending library staff out to them, did compensate, in part, for the loss of the outreach department. We were reaching children who were not likely to come to the library on their own, entertaining and educating them about the library, and encouraging them to check out books—just the things that outreach was designed to do. Further, we accomplished the additional and significant goals of actually bringing the children into the library for a series of visits and teaching them how to use the library to find items for recreational reading and school assignments. We think that these additional factors will increase the likelihood of program participants becoming regular library users. Our 21st Century partners were so pleased with our participation that not only have they invited us to partner with them again this year, but they also have asked us to develop a series of programs for middle schoolers, a request we were more than happy to accommodate.

There are some significant ways in which the outreach model was superior to the collaborations model: the number of children served and the number of books checked out were significantly greater in the outreach program. Although it would be difficult for the collaborations model—operating with much less in the way of library resources and staff time   to accomplish what outreach did in terms of these statistics, there are some steps we can take to move in that direction. First of all, we can work on expanding the program to include additional schools and continue to develop other collaborative relationships that result in getting more kids bussed to the library for regular programs. Second, we can emphasize the importance of getting the participating children library cards and offer them some time to select and check out books on their visits.

Highlights of Working with 21st Century to Get Kids to the Library

- Since 21st Century enrolls children who are significantly below grade level, working with this program allows us to specifically target kids who are having trouble in school. Many of these are kids who are not coming to the library on their own and who could greatly benefit from the library's resources and programs such as Homework Help.
- Orientation nights for parents allow us to draw the whole family into the library and give us a chance to encourage parents to get cards for themselves and their children.
- Regular visits enable kids to grow comfortable with the library and familiar with using its resources, making them more likely to return.
- Regular visits give library staff a real chance to establish positive relationships with children, which also encourage them to return to the library.

Some Potential (but Not Overwhelming) Challenges

- Identifying projects in the community to become involved with.
- Negotiating and compromising on curriculum and scheduling.
- Lack of credit: despite having its own goals met in a supportive, collaborative role, the library is not the grant winner or overarching director of these types of programs.

NEW MODELS, PART II: BRINGING ADULTS WHO WORK WITH CHILDREN TO US

When we realized that the library would no longer be sending out emissaries of early literacy, the children's and family literacy departments collaborated to develop a workshop for training childcare providers in the six early literacy skills of ALA's Every Child Ready to Read program. The hands-on workshop, featuring many books from the library's circulating collection, was designed to meet the goal of teaching early literacy skills to the children in our communities more effectively—by training childcare workers to teach those skills every day in their classrooms. Participants received continuing education credits through the North Carolina Division of Child Development for attending the class, which generated interest and bolstered attendance.

For Better or Worse: Old Model versus New

Evaluations of the early literacy workshops revealed that the program was a success and also indicated that providers felt prepared to apply what they had learned in the workshop in their classrooms. Throughout the course of the workshop, participants even contributed their own ideas for activities that would effectively support early literacy skills. Providers also expressed renewed interest in using the library's resources and suggested ideas for future workshop topics in the area of early literacy.

One powerful factor in the success of the outreach department was that it exposed early childcare providers to early literacy skills on a monthly basis. On the other hand, when providers attend our workshop, they receive only two hours of instruction. In the future, we can supplement this initial workshop with follow-up classes and additional workshops that cater to the needs and interests expressed by the childcare providers. Both attempts would further enhance providers' knowledge of early literacy and sustain relationships with the childcare providers themselves.

Another challenge we face is coaxing childcare providers accustomed to being visited by the library into visiting the library themselves. Encouraging providers to participate in library professional development opportunities establishes a good place to start. However, attaining the desired turnout may necessitate additional incentives. Free children's books for the provider's classroom, a light lunch for program participants, or even a few raffle prizes could increase participation.

Highlights of Offering Training Workshops to Childcare Workers

- Empowers teachers to use and teach early literacy skills.
- Workshop is cost effective, utilizing existing library resources from books to meeting room space.
- Reintroduces early childhood professionals to library resources, especially encouraging use of titles in the children's collection.
- Library maintains connection with the early childhood community.

- Teachers receive two contact hour credits for participation in the two-hour workshop.

Potential Obstacles

- Planning, marketing, and implementation of workshops require time and effort for full-time staff, who may be limited by other job duties.
- Securing incentives for participation such as continuing education credits, free books for the classroom, or complimentary snacks or lunch.

CONCLUSION

The outreach department served the library well for many years, extending library materials and services to the community outside our doors. The costs, however, proved to be too much when tough economic times prevailed. In response, we developed two basic cost-effective strategies to maintain

---

CONDUCTING WORKSHOPS FOR CAREGIVERS: DON'T FORGET THE LITTLE THINGS

Provide name tags to participants to create a sense of familiarity.

Create a recommended book list of all children's books covered in the workshop. Participants can later refer to titles of interest and check them out from the library.

Make sure providers know where the workshop will be held. Post signs outside of the building indicating the entrance and workshop's location.

Go through a trial run of the workshop the day before, making sure all audiovisual equipment functions properly.

Using library materials in your workshop? Make sure you check them out ahead of time to ensure they will be available the day of the workshop.

When preregistering participants, be sure to record their phone numbers. Then you can place reminder calls prior to the workshop, increasing the likelihood of greater attendance.

community ties, to promote use of the library, and to support early literacy skills development. Our collaboration with the 21st Century program invited children, their parents, and their teachers to come into the library, check out books, and enjoy programs. In many cases, first-time or infrequent users of the library got their first library cards during their visit. Our collaboration with early childhood centers motivated and enabled childcare providers to teach early literacy skills in their classroom and encouraged childcare providers to make use of library materials in their classrooms as well. To accomplish this, we did have to send some staff outside of the library, but instead of bringing library services directly to Union County citizens, they were tasked with building partnerships and forging the kind of connections necessary to bring patrons—both children and their caregivers—back to us.

The initial motivation behind these program changes, cutting library costs, was clearly accomplished. Average monthly costs for outreach had been around $16,000; average monthly cost of the two new programs was around $750 (2008 to 2009). Moreover, these new efforts work toward the main goal of library outreach—introducing services to citizens who might otherwise not experience them—while doing something else that we think is equally important: helping to restore and reinforce the identity of the library as a locus of learning and literacy in our community.

18

COST FACTORS IN DIGITAL PROJECTS
A Model Useful in Other Applications

Lisa L. Crane

THE CLAREMONT UNIVERSITY Consortium (CUC) is the central coordinating and support organization for seven independent colleges, known as the Claremont Colleges, located in Southern California. A centralized library is one of a myriad of services provided by CUC to the colleges. The library contains a digital production unit consisting of four full-time staff and several part-time student workers. The output of the unit is the Claremont Colleges Digital Library (CCDL). Established in April 2006, the CCDL provides the infrastructure to disseminate unique resources held by the Claremont Colleges and the Claremont Colleges Library.

In March 2009, the digital production unit was asked to provide the cost to put an item into the CCDL. Fortunately, the unit had been gathering data since the fiscal year began on July 1, 2008. Now there was an impetus to crunch the numbers. It took the digital production librarian about two full weeks sequestered behind closed doors, doing nothing but number crunching.

What follows in this case study is not a complete instruction on cost accounting. Rather, I introduce concepts and share the tools and methods used. The numbers in this case study are actual numbers and cover the period from July 1, 2008, through the end of February 2009.

THE VARIABLES

There are two major cost variables when it comes to digital projects: material type and funding/wages. As with most digital libraries, or digital projects, the CCDL contains a variety of source material that must be digitized, uploaded, and described through metadata, including photographs, glass plate negatives, lantern slides, 35 mm slides, videos, oversized materials, scrapbooks, monographs, and documents.

Costs also depend on the funding provided and the various wages paid to students. At the time of our cost analysis, the digital production unit was working with two budgets, three grants, and seven different wage rates:

Budget #1 included wages of $8.50/hour and $9.50/hour.

Budget #2 included wages of $15.00/hour.

Work study for some students cost 25% of Budget #1 rates.

Work study for other students cost 30% of Budget #1 rates.

Grant #1 included wages of $15.00/hour.

Grant #2 included wages of $10.00/hour.

Grant #3 included wages of $8.25/hour and $8.50/hour.

DATA COLLECTION

To do a cost analysis, you must know the inputs and outputs of the project. Inputs are the time spent on various tasks, the time spent on various collections, and the labor wages. Outputs are the results of the project—in this case, the number of items added to the digital library. To quantify the inputs and outputs, you must put methods in place to collect data. As previously mentioned, the digital production unit had been collecting data since the start of the fiscal year. This data collection can be categorized into three parts: a weekly collection report, various budget and grant tracking spreadsheets, and the collection time log. The first two were managed by the digital production librarian and the latter was the responsibility of the students.

Various Budget and Grant Trackers

A different spreadsheet for each budget and each grant was kept. Some were tracked on a weekly basis; others were on a pay-period basis. The spreadsheets (figure 18.1) were structured such that only the hours worked were entered; formulas calculated amount paid per pay period, amount paid year-to-date, and actual versus budgeted dollars. This is a useful tool for projecting work schedules to see how many students can be hired, how many hours each student can work, and how long the budgeted dollars will last. This information was used to calculate costs.

Collection Time Logs

Students received their own notebook, which remained within the digital production center. Notebooks contained a student's personal notes and other reference handouts, a log of equipment problems, and other information. The most important document in their notebook, however, is the collection time log (Pellegrino 2008). The log identifies which students are performing what tasks on which collections and for how long.

FIGURE 18.1
GRANT SPREADSHEET

Grant #2						
2008-2009			20	19	18	17
	Name		9/26/2008	10/10/2008	10/24/2008	11/7/2008
Hours	Student #28		0	0	14.5	6.5
	Student #29		12.25	16	14	15.5
		Total	12.25	16	28.5	22
Rate	Student #28		$10.00	$10.00	$10.00	$10.00
	Student #29		$10.00	$10.00	$10.00	$10.00
Expended	Student #28		$0.00	$0.00	$145.00	$65.00
per pay period	Student #29		$122.50	$160.00	$140.00	$155.00
		Total	$122.50	$160.00	$285.00	$220.00
Expended	Student #28		$0.00	$0.00	$145.00	$210.00
YTD	Student #29		$122.50	$282.50	$422.50	$577.50
		Total	$122.50	$282.50	$567.50	$787.50
Summary	**Budget**		$870.00	$870.00	$870.00	$870.00
	Expended YTD		$122.50	$282.50	$567.50	$787.50
	Refunded					
	Balance		$747.50	$587.50	$302.50	$82.50
	Hours YTD		12.25	28.25	56.75	78.75
	Year Remaining		77%	73%	69%	65%
	$ Remaining		86%	68%	35%	9%

Task Codes

As part of the collection time log, students entered a task code from a pre-determined list (Crane and Pellegrino 2008). Task codes helped to define tasks and kept data consistent. Task codes can be pretty detailed. Think of data used for cost analysis as being captured in buckets. It is always easier to capture data in the smallest bucket and then pour this information into larger buckets, or aggregate, as needed. If data are captured at a higher level, it is not as easy, and perhaps impossible, to break up the information into more minute detail should it become necessary.

Weekly Collection Report

The digital production unit uses CONTENTdm as its digital asset management software. One feature of this software provides a snapshot of the total items included within each collection at the time the report is viewed. Each week the numbers from this report were entered into a spreadsheet. Formulas calculate the change in totals from week to week, thereby providing the incremental additions each week. These weekly additions represented output, and the total for the analysis period was used to calculate costs.

DATA ANALYSIS

This is where the sequestered number crunching session began. Information from each of the student's collection time logs was entered into an entirely new spreadsheet. It is strongly advised that the available person with the most knowledge of the digital projects do the data entry; this allows for an intimacy with the data. One becomes familiar with how each student tracks their time, what tasks are performed, and what collections each student works on. Data quality is enhanced by catching errors, or inconsistencies, in the use of task codes. After all of the information was entered, there were over 2,100 rows of data in the spreadsheet. The data were then sorted by student name, then by collection, and then by task; the results were subtotaled by collection with total hours by student (figure 18.2).

Budget Data: Hours

The next step consisted of condensing those 2,100 rows of data into a single line per student and comparing the collection time log hours with the actual paid hours taken from the various budget and grant spreadsheets. Starting with a new Excel workbook, students were listed by name down the first column on the first sheet. Each collection was listed as a column heading across the same sheet. The total hours a student worked on a particular collection were entered into the appropriate cell (figure 18.3).

In many cases, the hours documented by the collection time log did not match the actual hours paid. Differences were then "plugged" and allocated across collections. This is where knowledge of the students and the collections they worked on came in handy. Finally, this provided total hours for each collection.

Budget Data: Wages

On a second sheet within the same Excel workbook, the students were again listed by name down the first column and each collection was listed as a column heading across the sheet. Formulas were built into each cell that

---

FIGURE 18.2
COLLECTED DATA

Data collected from Collection/Time Log								
Name	Collection	Task	Date	Start	Stop	Total Hrs	Completed	Hrs/Coll
student #3	cpo	ocr	12/5/2008	10.3	11.8	1.5	65	
student #3	cpo	ocr	12/10/2008	10.1	11.8	1.7	73	
student #3	cpo	ocr	12/12/2008	10.2	11	0.8	39	
student #3	cpo	ocr-cu	2/24/2009	10.1	11.8	1.7	5.5	
student #3	cpo	ocr-cu	2/26/2009	10.1	11.8	1.7	5	
student #3	cpo	ocr-cu	3/3/2009	10	11.8	1.8	6	
student #3	cpo	ocr-cu	3/10/2009	10.2	11.8	1.6	7	10.8
student #3	cwd	cp-rotate	2/17/2009	11.7	11.8	0.1	13	
student #3	cwd	me	2/19/2009	10.1	11.8	1.7	10	
student #3	cwd	sc	12/2/2008	10.5	11.8	1.3	20	
student #3	cwd	sc	2/12/2009	10.1	11.8	1.7	1	
student #3	cwd	sc	2/17/2009	10.2	11.4	1.2	22	
student #3	cwd	sc/cp	10/2/2008	10.15	11.55	1.4	14	
student #3	cwd	sc/cp	10/7/2008	10.1	11.55	1.45	22	
student #3	cwd	sc/cp	10/9/2008	10.35	12	1.65	28	
student #3	cwd	sc/cp	10/14/2008	10.3	11.55	1.25	??	
student #3	cwd	sc/cp	10/16/2008	10.3	11.55	1.25	22	
student #3	cwd	sc/cp	10/23/2008	10.1	11.3	1.2	26	
student #3	cwd	sc/cp	10/28/2008	10.1	11.5	1.4	23	
student #3	cwd	ts	12/12/2008	11.1	11.8	0.7	??	16.3
student #3	sca	me	12/2/2008	10.1	10.3	0.2	26	
student #3	sca	me/mn	11/4/2008	10.2	11.45	1.25	3	
student #3	sca	me/mn	11/6/2008	10.3	11.45	1.15	7	
student #3	sca	me/mn	11/11/2008	10.3	11.5	1.2	8	
student #3	sca	me/mn	11/18/2008	10.15	11.45	1.3	5	
student #3	sca	me/mn	11/20/2008	10.1	11.45	1.35	15	
student #3	sca	measuring	11/20/2008	10.1	11.15	1.05	31	7.5
						34.6		34.6

FIGURE 18.3
BUDGET DATA: HOURS

CCDL Costing March 2009

Budget Data - Hours

Collection alias →

Student Name	Total hours as of 02/27/2009	ck	aot	bce	bia	ccp	cdl	cmt	cpo	csa	cwd	dac-doc	da[illegible]	[illegible]m	nha	pap	per	phl	sca	twi	wsc-file	wsc-ocr	non prod	Total per Ntbk	Total per Other	Total Hrs	Total Hrs v. Budget
Student #1	278	0				19	5				5													247	30		
Student #3	36	0							11		16								9					35	1		
Student #7	69	0														5	65								69		
Student #8	150	0									127			3					8					155	-5		
Student #9	55	0									55													46	9		
Student #10	117	0									81								6				2	127	-11		
Student #12	110	0									30							9			18	19	2	77	33		
Student #22	29	0									29													43	-14		
Student #23	20	0	5								15													20	-1		
Budget #1	2,172																							1,372	800	2,172	0.00
Student #24	150	0		150																					150		
Student #25	64	0				64																			64		
Student #26	88	0				88																			88		
Student #27	85	0				85																			85		
Grant #1	387																							0	387	387	0.00
Student #28	21	0																							21		
Student #29	58	0																						22	35		
Grant #2	79																							22	56	79	0.00
Student #30	33	0																						43	-10		
Student #31	22	0																							22		
Student #32	66	0																							66		
Student #33	12	0																						19	-7		
Grant #3	132																							62	70	132	0.00
Student #34	386							368				18												386			
Student #35	676							555																676			
Budget #2	1,062																							1,062	0	1,062	0.00
Totals - Prod & Non-prod	3,833		5	150	6	309	5	924	11	2	675	18	[illegible]	3	74	5	65	92	26	1	26	19	136	2,519	1,314	3,833	
Less - Non-production	-136																					3697	3832				
Total - Production only	3,697																										

FIGURE 18.4
BUDGET DATA: WAGES

CCDL Costing March 2009																	
Budget Data - $$																	
					Collection alias →												
Student Name	Total hours as of 02/27/2009	Rate	%	Total spent	aot	bce	bia	ccp	cdl		nm	nha	pap	per	non production	Total sum of coll	Rndin di
Student #1	278	$9.50	100%	$2,636.25	$0.00	$0.00	$0.00	$178.13	$51.21	$0	$0.00	$0.00	$0.00	$0.00	$0.00	$2,636.35	0.1
Student #3	36	$9.50	100%	$339.15	$0.00	$0.00	$0.00	$0.00	$0.00	$0	$0.00	$0.00	$0.00	$0.00	$0.00	$339.15	0.0
Student #7	69	$8.50	100%	$586.50	$0.00	$0.00	$0.00	$0.00	$0.00	$0	$0.00	$0.00	$38.25	$548.25	$0.00	$586.50	0.0
Student #8	150	$8.50	30%	$382.50	$0.00	$0.00	$0.00	$0.00	$0.00	$0	7.65	$0.00	$0.00	$0.00	$0.00	$382.50	0.0
Student #9	55	$8.50	25%	$117.58	$0.00	$0.00	$0.00	$0.00	$0.00	$0	0.00	$0.00	$0.00	$0.00	$0.00	$117.62	0.0
Student #10	117	$8.50	25%	$248.26	$0.00	$0.00	$0.00	$0.00	$0.00	$	0.00	$0.00	$0.00	$0.00	$4.25	$248.20	-0.0
Student #12	110	$8.50	100%	$935.85	$0.00	$0.00	$0.00	$0.00	$0.00	$0	00	$0.00	$0.00	$0.00	$17.00	$935.85	0.0
Student #22	29	$8.50	100%	$246.50	$0.00	$0.00	$0.00	$0.00	$0.00	$	00	$0.00	$0.00	$0.00	$0.00	$246.50	0.0
Student #23	20	$8.50	100%	$165.75	$42.50	$0.00	$0.00	$0.00	$0.00	$0	0.00	$0.00	$0.00	$0.00	$0.00	$165.75	0.0
Budget #1	2,172			$16,468.35												$16,468.41	0.0
Student #24	150	$15.00	100%	$2,250.00	$0.00	$2,250.00	$0.00	$0.00	$0.00	$0	.00	$0.00	$0.00	$0.00	$0.00	$2,250.00	0.0
Student #25	64	$15.00	100%	$960.00	$0.00	$0.00	$0.00	$960.00	$0.00	$0	.00	$0.00	$0.00	$0.00	$0.00	$960.00	0.0
Student #26	88	$15.00	100%	$1,320.00	$0.00	$0.00	$0.00	$1,320.00	$0.00	$0	.00	$0.00	$0.00	$0.00	$0.00	$1,320.00	0.0
Student #27	85	$15.00	100%	$1,275.00	$0.00	$0.00	$0.00	$1,275.00	$0.00	$0	0.00	$0.00	$0.00	$0.00	$0.00	$1,275.00	0.0
Grant #1	387			$5,805.00												$5,805.00	0.0
Student #28	21	$10.00	100%	$210.00	$0.00	$0.00	$0.00	$0.00	$0.00	$0	.00	$0.00	$0.00	$0.00	$0.00	$210.00	0.0
Student #29	58	$10.00	100%	$577.50	$0.00	$0.00	$0.00	$0.00	$0.00	$	.00	$0.00	$0.00	$0.00	$0.00	$577.50	0.0
Grant #2	79			$787.50												$787.50	0.0
Student #30	33	$8.25	100%	$268.95	$0.00	$0.00	$0.00	$0.00	$0.00	$	00	$0.00	$0.00	$0.00	$0.00	$268.95	0.0
Student #31	22	$8.25	100%	$181.50	$0.00	$0.00	$0.00	$0.00	$0.00	$0	.00	$0.00	$0.00	$0.00	$0.00	$181.50	0.0
Student #32	66	$8.25	100%	$542.44	$0.00	$0.00	$0.00	$0.00	$0.00	$	00	$0.00	$0.00	$0.00	$0.00	$542.44	0.0
Student #33	12	$8.50	100%	$102.00	$0.00	$0.00	$0.00	$0.00	$0.00	$0	.00	$0.00	$0.00	$0.00	$0.00	$102.00	0.0
Grant #3	132	$8.31		$1,094.89												$1,094.89	0.0
Student #34	386	$15.00	100%	$5,790.75	$0.00	$0.00	$0.00	$0.00	$0.00	$5.52	.00	$0.00	$0.00	$0.00	$0.00	$5,790.75	0.0
Student #35	676	$15.00	100%	$10,144.65	$0.00	$0.00	$0.00	$0.00	$0.00	$8.33	$0.00	$0.00	$0.00	$0.00	$0.00	$10,144.65	0.0
Budget #2	1,062			$15,935.40												$15,935.40	0.0
Totals - Prod & Non-Prod	3,833			$40,091.14	$42.50	$2,250.00	$53.20	$4,241.38	$51.21	$13,8	7.65	$698.25	$38.25	$548.25	$1,273.35	$40,091.19	0.0
Less - Non-production				-$1,273.35													
Total - Production only				$38,817.79													

multiplied the hours from the first sheet ("Budget data—hours") with the hourly rate and percentage. This resulted in a total cost per collection at the bottom of the sheet (figure 18.4).

RESULTS

For each collection, the following were identified as part of this exercise:

- total items added over the fiscal year (taken from the weekly collection report)
- total cost
- average cost per item
- average rate per hour
- total student hours
- average items per hour
- average minutes per item

Of course, some information could not be determined. In some cases, the student labor and hours were tracked by another department and were not accessible for this exercise. In other cases, only digital production staff worked on the collection. Since they were not part of this exercise, these calculations were not done. But, for the most part, considerable information was identified (figure 18.5).

Data Correction and Validation

Some of the results seemed to be on the high side; they stood out and warranted further investigation. In a review of the data it became apparent that the total number of items added to a collection was too low for some of our more complex items, such as monographs. For example, forty-three monographs containing a total of 766 chapters were added to a single collection at a cost of $3,393. Because each chapter was digitized as a PDF and each monograph required descriptive metadata and digital assembly, a denominator of 809 (43 monographs + 766 chapters) was used, resulting in a cost per item of $4.19, which is too high. Once it was realized that the time it took to scan each page of each chapter was not taken into consideration, a new denominator of 7,025 (43 monographs + 766 chapters + 6,216 pages) was used, resulting in a more reasonable $0.48 cost per item. The $3,000-plus dollars represented the time and cost for scanning each page, running the scans through optical character recognition software, creating the PDF, uploading into CONTENTdm, and creating metadata for the single compound object, so

FIGURE 18.5
RESULTS OF THE ANALYSES

Digital Production Services
Costing
March 2009
Collection Data

Collection Name	Total new items added as of 02/26/2009	Total used for calculations	Note	Total Cost	Average Cost per Item	Average Rate per Hour	Student Production Hours	Average Items per Hour	Average Minutes per Item
Antiquities of the Institute for Antiquity and Christianity	533 (97 cpd/436 images)	50	Descriptive metadata only	$42.50	$0.85	$8.50	5.0	10	6
Bulletin of the Institute for Antiquity and Christianity	22 (1 cpd/21 pdf/92 pgs)	92	Scanning/full metadata	$53.20	$0.58	$9.50	5.6	16	4
Boynton Collection of Early Claremont	232	232	Scanning/full metadata	$2,250.00	$9.70	$15.00	150.0	2	39
California Water Documents	829 (43 cpd/766 pdf/6,216 pgs)	7,025	Scanning/PDF/OCR/full metadata	$3,393.12	$0.48	$5.03	674.7	10	6
Campi Phlegraei	111	11	OCR & OCR clean-up	$102.60	$9.33	$9.50	10.8	1	59
Chikanobu and Yoshitoshi Woodblock Prints	36	---	CCDL staff work				0.0		---
Claremont Colleges Photo Archive	980	980	Scanning/full metadata	$4,241.38	$4.33	$13.72	309.3	3	19
Claremont Colleges Sustainability Archive	38 (5 cpd/33 pdf)	5	Full metadata only	$15.20	$3.04	$9.50	1.6	3	19
Claremont Discourse Lectures	3	3	Videos	$51.21	$17.07	$9.50	5.4	1	108
Connie Martinson Talks Books	300	300	Videos	$13,854.90	$46.18	$15.00	923.7	0	185
Drucker Archives	172	151	Scanning/full metadata	$267.00	$1.77	$15.00	17.8	8	7
	---	21	Videos	$1,813.50	$86.36	$15.00	120.9	0	345
Early California Letters	621	---	Special Collections						---
Faculty Scholarship at The Claremont Colleges	55	55	U-SKIs prep work/metadata	$4,023.08	$73.15	$9.49	423.9	0	452
Fashion Plate Collection, 19th Century	222	222	Archival processing/ scanning/full metadata	$1,484.25	$6.69	$9.55	155.5	1	42
Growing a Digital Library	2	---	CCDL staff work						---
History of Jazz 109	14	14	Full metadata only	$43.70	$3.12	$9.50	4.6	3	20
Interface Journal Archive	1 (1 pdf/24 pgs)	24	Scanning/full metadata	$11.40	$0.48	$9.50	1.2	20	3
Italian Renaissance Manuscript Collection	53	---	Special Collections						---
Ken Gonzales-Day Collection	181 (161 items/18 pdf/437 scans)	616	Scanning/full metadata	$1,067.99	$1.73	$7.39	144.5	4	14
Larry Oglesby Collection	1,362	1,362	Scanning/full metadata	$1,669.73	$1.00	$8.66	192.9	7	8

the number of pages scanned had to be included in the divisor. This required a review of all the underlying denominators for each collection and resulted in a "total used for calculations" (see figures 18.4 and 18.5) that went beyond the original denominator of new items added to a collection.

Formulas

A variety of formulas were used to calculate each of the items identified above:

Total cost was derived from the bottom of the "Budget data: wages" sheet by collection.

Student production hours were derived from the "Budget data: hours" sheet by collection.

Average cost per item = Total cost ÷ total used for calculations.

Average rate per hour = total cost ÷ student production hours.

Average items per hour = total used for calculations ÷ student production hours.

Average minutes per item = (student production hours ÷ total used for calculations) x 60.

Additional Cost Factors

This exercise focused solely on student wages because their wages were considered direct costs of digital projects. If there were no digital projects, there would be no student costs. To do a complete cost analysis of digital projects, however, one must also take into account indirect costs, such as direct and indirect staff wages, hardware and software maintenance costs depreciation, and other overhead such as allocations for square footage and utilities.

CONCLUSION

After completing this project, the digital production librarian was able to answer the original question—"How much does it cost to put an item into the digital library?"—with "It depends." Because of the variety of material types and the range of funding sources and wage rates that characterize the inputs to the CCDL, it was difficult to provide an uncomplicated answer.

Once the results were in, many additional uses for this information became apparent. With some supplementary calculations, a cost by material type was determined and the time and cost for scanning and metadata creation for a particular collection were separately identified. Those libraries with projects utilizing fewer material types or a smaller wage variance should be able to derive a comprehensive result.

Managers who understand and quantify the inputs and outputs of a digital project and use some of the tools and methods presented in this case study have a place to start costing their own projects should their administration or external funding sources ask, "What do your digital projects cost?"

WORKS CITED

Crane, Lisa L., and S. Pellegrino. 2008. Task codes. http://ccdl.libraries .claremont.edu/u?/adl,48 (accessed February 26, 2010).

Pellegrino, Sharon. 2008. Collection time log. http://ccdl.libraries.claremont .edu/u?/adl,49 (accessed February 26, 2010).

19

DATA-DRIVEN CANCELLATION DECISIONS

Leslie Farison

DATA-DRIVEN DECISION MAKING and accountability are some of the buzzwords in today's environment, and evaluation of service provision is expected of all types of organizations including libraries. The global economic downturn has forced libraries everywhere to pare down expenditures in a period of diminished resources.

Recently public university libraries have seen sharp budget cuts resulting from major state funding shortfalls. Efforts to preserve jobs have resulted in materials budgets being especially hard hit. In most cases resources must be identified for cancellation and libraries must make realistic decisions about resources they can do without. Selectors are challenged to make difficult decisions that can be defended and that make optimum use of the scarce resources the library has available. The goal of any university library cancellation project must be to reach the targeted spending reductions while maintaining adequate support for research, teaching, learning, and outreach.

When asked to identify resources for cancellation, selectors often do not know the extent of the cuts they may be asked to implement. Administrators may ask the library to prepare various scenarios in anticipation of the state budget being finalized and approved. Selectors at Appalachian State University (ASU) in North Carolina used a priority scheme that identified 10 percent, 15 percent, and 20 percent target reductions in the materials budget

WHY EVALUATE?

Provide accountability for use of limited resources.

Provide legitimacy for decisions.

Find the best alternatives.

Increase cost effectiveness.

Provide transparency for stakeholders.

Enhance communication.

and developed corresponding tiers of cancellation lists. There is no one best way to approach this challenge, but the process outlined in this chapter worked well for ASU.

WHERE TO BEGIN

Initiating a project to review all continuing expense obligations can be overwhelming when you consider the sheer quantity of data involved. First you need a place to hold all of the data you will be gathering. When designing this tool, build in as much flexibility as possible so that it can be used by different users for various purposes. Excel workbooks work well since you can filter and sort the data in a variety of ways. The next step is to populate the spreadsheets with lists of all subscriptions including databases, journals, and standing orders. ASU divided subscription titles into these four workbooks:

Databases and Journal Packages

> Worksheet 1: All Databases/Packages to which ASU Subscribes
> Worksheet 2: Resources Provided through State Libraries and Other
> Providers at No Cost

Journals via Subscription Agent

> Worksheet 1: Single Title Subscriptions and Small Packages
> Worksheet 2: Membership Titles
> Worksheet 3: Titles in Big Packages

Direct-from-Publisher Titles

Standing Order Series

Initial column headings for the Databases and Journal Packages worksheet might look like this:

Database Name · Selector · Record # · Onetime Money · 08–09 Price · 09–10 Price · Date Invoiced · Fund · Subscription Agent? · Notes & Cancellation Rules · Publisher / Platform

For the Journals via Subscription Agent worksheet, they might look like this:

Title Name Subject Area Title Number Order Number Invoice Number Invoice Date 08–09 Price 09–10 Price Open Access Notes & Cancellation Rules Pub Group Pub Package

BIG-TICKET ITEMS FIRST

Spending on electronic resources has overtaken spending on mono-graphs by a significant margin, and with spiraling annual inflation rates for these items it makes sense to focus cancellation efforts there. Not only have electronic materials expenditures grown sharply, they have grown at a rate far exceeding that of library materials expenditures overall. The median ARL university library now spends 54 percent of its materials budget on electronic resources.

Median Electronic Resource Expenditures as a Percentage of Total Materials Expenditures

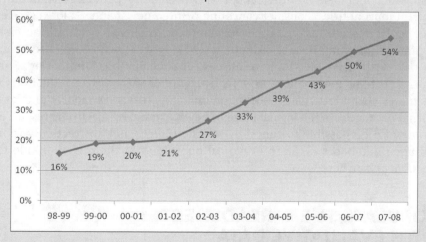

Source: ARL Statistics 2007–2008,
Association of Research Libraries, Washington, DC

DATABASE DECISION CRITERIA

Cost/use/cost per use

Title/subject/year coverage

Faculty research value

Curricular support

Interface

Ease of searching

Retrieval results

Ease of manipulating results

Vendor reliability

Licensing considerations

Populating the spreadsheet with descriptive data can be partially automated via your ILS, your subscription agent, and your vendors, but a good deal of the data gathering must be done manually.

LOW-HANGING FRUIT

If you have not already done so in previous serials review efforts, eliminating redundancy of format duplication is the easiest place to begin. High customer satisfaction with electronic journals, full-text databases, and the Internet has resulted in increased demand as well as increased expectations. In most disciplines, electronic formats exceed print in importance for research and scholarly activities, and students certainly prefer online access. Generally, once a resource becomes available electronically, the print format becomes a low-use item.

The impact of canceling duplicate items on teaching and research is minimal since the content is still available and few if any titles are lost. Be careful of situations in which you lose electronic access if you cancel the print version or in which membership titles cannot be canceled independently. In addition to print journal titles, consider canceling printed newspapers, indexes, reference tools, microforms, and other formats that duplicate electronic access.

After eliminating format redundancy, the most fruitful step is to evaluate more expensive electronic resources for cancellation. Eliminating a few big-ticket items may be a more effective way to meet target reductions in the materials budget than canceling many single titles. Databases and large journal packages are the logical place to begin examining electronic resources. It may also be possible to cancel electronic indices and abstract-only (non-full-text) databases if the information contained in them is available for searching elsewhere.

POPULATE THE SPREADSHEET WITH EVALUATIVE DATA

Although there are many criteria to consider when making value judgments about subscriptions, allowing usage statistics to guide cancellation decisions is one way of letting the market decide what resources are most valuable.

Allocating a library's materials budget in a manner consistent with proportional use increases the library's return on investment.

Having access to timely, consistent, and accurate usage statistics is critical for making retention decisions, but they are not always easy to gather. Your library may have already collected and organized the information needed to access usage statistics from the vendor, but if you need to gather it, allow time to do so. We started with a partial list of URL, log-in, and password information, but it took several weeks to update and complete the list.

For some subscriptions the log-in for administrative functions and the log-in to obtain usage statistics are the same. In other instances you may have to contact the vendor to obtain information needed to access the reports. ASU chose to add this information directly into the spreadsheets and added the following column headings.

URL   Log-in   Password   Abstract   Full Text   2008 Total Retrievals   Cost per Search   Action Recommended

MAKING SENSE OF USAGE REPORTS

In the early stages of electronic resource usage statistics, each content provider reported statistics in its own way. A lack of consistency and standards has persistently complicated our ability to compare usage statistics from

---

SINGLE-TITLE DECISION CRITERIA

Core title

Cost/use/cost per use

Curricular support

Available in aggregated database

Embargo length

Archive depth

Promptness in adding new issues

Held elsewhere in network/consortial/regional holdings

ILL/document delivery

COUNTER

COUNTER (Continuing Online Usage of Networked Electronic Resources) is an international initiative to improve the reliability of online usage statistics. It allows librarians to compare usage statistics from different vendors and make better-informed purchasing decisions. COUNTER's objective is to ensure that vendor online usage reports are credible, compatible, and consistent. Only vendors whose reports comply with the specifications of the codes of practice can be regarded as COUNTER compliant. For more information, see www.projectcounter.org.

different vendors. In the past few years, data are increasingly available in COUNTER format.

We have found "COUNTER Database Report 1: Total Searches and Sessions by Month and Database" to be of limited value. Definitions of searches and sessions are not applied consistently. More reliable statistics are those reported in "COUNTER Journal Report 1: Number of Successful Full-Text Article Requests by Month and Journal." Some vendors also offer additional statistics not required by COUNTER, such as Abstract Requests or Simultaneous Uses for the same time periods.

Current practice for statistics retrieval calls for library staff to go to each individual publisher's website and manually retrieve statistical data. Although data are reported monthly, ASU currently collects and reports usage only on an annual basis because of the tedious, repetitive, and time-consuming process of collecting the data manually. We hope to automate this process in the near future by gathering usage reports via the SUSHI protocol. This promises to be a huge time saver since once the automatic feeds are set up they require no attention. Data will be collected automatically on a monthly basis.

Some libraries have developed their own systems to manage electronic resources and may be able to incorporate the SUSHI protocol to automate collection of usage data. Newer versions of some commercially available ERM (electronic resource management) software systems used by libraries support the SUSHI protocol and offer automated request and response models for harvesting electronic resource usage data utilizing a web services framework.

ANALYZE, SYNTHESIZE, INTERPRET, PRESENT

Now it's time to turn the data into useful information. At this point the selector has information to nominate titles for cancellation. Usage statistics are triangulated with other criteria to determine relative value reasonably. The most logical approach is to nominate resources that have high cost per use unless there are mitigating factors. Look out for items that show zero use, since this may indicate that access to the resource was never activated.

Using a priority scheme like the ASU scenarios of 10 percent, 15 percent, and 20 percent materials budget reductions allows you to keep your options open. When you receive the finalized budget, you can implement the most appropriate level of cancellations.

Flat and declining materials budgets mean nothing new can be added unless something is canceled. If you have identified more than you really need to cancel, you may elect to eliminate some less useful resources voluntarily in order to make room for new items requested by current faculty, for new faculty research needs or new courses or programs, or to strengthen your overall collection.

ALTERNATIVE ACCESS

It is no longer possible financially to support the old "just in case" model of collecting resources for potential or future use—a model in which it was not unusual for a high percentage of materials in research collections to rarely or never be used. Key to cancellation decisions is the expectation that you can rely on effective interlibrary loan and document delivery services for continuing access to canceled titles. It is critical to increase funding in these areas to provide for the increased need for services.

SUSHI

Sushi is more than a delicious food offering from Japan. The Standardized Usage Statistics Harvesting Initiative (SUSHI) protocol is a way of harvesting electronic resource data automatically and is intended to replace tedious, repetitive, and time-consuming user-mediated collection of usage data reports. Release 3 of the COUNTER code of practice requires content providers to support SUSHI by reporting usage data in a standard COUNTER XML format, making the retrieval automatic and easier to use. For more information, see www.niso.org/workrooms/sushi/.

One of the cheapest routes to electronic resources is open access. Over the past few years the number and quality of open-access resources have grown and provided affordable access to some journal content. Key institutions and agencies that fund or support major research have started to encourage faculty and other researchers to publish research findings openly.

Another avenue that may prove to be cost effective is offering access to materials at the point of need. Strategies include providing on-demand purchase of articles and purchasing specified amounts of journal use in a database instead of subscribing to titles.

BENEFITS AND CHALLENGES

Few may view a budget crisis as an opportunity, but benefits can be realized from a cancellation review process. This type of assessment can give librarians tremendous insights into what already exists in a collection of resources and what may be needed to make the collection more responsive and relevant to the students and faculty. It can highlight how well a library's materials support the goals, needs, and mission of the library and, by extension, those of the university. Combining the access information with usage data provides information necessary to make highly accurate and responsible collection decisions and can build an overall picture of the strengths and weaknesses of the collection and target areas that may need development.

There are inherent challenges in obtaining both descriptive and evaluative data for resources, which are subscribed to in a multitude of ways. The tools available to gather and measure data about complex subscriptions are not perfect. A great deal of time and attention are needed to gather, clean up, and interpret the data. Electronic usage statistics for one item may be reported in a variety of different ways through various portals, and they are not necessarily unique. If a title is held in more than one database, how do you accurately measure access? Are you overcounting or undercounting?

CONCLUSION

Despite these challenges and shortcomings, the information gathered from the process outlined in this chapter proved to be extremely useful as we at ASU identified and nominated titles for cancellation. We met our own budgetary goals with a minimum of pain and impact on users and surprisingly few objections or complaints.

The financial constraints faced by higher education will most likely result in more and deeper cancellations in the future, and decisions will grow more difficult as collections grow increasingly lean. Having effective evaluative tools and processes to gather and analyze usage data allows selectors to have confidence that they are making prudent and objective decisions that can be justified to administrators and faculty.

20

GREEN INFORMATION TECHNOLOGY SAVES MONEY, SAVES RESOURCES

Sarah Passonneau

SUSTAINABILITY HAS A long history in the United States. Theodore Roosevelt made conservation a mainstream concept through the creation of the National Park Service. Today more and more libraries understand that green management practices conserve energy and save money. Depending on current organizational practices, green or environmentally friendly information technology (IT) processes can save a library thousands of dollars in energy costs and general resource expenses. At the Iowa State University (ISU) library, balancing the need to conserve resources because of budget cuts with the need to provide high-quality service has become a top priority. The simple green IT projects implemented at the library have saved substantial amounts of money while improving services, involving stakeholders, and creating new long-term community partnerships.

THE REALITY: BUDGET CUTS AND THE SUSTAINABILITY TASK FORCE

In the 2008/9 academic year ISU budget cuts precipitated a 5 percent reduction in library finances. It is projected that during 2009/10 through 2011/12 the university will continue to face severe budget reductions. The dean of the library called on all library staff to contribute money-saving ideas and also asked each department to review its practices. The creation of a sustainability task force grew out of a need to examine resource use. A summary of purpose, goals, and charge of the task force were as follows: assess best environmental practices (also known as green practices) through a participatory process involving the entire library community, review current policies and make recommendations, and promote the greening of library operations. Members of the task force came from all areas of the library. Each member provided important perspectives and information.

The sustainability task force learned that, in particular, green IT practices save money and instill smart management practices. Many businesses are looking at "smart," or green, IT. Green IT not only saves money but also encourages reflective and proactive strategic planning (Dunphy, Griffiths, and Benn 2009, 88; Esty and Winston 2006, 38, 46–57; Velte, Velte, and Elsenpeter 2008, 50–67; Webber and Wallace 2009, 49).

The introduction of new practices in any organization almost inevitably brings about internal change, and such change requires the support of the organization's members. Any library that wishes to introduce green IT measures should therefore build a team and develop internal community buy-in. Even in the most austere economic times, saving money is never solely the activity of an individual; it requires community participation. Community change agents or leaders should be identified who can engender community responsiveness (Miller 2006, 211). Teams that have effective leaders can conduct an IT audit and create actionable goals that either save energy or raise funds.

LEADERS AND TEAMWORK

Although the chair of the sustainability task force had chief responsibility for the library's green efforts, she worked closely with the library's IT officer, who was not a member of the task force, regarding the library's use of technology. Together, the IT officer and the task force chair facilitated intralibrary communication and the exchange of ideas and created efficient and inclusive processes that saved, and will continue to save, the ISU library substantial amounts of money. This chapter details two of these measures: public printing and computer usage processes.

Strategy: Think Green, an IT Audit

The sustainability task force fashioned goals based on the "reduce, reuse, and recycle" framework of the U.S. Environmental Protection Agency. Three of the

FIGURE 20.1
IT INVENTORY GRID

	MODEL	QUANTITY	AREA	PURPOSE	USAGE PATTERNS	MATERIAL CONSUMPTION	SETTINGS	REPLACEMENT PLAN
Computers								
Monitors								
Printers								
Computers								
Monitors								
Printers								

PRINTING AND SUSTAINABILITY

For a source of information that empowers community members by providing clear standards and methods related to printing and provides information and behavioral prompts for staff and faculty, see the University of Washington's Creative Communications website, www.washington.edu/admin/pub serv/printing/print.save.html.

goals were to assess and implement a plan to reduce waste, to assess and implement a plan to reduce energy consumption, and to assess and measure monetary savings.

These goals provided a framework within which the task force could proceed to assess building practices and develop actionable items. The sustainability chair created a comprehensive IT inventory grid (figure 20.1), which the task force filled with data. Looking at energy and material consumption as well as reviewing hardware replacement plans provided a wealth of details. Most important, the task force learned the purposes of the various pieces of hardware, their usage patterns, and their default settings. After the audit the library determined several interesting facts—among them that not all the printers could duplex print and that management of the public computers did not optimize energy savings. These facts informed several projects.

After completing the inventory, the group developed a five-step process:

1. Assess data.

2. Develop a list of actionable items.

3. Identify stakeholders.

4. Apply for funds (when applicable).

5. Implement best practices.

Two projects emerged from the data analysis, one dealing with public printing processes and the other with public and work-related computing.

First Project Action Item: Create Sustainable Public Printing

After learning that none of the fifteen public laser printers could duplex print, the sustainability task force, in conjunction with IT, developed an actionable item: retrofit all the public printers to reduce paper consumption and save money.

The library's budget made funding the project problematic. The sustainability chair took the lead to identify stakeholders or users of the public

COMPUTERS AND SUSTAINABILITY

Here are two resources that provide clear information regarding computer use; they are must-reads for anyone interested in green IT.

Climate Savers Computing Initiative, University of Michigan. Best Practices for Faculty/Staff @ the Office. http://climate savers.umich.edu/resources/Faculty%20&%20Staff/index .html#faculty_office.

University of Colorado, Boulder, Environmental Center. Green Computing Guide. http://ecenter.colorado.edu/energy/ projects/green_computing.html.

printers. A review of LibQUAL+ survey data showed that undergraduates constituted more than 50 percent of the visitors to the library. Over the past five years undergraduate visits to the library had increased by 2 percent. Total foot traffic in the library had increased by 5 percent every year during much of the same period. In addition, the sustainability chair conducted an environmental scan and found that in the public areas students processed more than 90 percent of the print jobs.

Having this information, the sustainability chair and IT officer agreed that the Government of the Student Body (GSB), as the voice of the student body, could be a potential project funder. The IT staff provided pricing and model numbers for the retrofit. The library submitted a request for funding to the student budget director of the GSB. The student director of sustainability reviewed the proposal. The student leaders felt that the project would be advantageous to students. Because the library had developed a well-crafted argument with powerful data, involved students, and clearly stated the need to retrofit the printers, the project was funded by the students for the students to support their needs as well as their interest in sustainability.

The goal to retrofit public printers to reduce paper consumption was thus negotiated by the IT officer and sustainability chair. They agreed on needs, involved library staff, and reached out to stakeholders. The retrofit project funded by the GSB cost $3,770. The library implemented the retrofit in October 2009. Although the total paper savings have remained unclear during the writing of this chapter, it is projected that the savings for one year could amount to 5,000 pounds, or 1,000 reams, of paper, for a cost savings of $3,650.

ENERGY AND MONEY SAVING TIPS

Set computers and monitors to "sleep" when inactive for more than a few minutes if no authentication process is needed.

Turn off office equipment at night, over the weekend, and during holidays.

Make duplexing the default for printers.

Use smart strips and unplug them when gone for the weekend or extended periods.

Implement thin client technology where and when appropriate.

Second Project Action Item: Reduce Computer Energy Consumption

The sustainability chair used a Kill A Watt–EZ power meter to determine how much it cost to run a computer for 24 hours a day. A Kill A Watt–EZ power meter measures the electrical use of electronic devises. The annual cost to run a computer was $49.91. There are a total of 275 public computers in the library, so it cost $13,725 to run all the computers annually. Then a second test measured costs when the computers and monitors were off for more than 30 minutes, such as when no one was in the room. The annual cost was $23.97 per computer. This showed that libraries could see more than a 50 percent savings in energy utility costs if the monitors and computers were shut down at night. The IT department had already set the computers to standby mode after 45 minutes, with the hard drive and monitor off after 20 minutes. But starting in the summer of 2009, the IT group powered down all public computers overnight.

Future Projects

Computer usage patterns will be assessed in the staff areas and recommendations made for library savings. A list of best practices for computer usage, photocopying, and printing will be posted for the library community via the intranet as well as in work areas. Where appropriate, building services will place energy-saving smart strips in work areas. Smart strips reduce phantom power draw. By eliminating phantom power draw, a library can save 5–12 percent in related electrical usage. The library is also exploring guidelines related to the production of instructional materials regarding the use of electronic equipment. A survey will be sent out to our library community to determine the staff's current computer usage and printing practices. Obtaining such community-wide input promotes inclusiveness and community building (Estes 2009, 77–91; Lamb 2009, 90–101). Assessing the survey results will inform internal educational needs. The library and IT staff are examining other measures such as a thin client implementation. Usually, thin client implementation involves servers host-

READ GREEN

There are many books riding the wave of green IT sustainability. One that covers human factors such as collaboration and governmental regulations and provides examples for businesses to save resources and money is John Lamb's *The Greening of IT* (2009).

ing programs, processing information, and conducting major functions. The desktop computer is merely a shell from which users access the computing power of an external source. It is possible this could save money and energy in public work areas.

More about Leaders

You can be become a local leader for green IT practices. If you are flexible and follow the five steps listed earlier in this chapter, you will move forward with your projects and improve workplace efficiencies. Any library interested in implementing an IT audit must create a team with a leader who can manage a variety of often opposing ideas and who inspires a sense of inclusiveness (Estes 2009, 169–177). Leaders generate ideas within the group. A leader is a facilitator who guides members along a path, but it takes a team to institute change and save money.

CONCLUSION: PRACTICAL APPLICATION FOR LIBRARIES

The ISU library's processes can be repurposed for different types of libraries. After completing an IT inventory, it is important to identify stakeholders. All libraries have stakeholders who are possible funding partners. A public library, for instance, can work with youth groups, Friends of the Library, or other groups to create a sustainability fund-raiser. Any library that receives local financial support should build relationships with city hall; this sows the seeds for potential funding of sustainability projects. School libraries can work with PTAs, PTOs, and school boards. Special libraries have constituents who could collaborate to fund green IT projects. Include your stakeholders while initiating smart resource management practices in these austere times.

WORKS CITED

Dunphy, Dexter C., Andre Griffiths, and Suzanne Benn. 2009. *Organizational Change for Corporate Sustainability: A Guide for Leaders and Change Agents of the Future.* New York: Routledge.

Estes, Jonathan. 2009. *Smart Green: How to Implement Sustainable Business Practices in Any Industry and Make Money.* Hoboken, NJ: John Wiley and Sons.

Esty, Daniel C., and Andrew S Winston. 2006. *Green to Gold: How Smart Companies Use Environmental Strategy to Innovate, Create Value, and Build Competitive Advantage.* New Haven, CT: Yale University Press.

Lamb, John. 2009. *The Greening of IT: How Companies Can Make a Difference for the Environment.* Upper Saddle River, NJ: IBM Press/Pearson.

Miller, Mike. 2006. "The Eagle and the Worm: The Active Society from a Community Organizer's Perspective." In *The Active Society Revisited,* ed. Wilson Carey McWilliams. Lanham, MD: Rowman and Littlefield.

Velte, Toby J., Anthony T. Velte, and Robert C. Elsenpeter. 2008. *Green IT: Reduce Your Information System's Environmental Impact while Adding to the Bottom Line.* New York: McGraw-Hill.

Webber, Larry, and Michael Wallace. 2009. *Green Tech: How to Plan and Implement Sustainable IT Solutions.* New York: American Management Association.

21

MANAGING STAFF STRESS DURING BUDGET CRISES

Lessons for Library Managers

Colleen S. Harris and Mary Chimato

GOOD MANAGEMENT IS always essential to the health of an organization, but during times of economic crisis it becomes essential to the existence of the organization and to the well-being of staff. In the current economic climate, when many organizations are cutting budgets and workforce to remain viable, our colleagues, administrators, and staff are all subject to the stress that accompanies uncertain times. Understandably people are worried about their jobs. To maintain a positive and productive environment, it is essential for managers to recognize and alleviate staff concerns to the best of their ability.

COMMUNICATION

Communication is the principal tool separating effective managers from ineffective ones. Particularly critical during times of instability and change, keeping staff informed alleviates anxiety and maintains focus on the library's goals. Communicating change reinforces the trust and support necessary to a healthy workforce and a productive organization.

Address rumors. Gossip and speculation about the future can distract and paralyze staff. Particularly during budget crises, no news is *not* good news.

Communicating the reality of the situation, dispelling rumors and half-truths, and making clear what has been decided and what is still in flux serve to keep staff focused.

The personal touch counts. Though e-mail is good for broadcasting messages widely, staff meetings and conversations with individual staff members are best to convey critical and complex information. They also humanize you as a manager.

Participatory decision making eases worry. When you consult staff for their input, inform them of the likely parameters of budget impacts and keep them updated about the status of unknowns. Staff are far more likely to feel comfortable asking questions instead of making up worst-case scenarios, and more likely to put forth their own recommendations for addressing the situation.

Ask the experts. Often the folks who know a process or service best are those who perform the task on a daily basis. Your staff should be instrumental in revising or replacing workflows and services. Brainstorming organizational change, giving staff a stake in the library's future, and including them in the vision of how the library plans to weather change and fulfill its mission with different resource allocations benefit both the library and its staff.

NURTURING STAFF

One of the most important, and perhaps most overlooked, facts about dealing with staff during organizational change and crisis is that kindness and

VOICES OF EXPERIENCE: NCSU LIBRARIES

Facing budget cuts in 2009, the access and delivery services department of North Carolina State University Libraries closed the Media and Microform Center, absorbed the technology lending program formerly stationed in the Learning Commons, and absorbed staff from other library departments. The following were essential to the smooth transition of materials, processes, and personnel:

- Committees comprising all stakeholders: librarians, staff, administrators, university faculty, and students.
- Documentation of new procedures and development of new training materials.
- Staff enthusiastic about change, developing and documenting new processes, and cross-training colleagues.

consideration go a long way. As a manager, you should care deeply about your staff—these are the people who get the work done, who hold most of the knowledge about how to make your library run, and who are a great repository of institutional history. It is not difficult to extend a caring and considerate attitude and take the edge off of the discomfort caused by economic uncertainties, and your staff will be far more effective and able to maintain a positive outlook. Some easy-to-implement but much-appreciated tips include the following:

Listen. Many staff members may be stressed and feel that they have no power over the library's situation. Be an attentive listener, not interrupting, and validate concerns. Ask questions as necessary, repeat the main points to make sure you understand the primary concerns, and make sure to schedule a follow-up discussion if it is called for.

Be transparent. Disclose as much as you can about the decision-making process, and ask employees for input and advice. If you are unable to act on that input, explaining why helps people feel they have been heard. Describe how decisions were made when it comes to announcing changes or other important decisions, as opposed to creating a "black-box" scenario in which it appears that decisions are made in a vacuum.

Be available. Creating an open-door policy in which staff feel comfortable stopping by to discuss things with you, offering opportunities for individuals or small groups to voice concerns, and simply knowing your staff as individuals help demonstrate how much you value their commitment to their work. Budget woes may exist, but this is still an opportunity to create trust and grow relationships.

EFFECTIVE PLANNING FOR THE CHANGING WORKPLACE

Doing more with less, reassessing services, and reallocating staff and resources are always a challenge. When you are making decisions about staff and resources, keeping the following in mind will reduce staff stress and provide a clear path:

Goal setting. Set specific goals. Goals should be challenging but not impossible to achieve and should be made through staff/management collaboration for maximum buy-in. Including target dates, deadlines, and expected time lines helps to keep everyone on track and provides a reference point when reviewing and altering goals becomes necessary.

Clear and concise expectations. During economic downturns, when there may be fewer people to perform the same amount of work, provide clear expectations, agreed-on deliverables, and the opportunity to ask for assistance, clarification, or further training to ensure that staff can meet the demands of their jobs. This approach will give them a firm grounding and control over their work.

Process breakdown. If you are looking to streamline workflows, detailing the tasks to be accomplished and breaking them down into process steps can be helpful. Engaging staff in this process ensures that no tasks or details are overlooked.

22

STUDENT ASSISTANTS
Maximize Effectiveness through Coordinated Training

Ken Johnson and Sue Hisle

IT SHOULD COME as no surprise that lean years arrive from time to time in libraries. Those who have worked long enough know that library budgets rise and fall with the economy. During a recession or any other time of funding cuts, maximizing the effectiveness of personnel takes on heightened priority. Academic libraries are often lucky enough to have a pool of student assistants. To maximize the library's assets, the assigned tasks of student assistants are worthy of review.

This case study outlines how staff and librarians at Appalachian State's Belk Library and Information Commons embraced a strategic challenge and prepared for anticipated budget cuts simultaneously. We tackled the challenge to make our student assistant workforce more effective through coordinated training efforts. This successful endeavor provided the library with a more productive student assistant pool and put us in a stronger position to absorb state-mandated spending freezes that occurred in April 2009.

DETERMINING THE TRAINING MISSION AND GOALS

In *Complete Guide for Supervisors of Student Employees in Today's Academic Libraries,* authors Baldwin and Barkley state that "in academic libraries, the number of student employees, in real numbers, often exceeds the number of regular staff. . . . it follows that academic libraries need to place a high priority on the effective management of student employment" (Baldwin and Barkley 2007, 3).

For the Belk Library and Information Commons these words ring true. Increasing the effectiveness of student assistants through coordinated or cross-training made strategic sense. Student assistants often are the public face of our library at service desks, especially during the night and weekend hours. We have 188 scheduled service desk hours per week across three desks and two service outposts, and student assistants participate in 128 (68 percent) of those hours. Our students also do much of the day-to-day processing of materials and shelf maintenance. Our focused effort to coordinate the student assistant training started with the creation of a student training task force.

The library administration created this task force in December 2007 and charged it broadly to improve the effectiveness of our student assistants through training in order to meet the library's growing service challenges. Made up of student supervisors from the circulation, periodicals, reference, document delivery, instructional materials center, stacks management, and distance learning teams, the task force represented nearly every library unit. The library administration appointed the reference team staff member as head of the task force to capitalize on this staff member's skills and passion. Early meetings produced a mission statement for the task force and four basic goals, as follows:

HOW MANY STUDENT ASSISTANTS IN U.S. ACADEMIC LIBRARIES?

2007 student assistant FTE staff as a percentage of total staff (median) (Varvel and Petrowski 2009a, 2009b):

Baccalaureate colleges: 29.41%

Master's colleges and institutions: 26.10%

Doctorate-granting institutions: 24%

Mission

We will provide our library student assistants with the tools to give exceptional public service to our patrons. Through a series of ongoing training sessions, they will acquire the necessary skills to assist those who pursue knowledge.

Goals

1. *Standardize the knowledge base and skill set among student assistants.* The skills gained in our student training program carry across the library and are useful in all student jobs. This common skill set builds variety into student job duties, for it allows students to work in almost any area needed. This not only gives the library the flexibility to position students where needed but helps students realize more job satisfaction. Individual teams still handle the specialized training required for a student to work within that unit.

2. *Set a common high-quality service standard.* Our patrons deserve high-quality service in a consistent manner. We are committed to standardize student public service expectations by training all students no matter where they work in the building. Students provide assistance beyond that at service desks where librarians and staff are working. Patrons often ask shelving students a variety of questions—from how to find a book to how to print, and even about library hours and policies. Students providing document delivery service receive questions from nearly all departments across campus. We expect setting a high-quality service standard to lessen the chance of patrons receiving poor service from our students that reflects poorly on the library as a whole.

> **DID YOU KNOW?**
>
> In a 2008 survey, access services supervisors identified nineteen core work tasks performed by their student assistants (Tolppanen and Derr 2009).

3. *Build technical skills.* With around 360 computer workstations and seven networked print stations, technical questions are commonplace in our library. Student assistants often field these questions first. Our three full-time technical support staff members cannot cover all four floors of the library at once. Student assistants provide a needed boost to our technical support efforts. Our technical services staff provide training to student assistants on tips, tricks, and quick troubleshooting. This gives the student assistants the confidence needed to answer technical questions before contacting the technical support staff member on duty.

4. *Share student assistants whenever possible.* Students who complete the coordinated training efforts have the ability to contribute on many different teams. This sharing builds variety into the students workweek and offers the opportunity for more hours—something all students seem to want. Supervisors have less anxiety about absences when they can pull available assistants from other teams. From an administrative perspective, this goal allows the

library to absorb absences and almost any budgetary problem handed to us short of a mandate for a significant reduction in force.

DEVELOPING THE TRAINING MODULES

The Belk Library task force developed its training modules through an evolutionary process. Early on, task force members agreed that students needed to learn basic employment guidelines and adhere to our high-quality service expectations. Over the next year, the task force identified and developed six additional modules based on student survey feedback and our own scrutiny. For specific topics, we invited the library's most knowledgeable people to conduct the sessions. These are the eight modules:

Student Employment Guidelines. This module introduces students to the basics of working for the library and is similar to orientation sessions at most jobs. Topics include attendance, absences, breaks, the pay period, evaluations, and grounds for dismissal. Conducted by the university librarian, associate university librarian, and task force members.

Public Service Expectations. This module establishes our high-quality service expectations, such as the importance of positive attitude, approachability, name badges, telephone answering etiquette, and dealing with difficult patrons. Conducted by the desk services librarian and desk services managers.

Technical Issues and Work-Arounds. Students learn solutions to the most common technical questions in the library. Topics include issues with saving files, printing, flash drives, downloading campus software, wireless access, and common software questions. Conducted by the e-learning librarian and technical support staff members.

Basic Processing and Research Tools: Catalog, Databases, and Other Answers. This module helps students understand the fundamentals of locating items in the library from the point of entry at the loading dock, through the cataloging and processing steps, and then onto the public shelves. In addition, students learn fundamentals of research assistance using the catalog and research databases. Conducted by the bibliographic services staff member, shelving manager, and reference librarian or staff member.

Safety Training. Students learn the basics of remaining safe, dealing with a variety of emergencies, and reporting workplace injuries to appropriate personnel. In addition, the session addresses issues of handling potentially dangerous patrons and other situations. Conducted by library HR staff and building manager.

Privacy/Confidentiality Training. Students gain knowledge of the privacy issues surrounding personal library records as well as confidentiality expectations in dealing with patron information and requests. We cover the ALA Code of Ethics and common scenarios encountered in libraries. Conducted by the coordinator of public services and instruction and desk services librarian.

Reference Interview Skills. We introduce students to the fundamental skills of fielding questions from library patrons, gathering general and specific information from the patron, providing assistance or instructions, and seeking feedback throughout the interaction. Conducted by the reference librarian or public services staff members.

What's New in Belk? This module serves as a transitional orientation to our returning student assistants. We update students on any important changes implemented over the summer or between semesters. Conducted by student training task force members.

CONDUCTING THE TRAINING

The task force agreed that the training sessions needed to be fun, engaging, and informative all at the same time. We believed the student assistants would appreciate a more active learning environment rather than a lecture-style session. The following list provides some of our best practices:

Pay the students for their time.

Play training games using i > clickers or other educational technology you have; it will be fun and introduce the library's technology.

Offer inexpensive or donated prizes; the library and the university bookstore provide our prizes.

Engage the students with role-playing scenarios.

Enlist students in planning or conducting a training session.

Schedule sessions at several times over several days to ensure maximum attendance.

Announce opportunities for additional hours so students present have first choice.

Limit sessions to 60 minutes.

Feed the students.

Allow library experts to conduct training sessions.

Ask trainers to introduce themselves and describe their roles in the library.

SUPERVISOR BUY-IN

Student supervisors in the library developed closer working relationships with one another by participating in the training efforts. Before the task force, supervisors hired and trained students to work in one department only and shared minimally. This old model contributed to a lack of understanding of the larger library organization among supervisors and student assistants alike. Early training sessions sometimes brought students and supervisors from different teams together for the first time. After a few training sessions, supervisors began to recognize the value of the coordinated training by observing the students' excitement in learning new skills. This was a huge step forward as we continued to solicit buy-in from more supervisors.

Expect all students and library personnel to wear a name badge.

Provide students with training folders and handouts.

GOING DIGITAL

After completing the first cycle of face-to-face training sessions, the task force agreed that much of the introductory basic training information could be adapted to an interactive and online format. The task force enlisted the assistance of our e-learning librarian to handle this conversion. Supervisors now require students to complete three online modules that cover employment guidelines and our public service expectations as a condition of their employment. Since we pay our students to attend face-to-face training, this was a cost-wise step that saved a supervisor's time. Find our online modules and other training materials on the Appalachian State library website, www.library.appstate.edu/elearn/student.html.

EVIDENCE IN SUPPORT OF TRAINING EFFORTS

Our advanced planning and training plan paid dividends in the spring and summer semesters of 2009. Because of tax revenue shortfalls, the state of North Carolina instituted two spending freezes that lasted nearly five months beginning in April 2009. This prevented the library from hiring new students to replace our graduating seniors. Certainly librarians and staff had to do more with less, but supervisors shared available students in order to cover gaps at service desks, reduce shelving backlogs, and complete document delivery workflows.

The student training task force sent online surveys to student assistants about the training. Survey responses were anonymous. Since the program began in 2008, about 40 percent of respondents have described the training sessions as somewhat valuable, 21 percent as valuable, and an additional 21 percent as very valuable. The technical support training session always ranked as the most valuable session.

Student supervisors provided anecdotal evidence that student job satisfaction and work quality improved as a result of the coordinated training. They report that the variety of jobs, availability of more hours, and opportunity to develop technical skills give our student assistants the kind of job satisfaction that keeps them working here. Supervisors also are happy to know they have a larger pool of trained students to complete the job.

LESSONS LEARNED

We discovered a great deal over the past two years of training and profited from overcoming the challenges. Here are a few lessons learned:

- Prepare for lean budget years before they happen. We really would have been in bad shape had the spending freeze hit without a pool of trained students ready to work wherever needed.
- Students are willing and able to learn just about anything you ask of them.
- Despite our best efforts, 100 percent buy-in from student assistants and supervisors has not happened. We need to accept the current level of participation and continue to build momentum.
- Burnout is possible. Share leadership roles and planning. Rotate membership on the task force to keep things fresh.
- Keep student training initiatives in perspective and realize that it is only a part of the whole package that makes a library successful.

CONCLUSION

When a recession hits and library budgets drop, library personnel may not have the flexibility to absorb the cuts without some advanced preparation and sound library practices. This case study described here demonstrates one model of how to improve student training while preparing for a smaller or frozen budget. In our case, coordinated student training improved the library's service quality at the same time it prepared us to handle recession-driven spending freezes. Let us all hope that the boom years are far more frequent than the lean years.

WORKS CITED ————

Baldwin, David A., and Daniel C. Barkley. 2007. *Complete Guide for Supervisors of Student Employees in Today's Academic Libraries*. Westport, CT: Libraries Unlimited.

Tolppanen, Bradley P., and Janice Derr. 2009. "A Survey of the Duties and Job Performance of Student Assistants in Access Services." *Journal of Access Services* 6 (3): 313–323.

Varvel, Virgil E., and Mary Jane Petrowski. 2009a. *2007 Academic Library Trends and Statistics for Carnegie Classification: Baccalaureate Colleges, Master's Colleges and Institutions*. Chicago: Association of College and Research Libraries.

———. 2009b. *2007 Academic Library Trends and Statistics for Carnegie Classification: Doctorate-Granting Institutions*. Chicago: Association of College and Research Libraries.

PART VII

On-the-Job Success

23

BIDDING SERVICE CONTRACTS IN PUBLIC LIBRARIES

Tom Cooper

ONE OF THE most insidious ways to waste money in a public library is to grow comfortable with service providers. Whether it's the people cleaning your building, hauling your trash, or servicing your network, you may get a better deal, and better service, by putting that work out for new bids every few years. This is not to diminish the work that good vendors of these services provide, but even good companies can grow comfortable, and they rarely offer to cut the fees they are charging. The opposite is more often true, and many service providers ask for incremental annual increases in their contracted payments.

When I became director at Webster Groves (Missouri) Public Library, the library was in fiscal straits. It had not benefited from a tax increase in nearly twenty years, there were no cash reserves, and the library was borrowing money on a line of credit at commercial rates to cover tax anticipation. In working to resolve these financial difficulties, I did not want to cut materials budgets or staff salaries any more than necessary. The first thing I did was to take every service contract we had out to bid.

Many libraries do not contract this sort of work; lawn maintenance, janitorial service, and more are done by employees instead. But salaries can be expensive, not to mention benefits. Webster Groves Public Library belongs to a consortium of nine libraries in which human resource budgets for FY

2009/10 run from a low of 59.8 percent of the total budget to a high of 70 percent. Outsourcing some routine work can be the fiscally responsible way to go, but you have to make sure you are getting the best deal. By rebidding all of these contracts, I got better or equivalent service and saved the library significant amounts of money (see table 23.1).

A total of $855 saved per month makes a big difference at my library, as I suppose it would at many libraries. In some service categories, the work now being done is almost identical to what the previous provider had done, and yet the new providers have been doing it for much less money. In others, such as network maintenance, the new provider was able to make the case that we could get along just fine with less rigorous oversight and a greatly reduced monthly payment.

This is not hard to do. It just takes time and a commitment to find the best deal. Ideally, the bidding process should be a team effort. If your staff include a business manager, a facilities manager, a systems administrator, or anyone else whose daily job involves the areas to be bid, those people should be involved. In assembling a team, you should not forget to solicit expertise among your board of trustees; many boards include active or retired business-people who are well versed in the practice of issuing requests for proposals and evaluating bids. The problem for many smaller libraries is that they do not have these people on staff, and their boards may not include anyone with relevant expertise. In such circumstances, the entire process falls to the library director, whose training in library science likely includes little or no grounding in these basics.

But be careful of resigning yourself to an overly "go it alone" attitude. There is almost always someone on staff you can ask to cast an objective eye over your request for proposals, just to ensure that they make sense and

TABLE 23.1
SAVINGS FROM NEW BIDS

	OLD VENDOR	NEW VENDOR
Janitorial service	$835 per month	$650 per month
Lawn maintenance	$165 per cut	$110 per cut
Computer/network maintenance	$650 per month	$80 per month
Trash hauling	$129 per month	$84 per month

CREATING A PROCUREMENT POLICY

If your library does not have a procurement policy, you should establish one, for a variety of reasons:

- Your auditors, and other observers of your finances, may question whether things are being done by the rules; those rules need to be specified.
- The policy establishes an amount above which you must take bids. You would rather have a reasonable amount specified, like $1,000, than have an activist board trustee insist that *any* expenditure must go out to bid. Some older procurement policies might need to be revised if they specify an outdated limit on no-bid expenditures.
- The policy establishes how many bids you need to consider. Three is the usual number. Of course you can take more, but you do not want to be forced into taking more just because there is no written policy in place.
- A procurement policy should note that your decision does not have to be based on cost alone. Many procurement policies specify that the decision will be made on the "lowest responsible bid," or language to that effect. This is useful in case a low bidder who does not get the contract complains.
- The policy should be written and approved by your board of trustees and added to your operating policy manual.

are free of errors, and a second pair of eyes looking over the bid packages is always helpful, even if that pair of eyes are not those of an "expert."

The steps in the bidding process are largely the same regardless of the type of service you are contracting for. There are three preliminary steps:

1. Check your operating policy to see what sort of requirements there are in the procurement process. Our operating policy requires that we take bids from three vendors for any item over $1,000; this applies to contracts that will cost over $1,000 annually.

2. Check your current contracts to see when they are up for renewal. Make sure to note what sort of advance notice they require prior to automatic renewal. Many contracts specify 30, 60, or even 90

days advance notice. Arrange the contracts you want to work with in order by these dates, so you can attack them one at a time. Going through the bidding process on several services at the same time can be overwhelming. Of course, if you have (or a predecessor has) purposely set all of your contracts to expire on the same date—say the beginning of your fiscal year—you may have no choice.

3. Assess whether you are just bidding the service as it has been done or would like to ask for new things to be done. Staff input is important at this point. Surely there are employees who have noticed if more cleaning needs to be done, or if the grass needs to be cut more often during summer. Hold a few meetings with staff to discuss these matters, and make careful notes.

Once you have decided which service you are going to start with and the parameters of the work you are going to ask for, it is time to prepare a request for proposals (RFP). The RFP is just a more-or-less formal way of telling vendors what it is you are looking for. It generally consists of four parts:

Introduction. Tell interested parties what you are looking for in general. It might read something like this: "Webster Groves Public Library is seeking bids from companies with the expertise and experience to handle cleaning its building at 301 E. Lockwood in Webster Groves, Missouri. We are looking for a company to work after hours three nights per week to clean this 11,000-square-foot building."

Job specifications. Spell out exactly what you need done. A good guide is the contract with the current vendor, but don't forget to add any new duties you want to have done. Enumerate specific duties, something like this: "Vacuuming all carpeting. Emptying all trash receptacles and recycle bins. Cleaning two public restrooms and one staff restroom . . ." To get the most realistic price estimates from vendors, it is important to be thorough with this part of the RFP.

Date by which you expect responses. This should be based on when the current contract expires, how much advance notice the current vendor requires for nonrenewal, and enough time for you to review all the proposals and make a decision.

Disclaimer. There may come a time when, for one reason or another, you do not accept any of the proposals from vendors. You must state up front that this possibility exists so that vendors are aware of it.

In addition to these four parts, your RFP should solicit the following:

- A list of references—where and for whom the vendor has done or is doing similar work.
- Verification that the vendor carries the necessary insurance coverage.
- Some states require verification that the vendor is using E-verify or can otherwise confirm that all of its workers are legally working in this country.
- Finally, let vendors know if you need more than one copy of their proposals.

Send the RFP to several vendors. It should not be hard to find vendors to contact; at my library hardly a week goes by without someone representing a service company stopping by to give me a card and a flyer. There are several ways to find qualified vendors: Ask colleagues at other libraries or similar institutions for recommendations. Check Yellow Page listings for vendors in your area. Talk to your local chamber of commerce. Check online business directories.

Unless you are seeking to replace a current vendor due to poor performance or nonperformance, you should include that vendor in the list. This just seems fair—even though I have never seen a vendor present a bid lower than what they are currently charging.

If you want bids from at least three vendors, it may be wise to contact five or six. Some will not respond or follow through with a bid. If in the end you get only two bids, most boards are comfortable knowing you made a sincere attempt to get more. Arrange to meet with each vendor at your facility and give them a tour and orientation emphasizing the duties that are enumerated in the RFP. If any vendor notes something that you have missed, and you add it to the list of duties to be performed, then each competing firm must be notified in writing of the change, so all responses are based on the same terms.

During interviews with vendors, do not offer any information about how much money you have to spend. Vendors often ask what you are currently spending, or what your budget is for this work. These are all ways for them to keep from having to respond with their lowest possible bid. If they know you are currently paying $600 per month for x, then they know they only have to bid a little lower than $600. But if they have no idea what you are paying, they have to sharpen their pencils. If they are truly professionals in the field, they know what this type of work costs.

You must be firm about the date for returning proposals. If the RFP stipulates five o'clock on Friday the 19th, you must refuse to accept a proposal that comes in on Saturday afternoon. Accepting a late proposal would not be fair to companies that worked hard to meet the deadline. Moreover, there is reason to doubt the professionalism of a company that cannot even get a bid proposal in on time.

As soon as you can, read through the proposals carefully to make sure vendors have responded to everything you asked for. This is especially true if one bid comes in significantly lower than any other. Remember that you do not usually have to decide based solely on price. Sometimes a vendor can present the lowest price because he runs a shoddy operation. You need to decide among the proposals you get which company looks like it can do the best job for the most reasonable price. This is a good time to involve another staff member. Reading multiple bids that all sound alike can be mind numbing, and another set of eyes may pick up discrepancies that you have missed.

It is a good idea to set up a scoring grid, so you know you are evaluating all of the companies on the same set of criteria rather than on subjective qualities. Perhaps you liked the salesperson and want to do business with that company. But remember, it probably will not be the salesperson coming to clean your building or cut your grass. In many cases, after the deal is done you will never see the salesperson again. Write up a more tangible list of criteria, something like this:

Number of years in business.

Do they have a good training program for employees?

Is the proposal itself clear, complete, and professionally done?

Do they have the resources (equipment, staff) to do the job well?

Do they list any qualifications nobody else listed?

Who will be overseeing the work done at your location?

Who are their other accounts?

How big is the company, and is it "right-sized" for you?

Once you decide which vendors are in the running, it is time to call references. Don't call references for all the bidding companies; call them only for the company you prefer prior to making your decision final, or if two companies are so close that you need the extra input. Assemble a well-thought-out list of questions:

How long have you used this company?

Is the service good or excellent?

Do they respond well to requests for extra work?

Would you rehire them?

Do they change who services your location frequently?

Have there been any problems of note?

If the references check out, proceed to the stage of notifying the winning company. Most bid proposals include a contract or agreement to sign and send in, making that part of the process very easy. If the proposal you accept does not, ask for a written agreement.

Notify the current vendor that you are not renewing their contract, if that is the case, and make sure you do it in time to prevent an automatic renewal. It is also crucial that both parties are certain of the date when the new provider will begin work.

Send letters to all the losing bidders thanking them for their time and effort. Some of them will call or e-mail you wanting to know why they did not get the contract. You are not obligated to tell them every factor that went into your decision, though you do have to let them know who won. It might be a good idea to prepare a simple statement, especially if you did not accept the absolute lowest bid. Something along the lines of "We chose one of the lowest bids from a company that has a great track record of cleaning public buildings" should be all you have to say.

Webster Groves Public Library is more financially fit these days. We ran a successful tax levy campaign in 2009. During the campaign we were able to claim honestly that we had taken every reasonable measure to save money. It also helped that during the leanest times we had not cut too deeply into materials or staffing budgets, and our patrons were still happy with our collections and service.

DIGITAL PROJECTS ON A SHOESTRING

Emily Asch

ST. CATHERINE UNIVERSITY Library in St. Paul, Minnesota, began creating digital collections within the past few years. And, like many small libraries, we have not been able to add any new personnel or invest in expensive equipment to support these new collections. Despite these limitations, and in the face of shrinking budgets, we have managed to create two strong digital collections that are still growing, and we have even begun to plan for new collections. Through this chapter I discuss the process of digitizing one collection, an extensive photograph collection, and review the success and efficiency of the project.

The university's technical services department began digitizing the archives' photograph collection four years ago. This collection totals over a thousand photographs, of which five hundred are now digitized. Over the years the library has used existing personnel as well as graduate assistants to digitize the photographs, describe them, and create CONTENTdm records for each one. Initially graduate students in the MLIS program digitized the photographs. The input of metadata into CONTENTdm, including subject headings, was done by the cataloging librarian, and editing of records was performed by the graduate assistants. A technical services specialist was responsible for overseeing and assisting in the digitization of the photographs.

In quick step form, generalized, the process of developing our digital project on a shoestring went something like this:

1. Plan.

2. Determine goals and make them transparent.

3. Determine personnel for the project.

4. Identify strengths and weaknesses.

5. Determine standards and guidelines.

6. Look at what others are doing.

7. Determine workflows.

8. Identify and strengthen communication channels.

9. Choose equipment and software.

10. Get the best with the limited resources available.

11. Evaluate goals.

12. Evaluate workflows.

13. Ensure efficiency and effectiveness.

PLANNING

Any new project requires planning, but special attention is required when projects need to be built on a shoestring budget. There is not much room, if any, for trial and error, as this can add additional costs to an already tight budget. Often decisions that are made must be adhered to because the costs associated with changing them would be too great. For example, if the specifications for digitizing photographs are changed, time (a.k.a. money) will need to be spent to redigitize the images to the revised specifications.

St. Catherine University Library identified three main areas in which planning/cost control for both the start-up and maintenance of the digital collections would be essential: personnel, standards and guidelines, and equipment.

Personnel

St. Catherine University was unable to hire new personnel to work on building digital collections. However, it was possible to take advantage of several in-house experts as well as existing funding for graduate assistants. Our

USING "OLD" PERSONNEL

What do you do when you can't hire new personnel? Look in-house for

Existing expertise and strengths

Time that can be dedicated to a new project

Ability to be trained/retrained

Openness to change

Delineate expectations of

Personnel duties and goals

Workloads and workflows

Project goals

cataloging librarian's expertise in creating metadata and her familiarity with existing standards were put to use. The technical services specialist assisted in the management of the graduate assistants, equipment, and other technical details. Graduate assistants were hired with existing institutional funds for student employment, allowing us to use students with an interest in digital collections as well as basic knowledge of libraries and collections. With this knowledge and interest they were able to perform some of the basic processes, as well as research, needed to create, understand, and continue building the digital collections.

Standards and Guidelines

Standards and guidelines had to be established for metadata as well as image specifications. St. Catherine University used existing standards from various organizations and schemas: for metadata we used Qualified Dublin Core; for digitizing standards we followed the Minnesota Digital Library (MDL) specifications. The use of the MDL standards would allow for any future migration or submission of our collections to be accomplished without the need to redigitize. By relying on existing protocols, the library was also able to save personnel time and energy creating local standards.

Equipment and Supplies

Several pieces of basic equipment are needed to support the creation of digital collections: scanner(s), computer(s), software, and a server (or server space).

USING CHEAP LABOR

Places to look for "cheap" labor:

Nearby institutions with relevant program for interns

Work study students

Graduate assistantships

Volunteers

Friends groups

And don't forget, there are pros and cons to "cheap" labor:

Pros
Cheap or free
Often enthusiastic
Building relationship between departments and institutions

Cons
Can require extensive training
No decision-making ability

Scanning. With advances in scanning technology, it does not have to cost thousands of dollars to purchase a good scanner. Fortunately, our library was able to purchase a robust scanner before budgets tightened, and it has survived without need for replacement for almost five years. We will, however, need a new scanner in the next year or two. The next scanner will likely be cheaper and still deliver the same quality, if not better, than what we currently receive.

Determining the desired specifications for your scanned images and digital objects is important so that you can purchase the right scanner. Keep in mind that it is often beneficial, as well as practical, to purchase equipment that will outperform your current projected needs. If you purchase the minimum needed to meet your specifications, you may be forced to upgrade earlier than you anticipated. Digitization may need to be redone or edited because of changing requirements or compatibility issues if you purchase equipment that can meet only a minimal standard. Again, look at existing standards to help determine your needed and desired specifications.

Computers. Thankfully our existing computers and monitors can be used for digitizing, as well as for storage of the digital images, eliminating the need to purchase special equipment for this purpose. Our technical services unit created a separate scanning station for students to digitize the photographs; that workstation is also available for other student worker projects when not

EXISTING STANDARDS AND GUIDELINES

Find digital collections with similar goals.

Find organizations that are dedicated to creating or collecting multiple digital collections, such as Minnesota Digital Library.

Look for best practices from sources such as these:

Digital Library Federation: www.diglib.org/standards.htm

Minnesota Digital Library: www.mndigital.org

Office of Digital Collections and Research, University of Maryland: www.lib.umd.edu/dcr/publications/best_practice.pdf

BCR's CDP Best Practices: www.bcr.org/dps/cdp/best/index.html

being used for digitizing. There was no need for upgrades or reconfiguration of staff workstations, since the required applications could be added to existing computers. For backup, there are readily available external hard drives and other options that make storage and backup inexpensive.

Server. A server is needed to store the digital objects. Often, depending on the size of the collection, this can be accomplished with a dedicated computer hard drive. St. Catherine uses a Linux server and currently takes up approximately 15 GB for the digital collection. Support of the computer and access to the objects on the computer require staff expertise.

Software. A vital component of digital collection creation is a content management application. St. Catherine University is fortunate to have subscribed to CONTENTdm and has continued to be able to retain this expense within our budget. If CONTENTdm is not a viable option, there are several other platforms available, including CONTENTdm Quick Start, dSpace, and Flickr, that cost less or are open source.

Although open-source content management systems are free up front, these options often require expertise and time for configuration, maintenance, and updates—and such available expertise may or may not exist at your institution. The ability to support any program, free or not, is directly related to your ability to bear "hidden" personnel costs that may not necessarily be evident at first. Setup and upkeep are requirements of any system and digital collection.

Photo editing requires another software application, one that allows photographs to be saved in an appropriate format and size as well as enhanced for better viewing online. A photo editing software package usually accompanies scanners. For this project it became necessary to purchase Photoshop

Elements, a program with fuller editing capabilities.

EVALUATION AND TUNE-UP

When I arrived at St. Catherine University as the new head of technical services, the digitization project was in its fourth year and it was time for evaluation. My primary focus has been to evaluate goals and priorities, personnel, and workloads.

Goals and Priorities

Having a good plan, goals, and rationale is particularly important during times of tight budgets. When cuts appear imminent, being able to articulate the goals of a project is crucial. Demonstrating why scarce resources should be allocated to the digital collections is critical for their survival and growth. For our library, the "why" is most clearly seen in our efforts to provide access to a rich yet underutilized collection of photographs to alumni, friends, researchers, and current students, faculty, and staff.

It is also important to keep your goals and plans clear and transparent in order to maintain an efficient and effective project as well as workflow. Ensuring that everyone involved has the same knowledge of the plan, expectations, and end product in mind saves time and frustration. Where there are clear goals and expectations, guidelines, and time lines, there are fewer problems with duplicating efforts, wasting time determining who has done what, and dealing with unnecessary downtime. This is particularly

CHOOSING A SCANNER

What should you know about before you buy a scanner?

- Optical resolution (PPI)
- Color depth
- Optical density
- Speed
- Connectivity (how it connects to a computer)
- Type of scanner
- Format (flatbed, slide, wide format)
- Accompanying software
- Photo editing
- Capture program
- Control of settings

FYI CAPTURE PROGRAMS

The ability to fine-tune an image when you capture it can save you time editing it later. You also get a better-quality master image if you control things like resolution, color, and rotation as part of the capture rather than trying to correct for them by editing the digitized image.

STRATEGY

If a specific responsibility is an explicit part of a job description, it is accepted and supported by administration. This ultimately helps ensure continued support, financial and otherwise, for work that has begun related to that responsibility.

important when the project is using staff members who have other primary responsibilities.

Personnel and Workloads

People are the most valuable and expensive resource of any project. As part of my evaluation of the digitization project, I had to make sure that the people working on the digital collections were able to do what was expected of them and had the necessary support. It was particularly important to realign responsibilities and to ensure as little duplication of effort as possible. I found that there was little duplication of effort, but there was quite a bit of downtime due to technical difficulties and the timing of the project. The digital collections were being worked on only during the spring semester when a graduate assistant was hired. Because only four months of the year was being devoted to digitizing, there was an annual need to retrain personnel on any technical upgrades, and each spring the new graduate assistant had to be trained before digitizing began again. This refamiliarizing took much time and energy, leading to frustrations and to goals not always being met.

After my evaluation, we also updated job descriptions and titles. The cataloging librarian's job description was rewritten to highlight her role as metadata librarian, providing moral support for her work with the digital collections. By adding specific metadata criteria to her job description we also marked a level of implied financial support for digital collections by the institution.

CONCLUSIONS

Initiation and maintenance of a digital collection can be accomplished within the constraints of a small budget. It may take a while, and it may require considerable effort on everyone's part, but it can be done. Good planning and the right people are critical to maintaining smooth operation of digital collections with minimal impact on the budget. There are equipment and management systems to be acquired and maintained, but there are means for acquiring these for minimal funds.

At St. Catherine University Library we are fulfilling our goal of digitizing priority collections with the OCLC CONTENTdm annual maintenance fee as the only annual output. Equipment costs were solely up front, and all work is done by existing personnel or student employees. As long as we keep our workflow efficient and minimize frustration, we will continue to add to our digital collections productively.

25

DEVELOPING PARTNERSHIPS FOR ADDED VALUE

Aline Soules and Sarah Nielsen

ACADEMIC LIBRARIANS HAVE long engaged in faculty liaison work in disciplines across their universities for a variety of purposes; however, those relationships, no matter how equal, have not necessarily been true partnerships. Based on a case study, this chapter focuses on how to develop and sustain true partnerships with the added benefit of doing so at no or minimal cost.

CASE STUDY: PICTURE OF A PARTNERSHIP

At California State University, East Bay (CSUEB), we (a professor of English and a librarian) have developed a true partnership. Combining our knowledge of TESOL (teaching English to speakers of other languages), information competency, organizational skills, and Web 2.0 capabilities, we have embedded information competency throughout the MA TESOL curriculum.

This project resulted from several concerns: Because of the rich diversity of our students, many enter the MA TESOL program without strong information competency skills. Yet TESOL graduates may teach in global environments with scarce information resources, requiring them to use information competency and ingenuity to stay current in their field. As students, they need heightened awareness of Web 2.0 options, which can help them become members of a professional community early in their careers. And we had to address these concerns for no or minimal cost.

We began our project by analyzing information competency needs. Although we considered developing a stand-alone information competency class for MA TESOL students, that would have resulted in additional costs for students and the university. Instead, we opted for sets of assignments sequenced across the program, a wiki to provide a central site for our information competency initiative, and an assessment process that includes a pre/post-survey and formal and informal feedback mechanisms. Throughout, we have met regularly to ensure that these processes continue to address pedagogical needs from both the TESOL and information competency perspectives.

SAMPLE ASSIGNMENT

We provided a model evaluation of a commonly consulted TESOL website and a set of evaluative questions. We asked students to find and research two ESL or EFL websites, one designed for teachers and one for language learners; keep a running record of their research process; write a brief description and evaluation of each website; and rate each website. They also gave a ten-minute talk to the class on the websites they evaluated. Because the results of their work were posted on a public wiki, students had an early career opportunity to share their ideas with their professional community. See the results of the sample assignment at http://tesolcsueb.wetpaint.com/page/Web + Evaluations.

After two years, we are seeing positive and exciting results. Students value information more, evaluate it more effectively, question more often, and seek assistance from the library more often. The quality of the research and the substance of their citations have improved significantly. Their reflective essays, which include an evaluation of the information competency assignments, further confirm the growth of their information competency and show us new areas for ongoing curriculum development. This expands the partnership, for the students have now become another

STUDENT PERSPECTIVE

"The question 'What tools have you used in teaching information literacy to ESL/EFL students?' was really shocking. I have never taught information literacy before. Yes, students should be taught how to deal with the flood of available information and distinguish the 'good' from the 'bad.'"

—Kinda Al Rifae

partner in the process. Although it is too early to know, we are hopeful that the MA TESOL students will enlarge this partnership themselves by helping their own students develop information competency.

GETTING A PARTNERSHIP STARTED

Prepare the ground. True partnership opportunities abound, but only if potential partners know you are out there and available. Before our partnership, we were aware of each other because one of us (the librarian) participates in the other's English department electronic discussion list and keeps up with the activities of English department faculty, lecturers, TAs, and the like. She knew when to jump in to remind participants of library resources and services and when to lurk and observe what was going on. Too much participation is intrusive; too little and you are forgotten. We both knew we were available and what the library could provide.

Find commonalities. A good partnership starts with shared interests, complementary knowledge, and a variety of skills. In our case, there was a problem to solve—the information competency capabilities of our MA TESOL students—and a good combination of capabilities with our TESOL, information competency, organizational, and Web 2.0 skills.

Plan together. Part one of the process is figuring out what you will do. Our planning resulted in a two-year pilot designed to evolve into a continuously improving process with one of us leading curriculum development in terms of appropriate assignments for future teachers and the other leading information gathering, evaluation, application, organization, and wiki development. These are not hard-and-fast divisions, for there is overlap, but it is important to know how the leadership is shared and coconstructed through the process.

Part two is identifying what you already have and figuring out what's missing. We were lucky to have the combination of knowledge and skills we needed to get started, but if we did not we could have sought additional partners, researched other resources, or signed up for additional training. A continuously improving process requires partners to re-research, retrain, and

> ### STUDENT PERSPECTIVE
>
> "Completing the information competency survey on-line educated me about the concept of 'information literacy' and opened my eyes to some defects in my abilities as a student and as a teacher. . . . The survey's questions . . . drew my attention to the fact that I do have trouble sometimes finding information and I need to work on that."
>
> —Kinda Al Rifae

reinvestigate options. We have come to realize, for example, that we can use some statistical expertise to help us analyze the pre/post-survey results over a growing number of MA TESOL cohorts and will seek that help from our statistics department on campus.

Part three is building in assessment. You may be at the beginning, but you need feedback throughout. If you don't build it in to begin with, you will find it hard to embed later on. We developed a pre/post-survey and, in each class, included the reflective paper assignment mentioned above. As one example, student feedback has led us to change the sequence of assignments in the initial two courses of the program.

Your project will likely unfold in phases. Create a periodic "check" at the end of each phase and adapt your plans as needed.

MAINTAINING MOMENTUM

Track, track, track! You need a written plan and careful records of your process; otherwise, you won't know where you are or what needs adjustment. Librarians can offer organizational skills for documenting processes, and that is how it tends to work in our case.

Leverage existing resources. In our case, we have access to Blackboard, our university's learning management system, Elluminate for synchronous learning, SurveyMonkey, and existing library resources. The increased use of these resources is an additional justification for their expense. If your university does not provide the specific resources you need for your project, free and open-source options exist. For example, SurveyMonkey offers limited free service. We set up our wiki (http://tesolcsueb.wetpaint.com) using a free site called Wetpaint, having decided to accept the advertising displayed on the site.

Schedule regular meetings (or, at least, periodic ones—you will get off track once in a while). Review your current status, accomplishments, revision needs, action items, and new issues on the horizon. Be flexible and willing to revise plans based on your observations, student feedback, and planned outcomes. We met weekly in our initial planning phase and twice a quarter as we implemented the pilot curriculum.

Focus on your outcomes. This helps you to be more flexible and prepared to "let go" and trust the process. Things will not be perfect, but they will be on a trajectory of continuous improvement and you will be headed in the right direction.

Seek community. Are there others who are trying something similar, and can you exchange ideas? Do a traditional literature search periodically. There are also plenty of blogs out there. Maybe one of them is for you.

Assess, assess, assess. You want feedback. Our student survey is given as students enter the program and again when they graduate. There is a reflective essay for both our and the students' benefit, and we have engaged in periodic informal discussions. Focus groups may also provide useful feedback. Postgraduation telephone interviews, if you have participants' contact information, are a way to measure the longitudinal outcomes. In our case, with globally scattered graduates, Skype is our best financial option, since costs are minimal. Regardless of your method, help your beneficiaries ask questions and provide feedback throughout the process. Openness is key.

Enable your partner. It is so easy to be the "main squeeze" for a topic, but, if you are wise, you will make sure that you and your partner can do as much as possible of each other's roles. About a year and a half into our project, it became clear that both of us needed to be able to teach information competency skills.

Be in the classroom. Although one of us is a primary classroom person, the other—the librarian—had to spend more time there as well. Because of the additional time spent in TESOL classrooms, she has become more sensitized to the strengths, needs, challenges, and determination of this group of native and nonnative English speakers, who need to be able to use information competency skills in an English-language environment and in their future teaching. An added benefit is the increased willingness of students to visit the library, overcoming a cultural stricture, for some students, to seek help.

STUDENT PERSPECTIVE

"The best thing I got from three assignments was to narrow down the distance I used to have with librarians."

—Sujin Lee

As your project begins to move into its "ongoing" phase, celebrate the project, even as you may begin to feel a sense of loss and are continuing to identify failures, planning ways to minimize or reduce their impact, and thinking up new ideas to move forward.

Although ours is a case study in an academic setting, the principles explained here readily apply to other settings, including public and school libraries. You could engage in similar partnerships with trustees, city government, key donors—the possibilities are limited only by your time and ideas.

MOVING FORWARD

Are there other projects to continue the partnership? You may find that you expand your existing project or branch out into something new. Some projects are onetime collaborations. In other cases, collaboration can continue for many years. Among the many advantages of our project are the emerging new opportunities.

First, we were invited to participate in a video that will be available throughout the California State University System to talk about the benefits of our partnership and alternative learning solutions for our students.

Second, we have proof that we can do this. Our pilot will be a great jumping-off point for the grant application we are considering. We can describe our accomplishments and the positive results.

Third, who knows what we will think up next?

CONCLUSION

We already see signs that our students are more aware of information issues and the challenges and benefits of gathering and evaluating information. Via their feedback on the first year of the pilot, students reacted positively to the information competency focus and helped in the redesign of the content and sequence of activities. Their ongoing feedback also indicates that they like sharing their web evaluations with a wider and real audience of TESOL professionals through the wiki.

With the positive reinforcement we have been getting, we are more motivated than ever. When you find that you can make a difference and help people learn and move forward with their life plans, you get an incredible jolt of satisfaction. There is nothing like it, as you will find out for yourselves. In addition, your institution will benefit from broader collaborative thinking, increased use of library resources, and new approaches to learning with no or minimal costs.

You don't need much money. You need time, marketing, and a good project. Above all, have fun. Do something worthwhile that will give you satisfaction. If you enjoy your project, so will your beneficiaries.

STUDENT PERSPECTIVE

"I learned that information literacy plays a very important role in the teaching-learning process. It is important for teachers to develop information literacy because their job requires them to research things all the time—good teachers are lifelong learners. Also, teachers are now being asked to prepare students who can demonstrate understanding as well as knowledge and skill. . . . Information literacy can be transferred across subject areas, improve research, writing, and critical thinking and help students interpret and understand the world. There is a need to educate students for lifelong learning in a time of exponential growth of information."

—Suzana Alves

26

ORGANIZING IN THE STREETS AND IN THE STACKS

A Grassroots Movement Saves Neighborhood Libraries

Edgar C. Bailey Jr.

ON JULY 1, 2009, in the city of Providence, Rhode Island, a newly formed, nonprofit organization named the Providence Community Library assumed full control of all branches of the Providence Public Library, effectively splitting the city library system into two separately administered parts. The central city library remained under the control of the Providence Public Library, a partially city- and state-funded private entity. The story of how this dramatic change occurred is both interesting and instructive for other urban library systems considering reducing services and closing facilities in the face of severe budgetary constraints.

BACKGROUND

Providence Public Library (PPL) was founded in 1878 as a private, nonprofit corporation. Within twelve years of its founding, the library began to receive modest financial support from the city and later the state. This support, although varying, increased over the years until it reached nearly two-thirds of the library's operating budget. In recent years, as the library continued to seek greater support, relations with the city became increasingly strained. City officials countered the library's claims of financial stress with assertions that the library should either engage in more vigorous fund-raising or utilize a portion of its large endowment to cover any deficit.

Formation of the Library Reform Group

In the summer of 2004, facing a threat from the city to level funding or possibly reduce appropriations, PPL laid off twenty-one staff members and significantly reduced hours of operation at the central library. This action precipitated two responses: the library staff initiated a campaign to unionize, and a group of concerned Providence residents organized the Library Reform Group, a coordinating committee seeking to change policies at PPL. This group organized protest rallies and began pursuing two significant initiatives. It sought to get publicly appointed members added to what was a largely self-appointed board of directors and also succeeded in getting legislation passed that made previously closed board meetings subject to the state's open meetings law.

Continuing Conflict

Seemingly finally recognizing that it faced serious and growing financial and public perception problems, PPL announced that it had created a strategic planning committee and had hired a consulting firm to assist it in developing a long-range strategic plan. In the meantime, the staff unionization campaign culminated in a successful vote to unionize. Throughout this process, the Library Reform Group maintained close contact with union organizers, who, in turn, publicly supported the group's goals.

In January 2006, PPL abruptly, and without prior notification to the neighborhood or to the city council member representing the area of the city, announced the closing of one branch due to structural problems with the building. Shortly thereafter, the Library Reform Group succeeded in placing three of its members on the PPL strategic planning committee, where they steadfastly resisted proposals to shrink the size of the library system further. Their position was supported at a series of focus groups, conducted by PPL, in which city residents, when asked which library services were most important to them, made it clear they considered all services important and wanted more. Less than two months later, however, the library announced that, in order to avoid a $900,000 deficit in its FY 2007 operating budget, it would be forced to close six of its nine branches and lay off additional staff. In the face of this threat, the Library Reform Group increased its efforts, utilizing petitions, rallies, public forums, press conferences, and op-ed pieces to mobilize public opinion.

The Library Reform Group continued to enjoy the strong support of the city council, many of whose members represented wards where branches were threatened. At the group's urging, the council appeared ready to pass an ordinance authorizing it and the mayor each to appoint four public members to the PPL board. However, in an attempt to defuse the tension the mayor requested that the council defer action. He announced the appointment of an outside consultant to undertake an independent examination of PPL's finances. The consultant conducted a thorough review and recommended that PPL eliminate its deficit by using a small surplus from the previous year, taking an additional $250,000 from its endowment, and level funding pension contributions for one year. In addition, the city would increase its support by $250,000.

City/Library Agreements

Although fully aware that these proposals were not a permanent solution, both sides accepted them. In an attempt to achieve a more stable future, the mayor appointed an advisory group to develop a formal agreement between the city and PPL. Because no Library Reform Group members were appointed to this committee, the reform group decided to create a task force, the Library Advocates Coalition, to do its own study of library service in the city. The coalition sponsored three forums featuring PPL representatives, the library consultant, and library directors from other small New England cities. In February 2007, the coalition formally recommended that the city slightly increase its support to PPL and that the library cut administrative salaries.

In June the city and PPL signed a one-year contract, the first ever formal agreement between the two. In it, the city agreed to increase its financial support in exchange for a promise from the library to reopen the branch closed for structural damage and to keep all other branches open. The agreement also called for the creation of a standing Library Partnership Advisory Committee to advise the library on operations and finances. Four Library Reform Group members were appointed to this committee by the city council.

The rest of the year saw no significant new developments until December, when the PPL administration announced a projected $1 million deficit in the FY 2008 budget. Proposed options for eliminating the deficit included closing six branches, asking the city to assume responsibility for all branch operations, and taking money from the endowment. There was no suggestion that fund-raising efforts might be expanded. In May 2009, the Library Partnership Advisory Committee recommended that the city maintain its current financial support and PPL maintain its current level of service while both sides engaged in yet another assessment of the library services with the goal of establishing a "sustainable" system.

In July the city and PPL agreed to a four-year plan that called for no reduction in service for the first year while planning for the sustainable system continued. After the first year, PPL would have the right, with six months advance notice, to close branches. If PPL exercised this option, the city could choose to keep branches open with supplemental funding, run them as a city department separate from the central library, or turn them over to another organization to run. The Library Reform Group studied the agreement carefully and realized that, as written, it committed the city not to reduce funding over the four-year period even if PPL decided to close branches or otherwise reduce services. As a result, a clause was added allowing the city to opt out of the agreement.

FORMATION OF THE PROVIDENCE COMMUNITY LIBRARY

The Library Reform Group assumed from the start that the "sustainable" plan that PPL produced would probably call for the closing of as many as six branches. The group began exploring the feasibility of creating a new nonprofit organization to run the branches with the existing level of city and state funding. A four-person executive committee, drawn from group members, was formed. Although no one on this committee was a librarian, one member was a former state legislator with many contacts in state government and another was a certified public accountant familiar with nonprofit finances. The committee incorporated, developed a formal proposal, including a proposed budget, and awaited developments. In December 2008, PPL did, in fact, announce plans to close five branches. The Library Reform Group countered with a press conference two weeks later at city hall announcing the formation of the Providence Community Library (PCL) and offering to operate all nine branches with existing levels of funding.

Without knowing whether its proposal would be accepted and with very little lead time, the fledgling organization had to begin planning for a rapid transition while continuing to pressure the city to accept this dramatic change. Thanks to earlier lobbying efforts, a majority of the city council were already committed to the new entity. The mayor, however, still hoped to find a way to preserve the existing system. PCL resorted to yet another series of public forums at which both PPL and PCL presented their visions. Attendees clearly preferred the PCL proposal.

Finally, in May 2009, the mayor sent a letter to the PCL board accepting its proposal to assume control of the branches. This precipitated an increase in an already frenzied level of activity. A hastily constituted search committee succeeded in hiring an executive director in less than two months. Temporary administrative offices were established at one of the branches, and searches commenced for additional administrative personnel. A formal agreement was

STRATEGIES IN COMMUNITY ORGANIZING

Cultivate city officials.

Cultivate allies in the press.

Keep the public informed: forums, press conferences, petitions, op-ed pieces.

Capitalize on opponents' mistakes.

Involve the right people: financial knowledge, political connections.

Maintain contact with library employees and union officials.

Coordinate with other community organizations.

Make use of Friends groups.

Organizational skills are more important than knowledge of library operations.

negotiated with the city. In spite of the extraordinarily short lead time, PCL officially assumed control of the branch system on July 1 in a surprisingly smooth transition.

LESSONS LEARNED

Although every city's library system is different and this six-year experiment in community organizing probably could not be replicated exactly anywhere else, some lessons learned from the experience may be generally applicable.

Finances

The primary concern, of course, was how to operate the full branch system with existing city and state funding. In fact, as the PCL administration well knew, they could not; they would have to be more successful than PPL had been in finding external funding. As a result, they budgeted for two full-time development staff. Realizing that PPL was top-heavy with highly paid administrators, they achieved significant savings by hiring a lean but strong administrative staff. They were also able to save some on maintenance and trash contracts.

Politics

Perhaps even more important than the issue of financing is the whole question of how PCL managed to persuade the city to gamble $3.5 million on a newly created organization with no track record. One significant factor, of course, was the long history of antagonism and mistrust between the city and PPL. Council members knew they would feel the wrath of voters if branches in their wards were closed. Also, the mayor, who planned on running for another term, did not want to be known as the candidate who destroyed the city's library system. Further exacerbating the situation was the widespread knowledge that PPL was sitting on a sizable endowment that it was unwilling to draw down even in difficult financial times.

Public Support

Negative attitudes toward PPL alone would not have been enough to produce such a radical change. Also necessary were the methodical efforts of the Library Reform Group to publicize the situation and cultivate the support not only of city officials but also of the general public. The numerous informational public forums sponsored by the group were well attended and, thanks to careful cultivation of the press, widely reported in newspapers and on television. The group also worked hard to form alliances with other neighborhood organizations. Friends of the Library groups, which had been allowed to languish, were reestablished at all branches and assured that they would have representation on the board of the new entity. Even some members of the board of PPL, frustrated by what they saw as the intransigence of their colleagues, became allies and supporters of change. Finally, throughout the whole process, the Library Reform Group maintained close contact with the unionized members of the PPL staff. These employees, understandably nervous about such a dramatic change, were continually assured that their jobs were not in jeopardy.

27

TURNING GIFTS AND DISCARDS INTO GOLD

Robert Holley

LIBRARIES OFTEN OVERLOOK the value of their unwanted gifts and discards. I know because I am a small Internet bookseller who makes some of his best finds at library book sales. I like nothing better than selling a trade paperback for $60 that I bought for 25 cents. I once sold a volume of sheet music by an obscure Irish composer for $160; the library had valued the volume so little that it put it on the "free table." In this chapter, I outline strategies for maximizing potential revenue from gifts and library discards. Even a small library can make upward of $5,000; larger libraries can make much more. Time is money, so I take into account the effort needed to implement each strategy to increase revenue.

ACQUIRING MATERIALS TO SELL

Gifts. Most libraries get gifts without even asking, since many people hate throwing books away. The library should have a written gift policy and be firm about rejecting gifts of no value such as magazines, condensed books, damaged items, and especially books with mold or pests. Such a policy, of course, does not work for bags and boxes left at the library entrance in the dead of night. To get more and better gifts, the library should make it clear what kinds of materials it wants, advertise this fact, and have some easily accessible location to leave gifts. Pickups are normally not worth the effort unless the gift is particularly valuable.

Library discards. Library items removed from the collection normally sell for much less than items that have never been processed into a library, but many have some value. The library can increase marketability of these items by being as gentle as possible with them and avoiding destructive actions such as tearing out pages. The library should also stamp discards to show that they are no longer library property so that the purchaser can resell or give away the items without suspicion of theft.

SELLING MATERIALS

I cover where to sell materials first because the selling method has great importance for setting prices. I stress that the following methods are not mutually exclusive. A library, for example, could have a book sale for common materials but sell expensive materials to a dealer.

Book Sales

Permanent book sales. The library has a space, usually on its premises, where books are regularly available for purchase. The spot could be a book truck in the lobby, a special room, or bookshelves in the library café. The library renews stock regularly with fresh materials and should cull or reduce the price of materials that don't sell.

Regularly scheduled book sales. The library holds sales on a fixed schedule and does not expect to sell everything during the sale. This option requires setting up and breaking down the inventory and storing the materials from sale to sale.

Sporadic book sales. The library sells or discards all materials collected since the last sale. Most often these sales occur once or twice a year. The library can hold this sale within the library or at another location such as a community or shopping center. The sale is often timed to occur during a community event that draws potential buyers to the location. This option brings up additional pricing options because the library wishes to obtain the maximum revenue in a short selling period.

Selling to Dealers

The library sells materials directly to a dealer. Some dealers specialize in purchasing large quantities of books and media as one big lot. Others prefer to consider only smaller quantities of more valuable items to add directly to

PREPARE YOUR LIBRARY FOR GIFTS

Brainstorm ways to acquire more and better gifts that would work within the library's community. Create a gift policy if the library doesn't have one. Train staff on how to deal with gift offers, including asking the right questions to learn whether the gift will be useful or not. Involve the Friends of the Library if they have any responsibility for dealing with selling library materials.

their stock. At the high end, rare book dealers are interested only in expensive items. One innovate strategy by a library in an area rich in book dealers was to hold a silent auction for books of good quality arranged by subject. The library should not feel cheated if the dealer offers around 25 percent of retail value, since some items may have hidden defects and others will sell slowly or not at all.

Consignment Sales

BetterWorld Books (www.betterworldbooks.com) and B-Logistics (www.blogistics.com) sell books sent by libraries, pay the libraries a negotiated percentage of sales, and then donate or recycle the unsold items. The advantage for libraries is that these companies are experienced Internet sellers who sell internationally in multiple markets and have sophisticated software designed to adjust prices dynamically to achieve the highest revenue. Both companies prefer to receive better-quality materials with greater marketability and have some exclusions. Libraries should check the company websites or speak to a representative to get the latest terms and procedures.

VENUES FOR SELLING MATERIALS

Book sales: permanent, regularly scheduled, or sporadic

Dealers

Consignment sales

Selling on the Internet

Direct Internet Selling

Some libraries sell directly on the Internet. This strategy has the potential to provide the greatest revenue, since the library receives the full purchase price minus the listing agent's commission. Selling directly also requires the most effort, since the library must list items accurately, price them correctly, ship them promptly, and take care of customer issues. Each day, someone must deal with sales, since listing agencies require prompt shipment. Half.com is the easiest place to get started since there are no listing fees and the commission schedule favors casual sellers. Amazon.com has higher visibility but charges a much higher commission at lower sales volumes. Other possibilities for serious sellers are Alibris.com and Abebooks.com. eBay, with its listing fees and limited selling period, is appropriate for items rare enough to attract buyer attention. Since items do not necessarily sell quickly, the library needs to have storage space and also a well-designed location system for finding materials.

VALUING MATERIALS

The major mistake that both inexperienced private sellers and libraries often make is to overvalue hardcovers and undervalue trade paperbacks. Hardcover best sellers from past years, even in pristine condition, most often have little resale value except as reading copies for book sale buyers. The same holds true for most beautiful coffee-table books; many are remainders with thousands of available copies and weigh so much that postage eats up any profit from Internet sales. On the other hand, quirky fiction; many trade paperbacks, especially university press titles; and gray literature are often far more valuable than hardcovers.

> **SEARCH EXERCISE**
>
> Select five books that you think might be valuable from the next batch of library discards or gifts. Search them through AddALL or BookFinder. Compare the results with your initial judgment. If you have time, search a random sample of the remaining books to see if you encounter any surprises.

Determining Values

Two Internet meta–search engines make determining book values a simple task. The two companies, AddALL (http://used.addall.com) and Book-Finder (www.bookfinder.com), provide federated searching of thirty to forty booksellers such as Abebooks.com, Alibris.com, Amazon.com, and Half.com as well as major foreign sellers. BookFinder claims to "compare prices on over 150 million books for sale." Searching is particularly easy for books with ISBNs. I prefer AddALL with the default sort set to price, because the results appear in one list with options available for further differentiation. Volunteers or student staff can quickly search large quantities of gifts or discards. The library can set a threshold value for review by higher-level staff to consider special handling or pricing.

Eliminating Categories to Value

Massmarket paperbacks and children's books, with some exceptions, are not worth the time required to determine special value. Exceptions might be paperbacks in pristine condition, science fiction, and older materials on popular topics such as astrology, sex, and popular culture icons. Certain classic children's works command high prices in the out-of-print market, but most modern imprints are inexpensive and don't sell well.

Pricing and Selling

PRICING QUICK TIP

Pricing books at double the regular rate during the first hour will not deter serious buyers. Monitor any patrons who stash books to buy later. At the end of the sale, selling books at $2 per grocery bag or box saves having to take the remainders to the recycling center.

Book sales. Especially for infrequent sales where the library wishes to dispose of all items accumulated over a longer period, the library should have a preview sale in which the prices are higher or access requires membership in the Friends group. Dealers show up at the beginning of sales and astutely select the most valuable materials quickly. Similarly, prices should be lower toward the end of the sale, including perhaps selling bags or boxes at a fixed price to help the library avoid having to deal with large quantities of unsold materials.

For continuing sales and regularly scheduled book sales with continuing inventory, a simple system of fixed pricing works best. Mass-market paperbacks should be cheap. Hardcovers and trade paperbacks should be sold at the same price. Media and other special formats should be priced according to demand, so DVDs will cost more than VHS tapes. Ex-library materials most often do not sell well unless they are very cheap. Variable pricing beyond these easily recognized categories complicates checkout and should be based on valuation as described above rather than on attractiveness. Any pricing tags should be clear but not destructive of the book's resell value, such as marking the book with a grease pen.

Some libraries prefer that dealers not attend their book sales, but dealers often buy large quantities of materials. Some bring scanners or cell phones that tell them an item's price in the out-of-print market. Treating dealers like other buyers is the best strategy unless they are rude to customers or damage materials in their eagerness to find the gems.

Dealers. Having a detailed inventory list with approximate valuations from Internet searching gives libraries greater bargaining power than showing the dealer a mass of mixed titles. If the library is clear about the rules, asking for bids from multiple dealers is appropriate.

Consignment sales. BetterWorld Books and B-Logistics set the prices, collect the money, and pay the library's percentage according to the agreement.

Internet selling. Selling on the Internet is the most complex option. Listing an item first requires describing it as accurately as possible; a more detailed description inspires increased buyer confidence. Pricing should be in line with other copies in similar condition for sale in the selected market. The lower the price, the more likely a quick sale. Most buyers will not pay more to support your library instead of purchasing from a commercial seller. The library should check for orders at least daily and mail them out promptly with secure packaging. The library should also respond quickly to patron inquiries or complaints. Most sites allow buyers to evaluate sellers and provide detailed comments. Having a satisfaction rating as close as possible to 100 percent makes buyers more likely to buy the library's copy.

Before getting started, the library should devise some sort of location code to find materials as they sell. Arranging items by date is one possibility, but a location code gives the option of adding new items in the same spot without shifting. Since it is doubtful that the library can afford the sophisticated automated pricing software used by large dealers, the library should devote some time to checking older inventory periodically to reprice items. Limits to the library's storage space requires culling items that haven't sold. Older inventory may sell, but more purchases will come from recently listed or recently repriced items.

STAFFING

Most libraries have lean enough staffing that using untrained volunteers or lower-paid employees such as student help makes sense for simple activities such as setting up book sales or packing boxes for the consignment sellers. Evaluating more expensive items, bargaining with dealers, and selling on the Internet require a higher level of expertise. For many libraries, Friends groups handle the disposal of gifts and withdrawn items. A dedicated core of volunteers is required to assure continuity, especially if the library wishes to sell directly on the Internet.

CONCLUSION

I suggest the following three steps. They require the least effort and staff time:

1. Sell trade paperbacks at the same price as hardcovers.

2. Evaluate materials with potentially higher prices on a valuation site and consider sending them to BetterWorld Books or B-Logistics or selling them to a dealer.

3. Use variable pricing including a premium for early purchases at book sales where the goal is to get rid of all items in a short period.

Although selling books directly on the Internet has the possibility of generating the most revenue, this strategy requires a commitment that is beyond the ability of many libraries. With some effort, most libraries can increase revenue by selling gifts and discarded materials.

28

A SMALL SCHOOL LIBRARY MEETS THE ECONOMIC CHALLENGE

Colleen Driscoll

WITH LITTLE BUDGETED income, school groups must raise money on their own. The library/media center is no exception. Though it competes for money being raised for athletics or other academic needs, most parents and students recognize the necessity of a well-equipped media center and are supportive.

This chapter highlights programs we have used at Kingsford Middle School and High School library/media centers with success. Kingsford is located in Dickinson County, in the western Upper Peninsula of Michigan. Part of Breitung Township Schools, our schools are relatively small (middle school enrollment, 375 students; high school, 620) but academically successful. Though both libraries are given a small budget, most materials are obtained through the efforts described here.

A key to the success of these programs is publicity and acknowledgment. It is imperative that people (individuals and groups) feel appreciated for their time and donations. Publicity also generates interest from others.

Having districtwide support is also fundamental. Individual schools within the district should not be in competition with each other. All library fundraisers are supported by all the schools. For example, the middle school library holds its book fair in the spring, the elementary school in the fall; this way, parents are able to support both fully. All library events are put on the announcements (announcements for our schools are sent to parents via e-mail) for all the schools, and often monies generated help all the libraries.

The events described here do not require much staff. In fact, almost all were done with one part-time media specialist and a handful of dedicated aides or volunteers.

FUND-RAISING

Fund-raising is essential to securing funding for the library. Monies allocated from our school budget are minimal; to secure the materials needed, money has to be obtained in creative ways. Here are some of them:

Book Fairs

Book fairs are the most successful fund-raiser for our middle school. As promotional material proclaims, everyone benefits: students acquire great books for their personal collections, and the media center profits monetarily.

Schedule book fairs when parents will be in the building; parent/teacher conferences are a great time. Or schedule an event that will bring parents into the school. For example, the elementary school in our district organized an event called "Night of 1000 Stars" and had local celebrities read to students during the fair. The middle school hosted adult author visits during the fair; community members who came in for the booktalks could then visit the fair.

Publicizing is essential. Offer contests, place advertisements and pictures in the newspaper, post displays in the hallways and school announcements, and send parents e-mail. Food, of course, is a great incentive; people will come if offered snacks. Put up balloons, make attractive displays, and generally use your marketing skills to make people want to buy the items available at the fair.

School Store

The high school library runs a school store, and all proceeds benefit the library. The store sells all school supplies students need, including basics like pens, pencils, and notebooks. Also for sale are items that students need occasionally such as flash drives, notecards, book covers, and construction paper. If a teacher requires an item for a project, we make sure we have it for sale: poster board, markers, rulers, and sticky notes are there. The music department needed assistance with its own selling activities, so the library now offers reeds, valve oil, and even socks. The library also sells display boards for the science fair and other presentations. This has the added benefit of bringing students into the library to see what else is offered. In addition, other schools, after finding out that we sell supplies, send their students over to get what they need.

Auxiliary Services

The library offers students the services of laminating, overhead transparencies, Ellison machine cutouts (for bulletin boards), and other needed services for nominal fees. We also recycle ink cartridges through a local store and receive a small fee for each container brought in.

DONATIONS

A way to secure items without raising money by direct sales is to seek donations.

Item Donation

Take donations of any item you can. Once the items are in the library's possession, they can be evaluated for use in your facility. If the items are not needed or appropriate, pass them on to an entity that can use them, perhaps the public library, teachers, or other schools. Our library accepts all donations of videos, books, magazines; we even accept old holiday decorations for use in making the facilities festive.

Our facilities have a small magazine/journal budget, so subscription donations are appreciated. In addition, we accept previously read magazines; the address information is cut off and the magazines are available to be read and checked out. A few days' delay in waiting for a magazine is better than not having it available at all. Magazines we simply cannot use are made available to staff for art projects.

In addition, some magazines offer gift subscriptions. Our library has been lucky enough to be the recipient of such gifts. A thank-you sent to the donor helps assure a donation in later years.

Time Donation

Having volunteers is beneficial in several ways. For one thing, staff simply cannot complete all tasks in their allotted time. Currently our district has three libraries and one certified staff member, who also is assigned classroom teaching time. Volunteers are a great help with shelving, filing, cleaning, and decorating. Volunteers are also great library advocates and inform others of the wonderful happenings taking place.

Some businesses reward their employees for volunteering. One of our volunteers works at Wal-Mart. If she has twenty-five hours of documented volunteer time, the library gets a $250 grant. This is a great way to earn money for a good cause—for an activity she would do regardless. Many companies (more than one might expect) offer this type of opportunity. Seek out such charitable contributions.

Give the Gift of Reading

Our Give the Gift of Reading campaign is a partnership developed between libraries and the local bookstore. Each library can choose a month (our middle school does February; our high school December), and any books bought at the bookstore during that month, for that library, receive a 20 percent discount. Anyone may buy the books (parents, students, community members, library staff). The bookstore collects all the books, along with the names of the people who purchase them, and the school picks up the books at the end of the month. Book donation plates are placed inside the books, and the books are added to the permanent collection.

The libraries make lists of suggested titles for purchase (though any book is appreciated) and gives the list to anyone interested. The library does most of the publicity (articles in the newspaper, school announcements, flyers, etc.) and the bookstore does a display. Thank-you notes are also sent to donors. This is a wonderful community event. See figure 28.1 for an example of a flyer used for this campaign.

Birthday Book Club

For several years our middle school offered a Birthday Book Club. Parents (or others) could purchase a book in a child's honor. That book was added to the permanent collection. A donation bookplate was placed inside and a sticker on the outside. This program adds books to the collection, and it automatically generates interest for the title.

This program, as may happen with others, generated much excitement in the beginning, but interest faded after several years. That reaction should not be taken as a failure. Simply reintroduce the program after a short hiatus when a new group of students is in the building and eager for something new. Our school will be reimplementing this program in the fall.

FIGURE 28.1
GIVE THE GIFT OF READING CAMPAIGN FLYER

Give the Gift of Reading ...

The "Give the Gift of Reading" Campaign is a partnership between **BookWorld** and **Kingsford Middle School.**

Interested individuals can purchase a book(s) from BookWorld as a gift to the KMS library/media center. All purchases for KMS will be given a **20% discount** during the month of February!

Not sure what books the library needs? Both the library and BookWorld have a list of needed titles.

All books purchased will have a bookplate put inside with the donor's name. Books can also be purchased in honor of someone—what a memorable and lasting gift!

Please consider purchasing a book for the KMS library/media center during this month of love. Stop by BookWorld in the Midtown Mall or call the KMS library/media center for more information.

Thank you for your generosity!!

Local Reading Programs

Our district participates in a local reading program called Reading Olympics (there are other programs offered in various parts of the country). As a participant, our schools get copies of the books that are involved in the program. These books then become part of the libraries' permanent collections. Not only are the programs worthwhile and great reading incentives, books are added to the shelves.

Another program that our library supports is Quiz Bowl. Trivia and library go hand in hand! Students come into the library for practices, and the books used become part of the library's collection.

Parent Groups

Our high school has an Academic Booster Club (ABC) that is active in supporting the educational efforts of our students. The ABC group often requires documentation for requests, but it supports demonstrated needs. This group has purchased curriculum-related books and calculators for the library.

The middle school has a Parent Partnership, similar to a PTO at elementary schools. It too actively supports the educational needs of the students, including library needs. This group, when asked, contributes money and items to the library. It is a good idea for the librarian to be a faculty representative on such groups; this gets the library's needs heard.

Foundations

Our school district has a foundation, which supports all academic programs, including library/media centers. Donations made to the foundation are tax deductible. The library directly benefits from monies contributed to this cause. See figure 28.2 for the page our library used in the foundation booklet sent out to potential donors.

Funds/Memorials

The library can benefit from monies donated to the school. Our school can spend the interest each year on one donated fund, and with it our library was able to get a wireless hub and Ellison machine. Also, when a former teacher's spouse passed away (a teacher himself), books were donated to the library in his name. Books are a wonderful way to remember loved ones because they are checked out and read again and again.

CONTESTS AND GRANTS

Individuals and companies offer funds if one applies for them. Take the time to try to win money for your library. Some grants are for large amounts of money and require much research, effort, and time. If I believe that our library has any hope of acquiring these grants, I try. There are numerous websites available that give grant-writing tips and help.

Our libraries have received several smaller grants, including the We the People Bookshelf Grant five years in a row. We have also received the Picturing America Grant and received a consolation prize in DEMCO's makeover contest (this is how we acquired shelving for our school store). I have also won maps for the school through Nystrom, a company that manufactures and publishes social studies educational materials. If a grant is available, *go for it.*

The same go-for-it philosophy is shared with staff members and students. Someone out there is going to get the grant or win the contest—why not one of us? Staff and students are encouraged to showcase their talents and promote their successes. The library keeps a website on contest/grant/sweepstakes opportunities (www.kingsford.org/khsweb/mediacenter/newcontests .htm). Students have won books and bonds, had writings published, and generally received recognition.

SOLICITATIONS

You may have to take the initiative to go out and secure funds on your own. Companies may not advertise that they have money to give, but if approached they may be willing to help your library.

Businesses

Many businesses are willing to donate in exchange for publicity. Our library has offered food coupons from local restaurants as prizes in reading contests. We have also solicited local businesses during the book fair to make matching fund donations.

Individuals

There are individuals in the community who are willing to help libraries. One community member, vocal about her love of reading and libraries, has brought authors in to speak to the students. The authors, in turn, often donate books to the library (sometimes autographed copies) or give books that can be donated to students.

FIGURE 28.2
FOUNDATION PAGE

KINGSFORD HIGH SCHOOL AND MIDDLE SCHOOL LIBRARY/MEDIA CENTERS

Did You Know?? A substantial body of research since 1990 shows a positive relationship between school libraries and student achievement. The research studies show that school libraries can have a positive impact on student achievement—whether such achievement is measured in terms of reading scores, literacy, or learning more generally. A school library program that is adequately staffed, resourced, and funded can lead to higher student achievement regardless of the socioeconomic or educational levels of the community. (Source—Scholastic Research Foundation)

Mission Statement. The mission statement of the library/media centers is to provide the resources and instruction for students and staff so that they will expand their reading interests and abilities, become effective users of information skills and technology tools, think critically, gain and create knowledge, and become lifelong learners.

Vision Statement. The Kingsford High School and Middle School Library/Media Centers will be the academic hubs of the building—the places where all student and faculty academic needs are met.

Services. Library/Media Center services include, but are not limited to: Books (fiction, nonfiction, reference, etc.); School Store; Computers (with Internet and database access, word processing, etc.); Ellison Machine; Copier; Transparency and Laminating; Contest and Grant information distribution; Contests; Displays; Equipment (TVs/DVDs/VCRs, CDs, projectors, etc.); Newsletters; Reports; Orientations; Mini-lessons; Book Fairs and other fund-raisers; Research assistance; Quiet, friendly, inviting atmosphere; Career library; Public Enrichment Foundation free book distribution; Textbook inventory and checkout; American Library Association–sponsored event recognition (National Library Week, Teen Tech Week, Teen Read Week, etc.); STAR and AR assistance.

Statistics. Over 15,000 students per year come into each library (based on sign-in data). In addition, over 4,000 students use the computer lab; the TV units are checked out over 1,000 times; projectors are checked out over 500 times; the mobile lab is checked out over 500 times; and over 300 classes come in to use the library and the computer lab.

Conclusion. The goal is to make the KHS/KMS Library/Media Centers learning environments, yet places where people want to be—questioning, bustling, comfortable, helpful, friendly, useful places that promote reading, research, and any other academic endeavors. However, the library staff cannot do it alone. For the Library/Media Centers to be the academic focuses of the buildings, it takes the cooperation of all members of our school community. Thank you in advance for your donations and support!! All monies donated will go to continue the important and varied services and activities listed above.

Groups

Our library receives books every year from a Women's Club that buys books in honor of its members. There are outdoor clubs that buy outdoor magazine subscriptions for our collection. When a group is looking for a way to give back to the community, the library is the perfect recipient—so many people benefit. Of course, thank-you notes and publicity are a must. Pictures in the newspaper may generate interest from others.

FREEBIES

Getting items for free is the best deal there is. Take advantage of all free opportunities that come your way. Those that come your way for free have to be evaluated, and not everything is needed or appropriate, but unwanted items can be passed on to others. Keep your eyes and ears open for opportunities for free books, bookmarks, and posters. Sign up for free newsletters and groups. Take advantage of every offer you can. Recently our library acquired books because students filled out a survey for a company. The surveys were anonymous and required just minutes of each student's time. Vendors often offer free items as incentive for purchase; apply for every e-mail offer you can. If you attend a workshop or conference, take the gifts offered at the booths.

SO WHAT CAN YOU DO?

Hold a book fair.

Start your own campaign. (Our Give the Gift of Reading campaign was not in existence until I met with the manager of the bookstore and we worked out the details.)

If your school does not already have one, open a school store.

Collect fines.

Seek out donations.

Look into corporate partnerships.

Join (or start) local reading programs.

Solicit your school's parent organizations.

Seek out grants.

Keep your eyes and ears open for any opportunity available.

Book Clubs

Our middle school offers book club flyers to students. The library compiles the orders and delivers the books to the students. The orders accumulate points, which the library can redeem for free books. These books are added to the permanent collection. These book orders have the added benefit of showing us what books are popular with the students; the library often orders a copy of the titles the students are purchasing.

Database Trials

Many companies offer free trials of their online databases. This allows the students and staff some time to use the resources without paying for them. If deemed worthy, the programs can be purchased at a later date. This also allows the library some publicity ("Take a look at this great new link on the library's links page! Let us know what you think").

Public Enrichment Foundation

Our local public enrichment foundation offers books to organizations in need, including our schools. Each year this foundation gives overstocked books to our students and staff. The library also gets a copy of each title offered. The foundation does this all for free, though thank-you notes are always appreciated.

CONCLUSION

Obtaining what your library needs does not always have to be an overwhelming, time-consuming, impossible task. Many small, doable projects can get you what is needed. Know your needs, seek out help, see what your community has to offer, be creative, and just try it.

PART VIII

Staffing

29

LEVERAGING INTERNAL RESOURCES TO FILL LIBRARY STAFF SHORTAGES TEMPORARILY

Marwin Britto

IN THE MIDST of the worst economic recession since the 1930s, higher education institutions in the United States have been facing unprecedented budget cuts, with more expected in the foreseeable future. Online sources are rampant with news reports of massive cuts in academic library budgets across institutions. These cuts have resulted in significant reductions in library collections, services, and staffing. A survey distributed at the 2009 national ACRL conference asked librarians to identify the leading issues facing them and their profession. Not surprisingly, the respondents (more than 1,300 of them) overwhelmingly reported that the main issues were budget cutbacks and funding constraints, which they indicated were having a considerable impact on staffing, collections, equipment, and facilities (Kniffel and Bailey 2009). To make matters worse, deeper library budgets cuts are expected in coming years, with no reprieve in sight. Desperate times call for creative solutions. In this chapter I identify often overlooked institutional resources that can be tapped to help fill library staffing shortages until the economy and budget recover.

Staff positions in academic libraries typically run the full gamut from well-experienced, credentialed administrators and heads of departments to entry-level staff with little to no experience. The responsibilities of some of these positions can often be temporarily filled at no direct financial cost to the library through identifying and leveraging internal institutional resources. Specifically, universities generally offer a variety of resources and opportunities, some obvious and some not, that are potential sources of temporary library staff. By creatively leveraging these opportunities, academic libraries can help address staffing shortages. The resources discussed here are available in most universities.

GRADUATE ASSISTANTSHIPS

A graduate assistantship is a type of financial award, often merit based, that provides a graduate student part-time work in a variety of support capacities including research, teaching, and administration/staff. Different types of assistantships often come with certain requirements and restrictions. For example, research assistantships, which are typically grant funded, have specific requirements and duties aligned to the fulfillment of the grant goals. Some instructional assistantships are for a specific teaching assignment, which may prohibit other responsibilities because of the time needed to fulfill the teaching obligation. Administration/staff assistantships offer the most flexibility, since these duties are not limited to research or instruction.

Although funding and availability of graduate assistantships vary, many are funded 100 percent through the institution's graduate school or academic departments. Graduate assistantships offered through an academic department may be limited to work in that department, whereas those offered through the graduate school may have more flexibility. Institutions that offer graduate-level programs in library and information science, library media, instructional technology, information systems, and other related areas provide a ready pool of potential library staff who, through their assistantship, may have the option of temporarily filling staff positions in the academic library. Depending on the library's needs and the students' skills and knowledge, these students can be used in a variety of ways. For example, they may be involved in instruction, information literacy and reference assistance, research support, circulation desk, web services, and information and instructional technology support.

FACULTY SERVICE OBLIGATIONS

Tenured and tenure-track faculty at higher education institutions have teaching, service, and scholarship obligations. The proportion of these three areas varies depending on the focus of the institution. Research institutions have a heavier emphasis on research; teaching institutions have a greater focus on teaching. Both types of institutions require their faculty to devote time to service, and the definition of service tends to be quite liberal. This fact, although often overlooked, gives academic libraries access to usually well-educated individuals to fill and support a variety of roles in the library while meeting their service obligations. The exact nature of the support is contingent on the skill set of a particular faculty member and the needs of the library.

Academic libraries must be proactive in recruiting faculty for these roles and flexible in finding a fit for them. The added advantage of this arrangement is that these faculty members often already have credibility with many of the library patrons, who may be their students and their peers in their discipline. And it is not unusual to find a few individuals with an MLIS background, since after earning that degree some individuals complete a PhD program and then pursue a faculty position in their chosen discipline. Having the opportunity to use their MLIS degree as part of their service obligation can be a win-win situation for the individual and the academic library.

CO-OP/INTERNSHIPS

The terms *co-operative education* and *internships* are synonymous at some institutions and denote different programs at others, but both imply a for-credit program in which undergraduate and graduate students can gain some relevant work experience. Some academic programs require these types of experiences as part of the curriculum; others offer it as a recommended elective. In addition, some academic programs offer the flexibility to students to create their own internship or co-op experience by locating an appropriate employer willing to assume the responsibility.

With the depressed economy and record unemployment in this country, a growing number of students are pursuing these opportunities for a variety of reasons. Specifically, they want to get some work experience, network, get a good reference, and delay graduation in the hopes that the economy will have improved when they are ready to enter the workforce. It is important to understand that this type of experience is an exchange: the library is receiving service in the form of work from the student in exchange for mentorship, guidance, and supervision. Consequently, although internships and co-ops are not paid, there is a cost to the library in terms of time invested to manage these students. Many MLIS degrees provide opportunities for internships, and with the growing number of MLIS programs available via the Web you may find a local individual enrolled in an online MLIS program elsewhere but available and willing to work at your institution in an internship capacity.

OTHER INTERNAL RESOURCES AND OPPORTUNITIES

The opportunities at institutions to meet library staff needs presented in this chapter are not the only ones. Others include individual and independent study, academic service learning, and senior capstone projects in disciplines such as information systems and computer science. These three options, like others discussed here, have specific stipulations that may make them feasible only in a limited capacity in an academic library. In addition, similar to internships and co-op experiences, students in these programs often require extra staffing time to mentor, support, and supervise them. Either way, these options are worth exploring, for the benefits might be worth the effort.

CONCLUSION

Academic libraries continue to struggle in this depressed economy with diminishing budgets. Fortunately, through internal resources and opportunities, many can address some of their staffing shortages. These resources are not meant as permanent solutions but simply as means to manage current library projects and provide necessary library support services until funding levels resume.

WORK CITED

Kniffel, Leonard, and Charles W. Bailey Jr. "Cuts, Freezes Widespread in Academic Libraries." 2009. www.ala.org/ala/alonline/currentnews/newsarchive/2009/may2009/academiclibrarywoes051309.cfm (accessed December 22, 2009).

30

MAKING GOOD BY MAKING DO
Using Student Staff to Drive Library Technology Innovation

Gwen Evans

A CADEMIC LIBRARIES WERE familiar with the exhortation to "do more with less" even before the recent economic crisis. As budgets tighten, the phrase "innovative and low cost" becomes a mantra, especially when it comes to technology. Creative use of low- or no-cost web applications and cloud computing environments can help fill the gaps, but sometimes libraries need custom software/database development. Short of hiring programming geniuses, what strategies or environments foster innovation in technology? Can "making do" in a resource-poor environment really turn into "making good"?

At Bowling Green (Ohio) State University, a research university of over 18,000 FTE, the University Libraries Information Technology Services (LITS) consists of web services, systems, digital initiatives, and desktop support—currently provided by three full-time staff positions. Plans to hire a full-time web application developer in 2007 fell afoul of hiring freezes and deepening economic troubles at all levels. Still, we needed to incorporate emerging Web 2.0 technologies into our existing services to meet user demand.

Rather than retrench and retreat, we decided to move forward with student staff as primary programmers in 2007. At the time, we employed a team of excellent undergraduate computer science students for desktop support and simple web maintenance. Their initial successes in developing test applications on our new LAMP server made using students to do more than just HTML coding and printer hookup seem plausible.

RISK, INNOVATION, AND THE "BETA LAB" MODEL

We were aware that this was a risky experiment. Our major concern was lack of continuity, since support would be "handed down" from one set of student employees to another. Outages during intersessions or weekends could mean long waits for support. No one on the permanent staff had the kind of programming experience to review and correct student code, making supervision complex. Students have their own set of challenges as they juggle course work and the work of growing up. We already had some older homegrown web and database implementations that were increasingly hard to maintain as user expectations shifted rapidly. We did not want to institutionalize more projects that could not scale, were difficult to migrate, and could not be abandoned.

All the same, our "making do" strategy is recognized as a proven improvisational design process in technology firms with a reputation for innovation. *Bricolage,* the process of tinkering or improvising solutions from what is at hand,

LAMP AND OPEN-SOURCE APPLICATIONS

LAMP stands for Linux, Apache, MySQL, PHP—an open-source server installation that runs many library-specific or library-friendly programs such as WordPress, Omeka, Libstats, Open Journal Systems, OsTicket, and Drupal. Computer science students learn MySQL and PHP (the basis for many open-source applications) quickly if they don't already know them. You don't necessarily need special server hardware to create a LAMP server—you can repurpose a desktop computer. Many web hosting companies also offer LAMP application hosting if you cannot run your own server. Bitnami is an open-source installer that installs an all-in-one "stack"—server software and open-source applications—to make installations easy. At this time, these stacks (which include other server configurations besides LAMP) include Moodle, Joomla, WordPress, and more. For more information, see http://bitnami.org. WordPress in particular can do more than support a blog; it is an excellent lightweight content management system that can be a full-fledged website or multimedia database.

requires allowing and even encouraging tinkering by people close to the operational level, combining and applying known tools and routines to solve new problems. No general scheme or model is available: only local cues from a situation are trusted and exploited in a somewhat blind and unreflective way. The aim is to achieve ad-hoc solutions by applying heuristics rather than high theory. (Ciborra 2004, 45)

The concept of bricolage is familiar to cultural anthropologists from Claude Levi-Strauss's classic *The Savage Mind,* and the concept has been incorporated into disciplines as diverse as linguistics, literary theory, and research on organizational improvisation and technology. Karl E. Weick, describing bricolage in organizational improvisation, notes that "invariably the resources are less well suited to the exact project than one would prefer but they are all there is"—a succinct description of our situation (Weick 2001, 62).

A study by Shona Brown and Kathleen Eisenhardt describes the characteristics for innovation as a limited structure around responsibilities and priorities, extensive communication and design freedom, and improvisation within current projects. Strategic alliances, experimental products, and a "wide variety of low-cost probes into the future" also characterize successful firms. Neither planning nor reacting is as effective as a flexible structure emphasizing adaptation and experimentation (Brown and Eisenhardt 1997, 1).

In many ways it is easier to create this environment with student staff. The official name of the student work unit is "LITS Labs"—homage to other famous experimental groups. We discuss project suggestions from library staff, assess applications that we admire from other libraries, and generate speculative "blue sky" ideas. We argue about librarian subculture and work practices and discuss our different experiences of user behavior.

PERPETUAL BETA

Free analytics programs like Yahoo Analytics and Google Analytics provide an incredible amount of user information beyond simple web hits. An increasing number of other low-cost or free programs can capture exactly what users are doing on a page without formal usability testing. Some popular ones are Loop11, Userfly, ClickTale, fivesecondtest, Google Website Optimizer, and Chalkmark, among others. Almost all of the paid services allow a low-volume free account or free trial. Spending money for good data is cost effective; long committee discussions about user behavior based on anecdotal evidence or opinion can eat up hundreds, if not thousands, of dollars of staff time to less effect.

The students are responsible for researching techniques, platforms, and coding languages for any given project, experimenting with possible solutions, and presenting the options to the group. We search aggressively for open-source or free Web 2.0 technologies that we can adapt for our purposes, and we ask other libraries for their homegrown code.

The students introduced us to Agile software development and Extreme programming, and we adopted and adapted where we could. They self-organize, assigning tasks according to skill, and make incremental iterations in close collaboration with the requesting library "client." Short, simple programming cycles are much easier to manage with student coders. They work directly outside our offices, ensuring a free flow of communication and consultation. During the alpha stages of development, we invite all library staff to "break this application." This allows early feedback from a wide variety of users. We have discussed Tim O'Reilly's (2005, 4) idea of Web 2.0 software development as "perpetual beta" across the library so that staff are aware of the explicit foundation of the model and are not surprised or impatient if we tinker with the functionality on a constant basis. We use analytics from a variety of sources to determine current use patterns, especially if we get requests for added functionality for a particular module or feature.

RETURN ON INVESTMENT

In the initial eight months, our students created a popular stack map integrated into the OPAC; a library tutorial that embeds text and multimedia and calculates simple statistics for assessment; a library hours database; and HueTunes, an experimental color tagging and search application for music, among others. The first year cost $16,000 in student wages. Is support still an issue? Yes, we still have nightmares about applications crashing over Thanksgiving break. Occasionally an application is off-line longer than we would like. Are applications less polished than those produced by full-time developers? Sometimes, but many in-house library applications (or commercial products, like OPACs) look rather "Web 1.0" when compared to newer applications. We receive requests for our applications from other libraries and feel we compare well.

GUIDING PRINCIPLES: THE PROJECTS

Some of our guiding principles are tried and true in software development, but they are particularly salient when working with a student team:

KISS—Keep it simple, stupid. One of the biggest killers of any software or technology project is scope creep—the external pressure or internal temptation to add features. Concentrate on core functionality; be ambitious, but keep it streamlined and highly focused. A polite but firm "no, that's too complicated for students" usually makes sense to staff without making the department look obstructive. Know when to quit too. Look for another open-source or commercial solution if progress isn't brisk.

The perfect is the enemy of the good. Obsessing about minor flaws or waiting for full features can hobble production. Deploy the applications fast and tinker as you go. If the project needs to endure for ten years, you should not be using student staff to develop it. Appropriate projects are those that you can already foresee as replaceable; a better platform will come along, or the need will disappear as user behavior or service models change. Virtual tours are a perfect example; there are dozens of ways to create one, including Flickr photosets, YouTube videos, and complicated Flash applications.

Bricolage. Mash up what is available—open-source applications, cloud applications, and student talent. The constant flow of free web and cloud computing applications is making this mash-up/bricolage approach even easier. Although it may make your administration (and IT staff) nervous to rely on Google or Conduit or Flickr, if the choice is between something and nothing, shouldn't you choose something?

Robust administrative interfaces. Because many applications are database driven and change frequently, we design every application with an easy-to-use administrative interface that requires no programming for routine updates or changes. Library staff can modify the ranges and maps in the stack map application themselves during a stack shift or update the hours database. Designing the back end is usually the most difficult task, but it is critical to application self-sufficiency and sustainability after the original programmer has graduated or gone home for the holidays.

THE RIGHT STUDENTS

Success depends on hiring the right students and managing them well. Recruit actively, maintaining relationships with appropriate departments and faculty for referrals. Turn your students into talent scouts with a handful of your business cards; weekend coding raves, online gaming tournaments, and class projects are all recruitment opportunities. Our student team members participate in interviews for new hires to assess coding ability and teamwork skills. Foster your students' personal pride and investment in the projects, and they will want to find someone who will do justice to "their" application.

Although the "lone wolf" genius is an IT stereotype, we have found it more productive to hire students with well-developed communication and social skills, and we have noticed that undergraduates tend to have more polymorphous talents than graduate students, who have often already specialized.

Stagger your hiring so that freshmen and sophomores are working alongside juniors and seniors; it ensures continuity of support and helps with supervision. The juniors and seniors are told that their job descriptions include coaching and teaching less experienced students.

Be explicit about the expected trajectory of employment in the job interview—from underclass newbie to upperclass project manager—and hire students who recognize the opportunity to grow rather than those who seem daunted.

At least one student needs CSS/HTML and Photoshop skills, unless you already have those on staff. Hire students interested in usability issues and user testing, or assign that aspect of development to one of them.

Esprit de corps is important. Schedule the students so that they work as a team. For students especially, development in this "beta lab" environment is learning and problem solving, so don't expect them to work as though they are doing data entry. Playing, experimentation, and unexpected sources for inspiration foster innovation. For example, gaming maps sparked a still-running discussion about virtual tour and stack map navigation. Food, the classic student encouragement tactic, works too.

Professionalize your students' environment and work practices, so they act like professionals. Make sure they comment their code extensively and write documentation. We rely on campus IT services to help us with periodic security audits. We upgraded the student work area with height-adjustable desks and two large monitors for every computer.

STUDENT TALENT FROM ELSEWHERE

Not an academic library? Your local campus, community college, or vocational school is a great source for potential student or part-time employees. Many campuses have co-op and internship programs to match students with employers. Depending on the internship or co-op program, a site coordinator or program officer can help define expectations, match skills, arrange interviews, and mediate if there are problems. The students get academic class credit, which helps keep them focused.

CONCLUSION

We have been developing for three years with a changing team of students. We have updated and refined the original applications and added more. We have not stopped worrying about support issues and continuity (every graduation gives me the jitters). Supervising students is more time intensive than supervising permanent staff—a cost that is hard to calculate. Occasionally the students are frustrating, more often inventive and delightful. All have gotten professional jobs after graduation. Not only do we give our open-source code away on request, we encourage the students to look at jobs in libraries, with library software vendors, or graduate school in library and information science—another way of giving back to the library community. By making do, we have managed to do good not only for ourselves but for our student employees also.

WORKS CITED

Brown, Shona L., and Kathleen M. Eisenhardt. 1997. "The Art of Continuous Change: Linking Complexity Theory and Time-Paced Evolution in Relentlessly Shifting Organizations." *Administrative Science Quarterly* 42 (1).

Ciborra, Claudio. 2004. *The Labyrinths of Information: Challenging the Wisdom of Systems.* Oxford: Oxford University Press.

Levi-Strauss, Claude. 1966. *The Savage Mind.* Chicago: University of Chicago Press.

O'Reilly, Tim. 2005. What Is Web 2.0? http://oreilly.com/web2/archive/what -is-web-20.html (accessed June 13, 2009).

Weick, Karl E. 2001. *Making Sense of the Organization.* Malden, MA: Blackwell.

31

TIERED STAFFING FOR TECHNICAL SERVICES

Mary S. Laskowski and Fang Huang Gao

THE UNIVERSITY LIBRARY at the University of Illinois, Urbana-Champaign, is, like many large academic libraries, facing unprecedented budget constraints. Plans for long-term efficiencies, however, often require prioritization of short-term, large-scale collection management projects. In this chapter we discuss the tension between the need for skilled, permanent staff and a budget environment that can support only the use of temporary staff. Using two examples of recent large-scale collection management projects in an academic library setting, we hope to identify the challenges and benefits of making the most of tiered staffing plans, maintaining quality while increasing flexibility. Our experiences stress the importance of creatively adapting workflows to fit current project priorities and recognizing the changing nature and scope of ongoing work.

DEFINING THE PROBLEM

The need for creative staffing is not a new phenomenon, but bad budgets can in some cases provide the necessary impetus for positive institutional change. When under pressure to come up with a new solution quickly, however, it is often easy to ignore long-term goals of sustainability, reduction of duplicative effort, and the like. Much of our institutional budget is invested in people, and thus any change that affects permanent staffing levels is difficult and time consuming to adopt. As we move forward with new plans for technical services in bad budget times, it is increasingly important that we increase flexibility while maintaining the quality of work and expertise necessary to provide long-term support for collection needs. Clearly, as long as the institution performs technical services in-house, some level of permanent staffing with high levels of expertise in a variety of technical services work is vital, but if staffing at peak levels is not possible in tight budget years there may be underutilized models of staffing that prove equally productive and allow for prioritization of projects as they occur.

BALANCE PEAK PROCESSING PERIODS AND HIGH-IMPACT PROJECTS

Consider looking across library units to find efficiencies of scale. Staffing for peak processing in one area can lend itself well to utilizing those same staff for project priorities in down times. For example, staff who may be busy with cyclical responsibilities such as reserve processing during certain times of the year may be able to make use of many of the same technical skills at other points in the academic year working on such tasks as collection transfers.

TWO COLLECTION MANAGEMENT PROJECTS

Two recent major collection management projects provided us new opportunities for investigating flexible staffing models: redistribution of a small departmental library collection to other locations within the library system, and a major transfer of items from the central stacks to an off-site storage facility. Two units from the library's technical services division—information processing and management (IPM) and content access management (CAM)—assumed much of the responsibility for these collection moves. The work involved included retrieval of physical items from the shelf, checking that the catalog record matched the piece in hand and conformed to standards, fixing cataloging errors and creating new records when necessary, changing item locations and statuses in the online catalog, checking condition of the pieces for possible conservation work, and shipping as appropriate to new locations. Because both projects were on tight deadlines, the workload could not simply be distributed to existing permanent staff but required a new staffing plan.

The smaller of the two projects, completed in June 2009, afforded us the chance to test out new staffing models. As the unit less vested in skilled

> ## COMMUNICATION IS THE KEY
>
> To facilitate smooth operations and avoid bottlenecks in large projects, it is critical to have communications among different teams and among members on the same team. The former helps adjust the workflow, and the latter helps guarantee the quality and consistency of the work.

cataloging staff, IPM assumed responsibility for physical shifting of the materials, performing triage regarding the type and level of any cataloging and conservation work needed. To give a sense of scope, the first project involved moving/processing over 37,000 items, and the second, larger transfer project handled over 120,000 items. For the second project, IPM assumed responsibility for pulling items from the stacks, again performing triage regarding the type and level of any cataloging and conservation work needed; marked and shipped the materials appropriately for transfer to the off-site storage facility; but did not reshift the remaining collection within stacks. In both instances, it turned out that IPM was able to process from start to finish more than 70 percent of the materials without sending the items to other units for more in-depth cataloging work.

HIRING AND TRAINING

A large part of what made both projects a success from the processing perspective is that we were able to pursue temporary staffing hired and trained specifically for the projects. Though these people had little to no prior training in technical services work, their skills were focused solely on the needs of the project, creating a great deal of efficiency.

CONSISTENT TRIAGE OF COLLECTION NEEDS

One significant change in workflow for these projects was that a concerted effort was made to assign as much work as possible to the less skilled hourly staff, reserving the time of experienced permanent staff for complicated problems. IPM hired recent graduates as academic hourly employees; they could work close to forty hours per week. Working with hourly employees rather than undergraduate students greatly simplified the scheduling of the project and also meant that fewer people could receive more training more efficiently. The result was a highly effective, relatively small workforce that excelled at both physical retrieval/condition checking and triage of records for cataloging problems. Those same staff alternated physical work with processing of materials online, only forwarding problems as necessary to permanent staff. Processing included matching physical items in hand with existing catalog records, making location and status changes, fixing errors such as missing bar codes or call number mistakes, and identifying records that needed to be replaced or enhanced before transfer to the off-site storage facility.

Training Skilled Catalogers for Complex Maintenance

Any materials not able to be handled by the temporary team in IPM were forwarded to CAM for more in-depth review. Therefore, in addition to existing permanent staff, CAM needed to increase skilled staff available to work on these projects. Because of the complicated nature of serials and the time constraints placed on these projects, we needed people who could be trained quickly. Fifteen hourly staff were hired, some of them graduate hourly employees who are currently pursuing library degrees. The rest of them were academic hourly who had received their MSLIS recently but were still out in the job market. All had taken a cataloging and classification class and had a good understanding of AACR2 and MARC21 but had not had the opportunity to put their classroom learning into practice.

A key element in implementing any new staffing plan is a well-structured training program that can efficiently and effectively get new people up to speed. First we let the hourly employees understand what they would be dealing with. We want every item in our collection to have a full bibliographic record, a holding record with correct location, call number, and copy number, and an item record with correct bar code. When there were issues, such as items having duplicate call numbers or titles with incorrect bibliographic records, the physical items were pulled from the shelves and sent to CAM for review and correction. Therefore, the hourly staff needed to be trained in the following areas:

Working in OCLC Connexion client interface and Voyager library integrated system. Although all the hourly employees had taken a cataloging class, they had not had a chance to import bibliographic records from OCLC into Voyager. We showed them how to set up preferences in both OCLC Connexion and the Voyager Cataloging Module and how to create an export file in Voyager. We also showed them how to search OCLC for the correct bibliographic record to bring into Voyager, to replace the short circulation-like record. If no bibliographic record was found in OCLC, original cataloging was performed.

Understanding ANSI/NISO Z39.71 Holdings Statements for Bibliographic Items and MARC 21 Format for Holdings Data. For serials, holding records are important, since they show what issues the library has in the summary statement and the holding lines. Therefore, we need to make sure all the

FLEXIBLE STAFFING REQUIRES FLEXIBLE TRAINING

It is effective to provide training in different ways: both traditional face-to-face lecture style and creating and using screen-capture videos as training tutorials; both supervisor-to-student mentoring and peer-to-peer mentoring.

pieces on the shelves are included in the holding record. When creating and modifying holding records, we follow ANSI/NISO Z39.71 Holdings Statements for Bibliographic Items and MARC 21 Format for Holdings Data, with enumeration and chronology information reflecting what issues we have in our collection. That information is displayed in our OPAC, so library users know whether the issues they need are in the library collection.

Understanding cataloging and acquisitions modules in Voyager. For most of our ongoing serials titles, there are purchase orders and check-in records attached to the bibliographic records and the holding records. Not only does the holding information from the holding record go in the online display, but check-in information from the acquisitions module also forms part of the holding display in the OPAC. As each new issue arrives, it gets checked in and the OPAC shows which issue has been recently received. For staff working on our projects, this means that when there is a title change they need to make sure the new purchase order and check-in record are relinked to or created for the new bibliographic record so that the new issues are checked in under the right title, thus displaying correctly in OPAC.

Dealing with different types of library resources: monographs versus serials. Both monographs and serials are involved in our projects. For monographs, the processing steps are pretty straightforward. For serials, we point out their dynamic and complex nature and show our hourly staff how to trace all the title changes for a serial title; what to do when there are changes in place of publication, publisher, publication frequency; and more.

Different Ways to Train

At the early stage of training, we tried to get everyone together and went over steps to be taken for the project. However, since our hourly employees had different work schedules and different levels of cataloging experience, we soon realized that we should have training materials and documentation available for consultation in addition to the face-to-face lecture-style training. With the help of a graduate student, we used the screen-capture software Camtasia Studio to record different aspects of cataloging activities; staff could refer to these online tutorials at any time and as many times as needed.

As the project went on, some graduate assistants obtained their degrees and left for professional jobs, so new people were hired. We encouraged those who had been on the project longer to serve as mentors to new hires. If they came across issues too complex to resolve themselves, they checked with the supervisor.

WHAT WE LEARNED:
THE ADVANTAGES OF TIERED STAFFING

The University of Illinois library is undergoing restructuring, both to better serve current and future library patrons and to increase efficiencies to make the best use of our limited budget. As the budget crisis continues, the library and its host institution have offered retirement and separation incentives, and hiring freezes severely limit opportunities for the addition or even replacement of permanent staff. As a result, more positions are or will become vacant, though the amount of work needed remains the same. Therefore, the demand to think creatively and take advantage of tired staffing models has greatly increased.

Tiered staffing, specifically temporary tiered staffing hired for special projects, offers several advantages. Tiered staffing can allow the library to continue to investigate and test various options before making commitments to permanent staffing that are arduous to change. Hiring and training to address particular needs allow permanent skilled staff to spend their time as efficiently as possible, taking advantage of their experience and skills while temporary staff absorb as much of the mainstream work as possible. Careful assessment of project needs, such as particular language skills, coupled with appropriate hiring and training practices maintains excellent quality control while allowing for fast, large-scale results. We expect to continue to pursue various tiered staffing models for the foreseeable future and by doing so expand our capabilities within our budget constraints, revitalizing the work of permanent staff in the process.

MANAGING THE WORKFLOW

It is difficult to incorporate special projects into existing technical services workflows. But this does not mean that you cannot have experienced full-time staff help with training and managing the workflow for these projects. Encouraging permanent staff to take a supervisory role in the management of special projects, including supervision and mentoring of temporary staff, can help revitalize the work of existing staff members.

32

WE'RE ALL IN THIS TOGETHER
Solutions for Creative Staffing

Heidi Blackburn and Erin Davis

IN THESE DAYS of budget cuts, librarians have been called on to engage patrons while doing more with less and less. Because of massive reductions in funding, many libraries have become creative with their staffing, leading to greater need for effective and economical information technology so that the library's presence does not fade away. In this chapter we present two case studies that feature different approaches to this situation. Through creative staffing and innovative technological solutions, both the Utah State University's (USU) Merrill-Cazier Library and Kansas State University–Salina's library have maximized productivity efficiently while maintaining a high level of commitment to serving patrons during a period of economic restrictions.

KANSAS STATE UNIVERSITY AT SALINA LIBRARY

The most recent state funding for Kansas State University has been reduced by 12 percent from 2006 funding levels. For the Salina campus, these cuts have resulted in (or are expected to) a 2 percent reduction in student salary funds, and operating budgets were decreased 10 percent for administrative departments. Even before the budget restrictions, the Salina campus library had already reduced the number of student worker positions. In 2009 only five workers were scheduled, none were hired for the summer, and only six were rehired for the fall. During this transition, the staff—one director, one reference/instruction librarian, and two staff members—struggled to perform the day-to-day tasks of four full-time positions and to cover the circulation desk. The most drastic move of not hiring student workers in the summer resulted in reducing the circulation desk from 61 hours a week coverage to zero, in order to retain a budget that could accommodate a reduced number of student workers in the fall of 2009.

To find a balance between meeting the needs of students and complying with budget restrictions, library staff members agreed to stagger their working hours during the summer, with each person taking a 10 am–7 pm shift one day a week, Monday through Thursday. This allowed the library to stay open later while keeping employee morale high, since no one was forced to alter her schedule completely. With disparaging talk about restrictions, budget cuts, and the economy, this was essential to maintaining positive attitudes in the workplace. Although monitoring the desk is not a challenging task in a library of this small size, it has had an effect on the staff in two distinct ways: increased responsibilities, and, consequently, some projects being put on hold.

Increased responsibilities have come in the form of handling new tasks at the desk, such as answering calls, selling coffee, checking in materials, and other public service duties. Although the librarians have always stepped in and helped during a sudden rush of patrons, they are now expected to leave their desks when a patron approaches. This puts their own daily tasks on hold and therefore pushes back other responsibilities. For example, the acquisition of e-books has been a project the library wishes to implement, but researching vendors and assessing the library's needs have moved to the bottom of the priority list because daily tasks like cataloging and interlibrary loans take priority.

In the fall of 2009, the Salina campus library staff hired six student workers to cover the peak operating hours, which included opening and closing shifts. Still, because the library faces a continued shortage of staff and simultaneous expectations to maintain the expected level of excellent customer service, the staff have adopted new methods to keep everything running smoothly. Here are a few of them:

- Adopting Google Calendar as the official office calendar software so that each librarian can quickly see who is scheduled to be in or out before making appointments, booking bibliographic instruction sessions, or planning meetings, thus ensuring fewer scheduling conflicts.
- Mandating cross-training so all staff are capable of such tasks as setting up the laptop/projector for meetings and running the coffee shop.

- Holding weekly staff meetings (instead of biweekly), which enables staff to be more informed about changes and upcoming activities in the library.
- Creating additional online tutorials and posting them on the library's blog, which gives instructors the option to use the tutorials in lieu of a full instruction session.

The library was already experiencing cutbacks before the term *recession* started being thrown around in meetings in early 2009 and was thus prepared to face changes. Some organizations might have despaired at the idea of making additional adjustments throughout the year, but the Kansas State Salina campus library was already in "budget mode." Although the restrictions made in the fall were by no means ideal, the library was prepared to accommodate reductions, having already survived the summer semester without student workers. With further university-wide budget cuts under discussion, the library may have to resort to another hiring freeze on student employees. Even though the library would regret the loss of additional employees, by applying methods previously adopted, the staff are better prepared for such a situation.

UTAH STATE UNIVERSITY LIBRARY

The economic crisis had a significant effect on students, faculty, and staff at USU. The state budget cuts for the university have added up to $27.5 million (Fall 2008–July 2010). Personnel were given the option of joining the Voluntary Separation Incentive Program, a onetime offer that allowed employees to discontinue their employment at USU. This program combined with the budget cuts directly impacted the Merrill-Cazier Library's reference department, reducing staffing by 1.5 FTE librarians and 1 FTE staff member. Another position was already vacant because of a librarian's retirement the previous year. To further complicate matters, the library was purposefully postponing hiring because of budget uncertainties, so the 2.5 FTE reference librarian positions remained vacant.

All told, the Merrill-Cazier Library's reference and instruction department consists of eight full-time librarians, two half-time librarians, one teaching assistant, and three library peer mentors. During the 2008/9 academic year, librarians taught over 1,000 instruction sessions, reaching some 10,648 students. To sustain the heavy teaching loads, the library became creative with staffing. Below we highlight some of those adaptive solutions.

Creative Staffing

Library peer mentors. Library peer mentors (LPMs) are student employees trained to provide reference and instruction assistance to students. Three students were hired to work during the 2008/9 academic year in the reference department. The LPMs play an important role in the library, teaching library instruction classes, staffing the information desk, and assisting with assessment projects for the reference department. Hiring the LPMs freed up staff time for other professional responsibilities and proves to be successful year after year.

Hire a teaching assistant. The library has found that hiring a teaching assistant is a great way to maximize funds while helping to ease the workload for other librarians. The library administration approved redefining the job description for the reference library assistant so that responsibilities now emphasize teaching assistance for librarians. This helps ease the teaching burden for the other librarians, particularly with the vacancies resulting from multiple retirements. The teaching assistant not only teaches but also keeps track of instruction statistics, helps manage the reference collection, and provides office support.

Instruction classes. The library implemented several changes in the instruction department to help sustain teaching demands. One change included limiting the number of English 2010 classes to three per semester with assigned professors. A second change involved reevaluating lesson plans to include only the most essential learning activities that concentrate on integrating research within the writing process.

> **INTRODUCING . . .**
> **YOUR VERY OWN**
> **PERSONAL LIBRARIAN**
>
> The USU Library found that when each class is assigned a personal librarian, students are more likely to return to the library and ask for help. Students seem to prefer the high-touch approach, since a hands-on learning component is always incorporated in which students can receive one-on-one research assistance.

In the past, librarians had scheduled anywhere from five to ten sessions with several sections of English 1010 and 2010. Now, although a class may meet with a librarian only one to three class periods per semester, students are strongly encouraged to contact their librarian, to visit the information desk, or to use the library's e-mail help resource for additional assistance.

Reevaluate. We also evaluated individual teaching loads, and the library experimented with a new staffing model in which one librarian is assigned a lighter teaching load each semester. The hope is that this teaching librarian can use the additional time to work on research projects for tenure and promotion requirements. To help pick up the slack, the teaching assistant and library peer mentors are assigned the extra classes, including online classes.

Write Now! drop-in workshops. The library recently started holding drop-in instruction sessions at the end of each semester called "Write Now!"—which offer both writing and research assistance. In these sessions, students obtain assistance with research papers from writing center tutors and library peer mentors.

Innovative Technologies

In the face of massive budget cuts, along with creative staffing libraries are relying on innovative technological solutions more than ever. The need for effective yet economical tools, such as Web 2.0 technologies, LibGuides, chat services, and other outreach activities are critical in these tough economic times. Libraries are doing what they can to stay afloat so that their online presence keeps up with current technology.

LibGuides. Instruction numbers have gone up as LibGuides and other innovative technologies are increasingly used to personalize the student's library experience. LibGuides are online websites designed to enhance classroom instruction and point students to relevant resources; they enable librarians to connect with students even after the class has ended. LibGuides are ideal for both one-shot and course-integrated classes, since the students can still connect with a friendly library face and have a research guide tailored specifically to their class. Some students even continue to use the LibGuides as their point of reference instead of the main library website long after their initial library instruction. Other students discover them when searching the library website and use them, even if they are not enrolled in a class. LibGuides are an excellent example of maximizing productivity while effectively serving patrons' research needs.

Meebo. The embedded chat feature within LibGuides is yet another way to serve patrons at their point of need.

HOLD AN INSTRUCTION SANDBOX

Instruction sandboxes are a fun way to collaborate with colleagues to learn about a new digital tool together in a relaxed, informal way. The USU Library reference department holds one at the end of each semester to update LibGuides, share tips, offer mutual support, and celebrate the end of a hectic semester. This approach not only boosts staff morale but enlivens general excitement toward jobs and new technology.

Meebo, a free chat widget, is installed on the main library website and on each LibGuides page. Some librarians enable Meebo to default to the reference desk chat account so that a librarian is always available for instant messaging. Patrons then have the capability to chat with a librarian any time during the information desk hours.

Web 2.0 tools. Web 2.0 tools have transformed libraries and the way people communicate with each other. Incorporating these innovative technologies into the classroom encourages an interactive, hands-on library experience without breaking the library's budget. Many of the technologies are free tools and require only minimal training for staff, including these:

Collaborative web technologies (e.g., the social bookmarking site Del .icio.us)

YouTube (e.g., showing Stephen Colbert's "Wikiality" clip)

Podcasts (e.g., students can record a review of a source and post on Blackboard)

Wikis or blogs (e.g., librarians can create a wiki for the class, so students can comment on each other's research ideas)

CONCLUSION

There are economical options available to those librarians willing to try them to enhance library services. The library at Kansas State University–Salina has suffered repeated losses of student employees each year yet maintained a strong commitment to customer satisfaction through flexible summer scheduling, increased communication channels, cross-training, and online modules. Utah State University's Merrill-Cazier Library has also implemented creative staffing such as peer mentors, teaching assistants, and the use of online technology to balance face-to-face teaching with online assistance to improve productivity and maintain high-quality service to patrons. Both libraries, though differing in size and patron needs, have managed to keep their staff active and engaged with patrons despite financial restrictions by seeking creative solutions to their ever-changing needs.

PART IX

Professional Development

33

BUILDING SUSTAINABLE PROFESSIONAL DEVELOPMENT OPPORTUNITIES IN TECHNOLOGY LITERACY

Marwin Britto

EDUCAUSE, A NONPROFIT association dedicated to advancing higher education through the intelligent use of information technology, recently released the Top Teaching and Learning Challenges List of 2009. The list (www.educause.edu/eli/challenges) is the result of surveys, brainstorming sessions, and a community vote among those directly involved with teaching and learning matters in higher education. Notably, the issue of faculty becoming technology literate in teaching has been one of the most persistent elements in the list over the past several years. The challenge of accomplishing this in a period of reduced budgets emerged as an issue in 2009. Making the situation even more challenging is that, in spite of the budget cuts, the demand for use of information technology for instruction continues to rise (Green 2009).

The responsibility of helping faculty learn to utilize technology often involves the institution's academic libraries. At our institution—Central Washington University—this is certainly the case. Like our main campus library, our Educational Technology Center (ETC), a library dedicated to the education program, has been subject to budget cuts over the past few years. The ETC is also the primary library dedicated to assisting faculty learn how to leverage technology effectively in the classroom. Consequently, in 2006 the ETC established the goal of building a sustainable model for professional development opportunities in technology literacy with little funding. In the hopes of helping others replicate our success, we share our processes and results here.

A TECHNOLOGY ADOPTION MODEL AS A FRAMEWORK

Past research has demonstrated that faculty typically undergo progressive stages of development in technology adoption when introduced to a new technology (Apple Computer 2000; Russell 1995). Anne Russell's model, shown below, consists of six progressive stages. We use this model as a framework for assessing technology adoption levels for our faculty and subsequently creating professional development opportunities aligned to these levels.

Stage 1: Awareness

Stage 2: Learning the process

Stage 3: Understanding and application of the process

Stage 4: Familiarity and confidence

Stage 5: Adaptation to other contexts

Stage 6: Creative application to new contexts

Not surprisingly, anecdotal evidence from the ETC help desk and informal assessment indicated that most of our faculty were primarily at the early stages of technology adoption. The next-largest group clustered around the middle to latter stages of the model. These findings suggested that, to support both groups, we needed to develop both basic "how-to" professional development opportunities in technology literacy and more advanced offerings.

AN ONLINE TUTORIAL SYSTEM FOR TECHNOLOGY LITERACY

With limited ETC staff available to provide training in technology literacy for faculty, we decided to build an online system of tutorials of technologies used at our institution to meet stages 1 and 2 of Russell's model. Through discussions with faculty, we knew that many of them would be willing to learn how to use various technologies through static and video-based tutorials online. Throughout the development process of the website, we solicited faculty feedback. This was most useful in developing the system to ensure it was meeting faculty needs. Some of the feedback we received included these suggestions:

- Do not require a username/password to access the system.
- Provide pictures of all the technologies.
- Provide a Word document with detailed screen captures of how to use the technology.
- Provide VHS and DVD copies of the tutorials available for checkout at the ETC.
- Create a mechanism to schedule one-on-one assistance for faculty using any of the technologies.

Within a year, with the help of open-source tools (e.g.,. PhP/mySQL), we had implemented our website and incorporated the faculty suggestions listed above. The website is currently accessible to anyone and offers tutorials on sixteen technologies that are in use at our institution. The large number of website visits and scheduled one-on-one sessions are evidence that this resource is being used frequently by our faculty. This resource can be found online at http://websolutions.cwu.edu/ctlassistance/.

We also needed to address faculty at stages 3, 4, and 5 of Russell's model. These individuals had mastered the basic technologies and were interested in learning how to integrate them into classroom teaching. Most believed that a hands-on workshop led by a faculty peer would be the best way of learning this. The ETC faced two obstacles in meeting this need. Specifically, we did not have additional staff who could manage registration and outreach for the workshops, and there were no stipends or other financial incentives available to the workshop facilitators. A web-based self-registration system was the most feasible way of addressing the first obstacle. Using open-source tools, we built a workshop registration system online through which faculty could self-register.

During the development process, we asked faculty for their input on how the system could best suit their needs. These are some of their suggestions, which we incorporated into the website:

- Do not require a username/password to access the system and register for workshops.
- Design the system to confirm registration automatically through e-mail and send those who register a reminder just prior to the workshop.
- Archive all previous workshops.

Identifying faculty who were willing to lead workshops without compensation was challenging, but through extensive networking and support from department chairs and academic deans we have been successful in this endeavor as well. Many faculty who led these workshops did so as part of their service requirement.

With ongoing faculty feedback, we continue to improve our system through additional features and functionality for our faculty. On the administrative side, we added functionality to allow us to invest only a few hours a week to prepare for our weekly workshops. The system automatically prints out a workshop registration list and evaluation forms and reports workshop participation by college, department, and individual.

Our weekly faculty professional development workshop series has been a resounding success. From January to March 2010, we offered our tenth such series. This resource can be found online at http://websolutions.cwu.edu/ctl_workshops/index.php.

CONCLUSION

Despite budget shortfalls at the ETC, we have managed to increase professional development opportunities for faculty interested in technology literacy. This has been accomplished through the development and implementation of two well-utilized resources—an online tutorial system for faculty at the beginning stages of technology literacy, and face-to-face faculty-led workshops for more advanced faculty. As we face even deeper cuts in the next few years and as new technologies emerge, we expect to expand our two resources further and make them of even greater benefit to our faculty.

WORKS CITED

Apple Computer. 2000. "Apple Classrooms of Tomorrow Library." www.apple.com/education/k12/leadership/acot/library.html (accessed April 21, 2001).

Green, Kenneth. C. 2009. "The 2008 Campus Computer Project." www.campuscomputing.net/survey-summary/2008-campus-computing-survey (accessed October 15, 2009).

Russell, Anne. 1995. "Stages in Learning Technology." *Computers in Education* 25:173–178.

34

$40 A DAY, OR ATTENDING LIBRARY CONFERENCES ON THE CHEAP

Regina Koury

WHY GO TO conferences? Conferences are a great way to refresh our attitudes toward the profession and connect with peers in a relaxed atmosphere. Sharing your library's challenges and successes with fellow librarians at the dinner tables, exhibit halls, or session breaks is a great morale builder. Attending library conferences to network with my colleagues and keep up to date on the latest ideas is vital for my job as an electronic resources and reference librarian. As tenure-track faculty I, as well as many academic librarians, am expected to present and publish to build my portfolio. Conferences offer excellent venues for publishing and presenting research.

Unfortunately for me, in this economic recession Idaho State University's library travel budget was cut. In response, I used several strategies that allowed me to attend four national library conferences in 2009 without paying for them myself. One of them was subsidized by my library, two were funded by the scholarships, and one was possible because of its geographic location. Why $40 dollars a day? That's how much I ended up spending when going to the conferences. Travel, registration, lodging, food, and transportation are just a few of the areas I look at in planning ahead for my conference year.

APPLY FOR SCHOLARSHIPS

Start by looking for scholarships. Pretty much every library conference has a list of scholarships—from student to recent graduate to need-based grants. Plan ahead and write down your due dates. Most ALA annual conference scholarship applications are due at the beginning of December. Apply even if you have done so many times before. For every ten rejections, you will eventually win one. A colleague of mine had been applying for the ALA 3M/NMRT Professional Development Grant several years in a row before he finally won one. Talk to someone in your organization who has won similar scholarships for helpful tips and techniques. Ask someone whose writing you respect to proofread and edit your application.

In 2009 I had applied for every ALA, ACRL, ER&L (Electronic Resources and Libraries), NASIG (North American Serials Interest Group), and Charleston Conference scholarship and local Idaho LSTA grant for which I was eligible. Sure, applying for a scholarship is a lot of work and rejection hurts, but winning one makes you feel at the top of your world. I won an ER&L recent graduate scholarship and LSTA first-time attendance grant to attend the Charleston Conference. Determination and patience are the keys in this process.

SUPPORT FROM INSTITUTIONS

Institutional funding for travel is declining. According to ARL SPEC Kit 315, Leave and Professional Development Benefits (2009), 92 percent of the responding institutions reported some financial support for conference registration or travel and accommodations for conferences that librarians attended primarily for their own personal professional development. Although only eight respondents (11 percent) pay full registration and full travel expenses, half of respondents pay at least part of the registration and travel costs. Only six respondents (8 percent) offer no financial support.

REGISTRATION

Registration can be pretty expensive. Many conferences waive your registration fees if you are a presenter. If they do not, work with conference organizers and explain to them your financial constraints. See if you can negotiate a reduced rate or other helpful arrangement. I found that conference organizers are pretty reasonable and open to finding solutions. For instance, my colleagues and I presented a poster session at the LITA National Forum in

Salt Lake City in 2009. Because this event coincided with the Idaho Library Association annual conference, we received comp registration for poster sessions that day only. True, not being able to go to the keynote addresses and concurrent sessions was frustrating, but at least we got to look at other poster presentations and get useful feedback for ours. This is so much better than nothing. If you are not a presenter, register for one day only; if you are a student, register at a student rate. ALA conferences also offer the option of registering for less expensive Exhibits Only or Exhibits Plus. Do what you have to do to get in.

AIR FARES

According to farecompare.com, generally the cheapest day of the week to fly is Wednesday, then Tuesday and Saturday. Airlines often file cheaper airfares that are good only on these three days. "The cheapest time to fly is typically the first flight out in the morning—yes, that means you have to get up at 4 am. Next best times are flights during/after lunch and flights at the dinner hour" (Seaney 2010).

TRAVEL

For me travel consists of two parts: getting to the conference location, and traveling within the conference city. Because I had only $500 to attend the 2009 ALA annual midwinter meeting in Denver, I was stretching every penny. I bid and named my own price for the round-trip flight from Salt Lake City to Denver for $109 through Priceline.com. Priceline.com and Kayak.com are my personal favorites to search for best deals on flights and hotels. If you are flying, take one carry-on bag. Save yourself a headache and an extra expense and pack lightly. For a recent trip to Charleston, I had my laptop bag and a carry-on bag in which I stuffed my purse. The goal here is to be cheap. Unless you are presenting—and even then you can get away with one suit—two pairs of jeans and a few tops should do it for you. Make yourself comfortable with SeatGuru.com, which shows you the chart of seats and how much leg room you will have.

Another suggestion is go to the events in your region and consider driving, especially if the conference is not that far. Location, location, location! This year the LITA National Forum was in Salt Lake City, about two and a half hours from Pocatello. I and two colleagues drove and split the price of gas. We brought snacks and water to save on lunch, and the only meal we had was a dinner at a reasonable Greek restaurant. That's how I was able to attend my third library conference. Once in the city, use public transit and take advantage of conference-sponsored transportation, whether it is from the airport or within the city.

LODGING

I like to network and see which of my colleagues are going to the same conference I am. Sharing hotel costs is such a savings. At the recent Charleston Conference I shared a room at the Embassy Suites Historic Downtown with three colleagues. We had to decide who would sleep in the guest room and who in the main room. As librarians we negotiate with vendors and pacify patrons on a daily basis; I find that negotiating with my library colleagues as roommates is so much easier.

Many cities are famous for their hostels—Chicago and San Francisco, to name a few. Take advantage of them. Other cities—Seattle and Boston, for example—are pedestrian friendly, so you don't have to book your hotel right next to the conference facility. I booked my hotel in Seattle in the Space Needle neighborhood and was perfectly fine walking back and forth to the Convention Center for the conference sessions.

Look for the availability of courtesy shuttles. In Philadelphia my Comfort Inn Downtown Historic Area hotel was closer to the Benjamin Franklin Bridge than to the Convention Center. But the hotel had a courtesy van that took me back and forth to the Convention Center. And there are ALA shuttles. I usually print a map of the official hotel routes and use it for my planning. Every conference you plan to attend will have a wiki or blog for housing details. For instance, ALA conference wikis usually have a roommate requests section, and ER&L has a section on Facebook and on the conference wiki for such requests. E-mail electronic discussion lists to see if anyone is willing to share accommodations with you.

FOOD

I love signing up for the vendor-sponsored breakfasts, lunches, and dinners. I went to EBSCO, which offers wonderful Academic Libraries and Public Libraries lunches where you can have complimentary food, network with your colleagues who use EBSCO services, and learn about new products. This is also true for Blackwell Book Services and other vendors, who send their customers an invitation around major library conferences. Don't have an invitation? Don't despair: ask colleagues who are not attending to kindly send you theirs if they received one. The 2009 Charleston Conference and ER&L conference at UCLA did outstanding jobs with vendor-provided snacks for breakfast and lunch, and free evening receptions at both conferences had plenty of food, drink, and opportunities to reconnect with colleagues. The ALA midwinter conference exhibit opening reception always guarantees great snack food. Also check the ALA conference wiki for the Events with Food section. Line up receptions with food and go from one to another. This strategy guarantees that you will get enough food for your dinner. Don't be shy: everyone does it. And you may find that conversations over food are the most productive for some of your colleagues.

Another favorite tactic is staying in the hotel that provides complimentary breakfasts or has a refrigerator in the room. For example, Embassy Suites Hotel in Historic Downtown Charleston serves terrific free breakfast and a happy hour. I have experienced free basic breakfast at Courtyard Marriott hotels, and Motel 6s serve morning coffee and bagels or some kind of pastry.

> **FOOD FOR THOUGHT**
>
> Smaller library conferences usually have sign-up dinners. This is an excellent opportunity to meet new people, network with your colleagues, and try new food. And you can do that with the money saved on breakfast and lunch.
>
> Or save on dining expenses with coupons and redeemable credit card points. Stephanie Nelson, an author of the Coupon Mom website and frequent visitor on ABC's *Good Morning America*, suggests using Restaurant.com. This website offers gift certificates to the major restaurants throughout the country at a discounted price. You can save even more when coupon codes are available on the Coupon Mom website, paying as little as $3 to $5 for a $25 certificate.

If your hotel does not provide food, then there are always grocery stores or 7-Elevens around: look them up before you go. If you decide to eat out, go out for lunch; the prices are less expensive than at dinnertime and you can bring back the leftovers and store them in your room's refrigerator. Most restaurants also have menus and prices available online. Look before you go and decide which one is for you. Check restaurant reviews online. Trip Advisor.com and Yelp.com are just a few of my favorites for checking food and hotel reviews. For me they are always correct.

WHY GO?

Attending library conferences is also about having a great time. In a survey of 794 people, Robert Vega and Ruth Connell (2007) found that the two most cited reasons given for going to conferences were professional rejuvenation and networking, with expense and travel listed as the conference negatives.

Leonard Kniffel remembers his first ALA annual conference, which he attended in 1985 in Chicago:

> In those days, I never dreamed that one day I would actually live here. Since the library where I worked did not pay my conference expenses, I did the conference on the cheap—driving in, staying in a shared room in a low-end hotel, eating hot dogs, and generally having a grand time attending only programs that interested me and behaving like a conventioneer should: meeting people and having fun, falling in love with the city. It's not fancy hotel rooms or expensive meals that bring back the fondest memories, it's the people and the local venues. (Kniffel 2009, 4)

There are numerous articles on the benefits of attending library-related conferences. As library and information professionals, we have to expand our knowledge and grow professionally. Whether you are a seasoned librarian or someone just assuming new duties, attending conferences will always guarantee a good return on your investment. You never know if a connection you make or a new idea you hear will "pay dividends" now or down the road. Conferences are the best places to share concerns and get feedback from peers, learn new ideas, and build new collaborations.

The problem is financing your trip in these budget-tight times. If you really, really want to go, you can find a way. I know it is easier said than done, but there are librarians and information professionals out there who have done it. Determination, patience, and planning ahead will get you where you want.

WORKS CITED

ARL Association of Research Libraries. 2009. Leave and Professional Development Benefits, December 2009. ARL SPEC Kit 315. www.arl.org/bm~doc/spec-315-web.pdf.

Kniffel, Leonard. 2009. "Sweet Home Chicago." *American Libraries* 40:4.

Seaney, Rick. 2010. "Cheapest Days to Fly and Best Time to Buy Airline Tickets," June 25. www.farecompare.com/articles/tips-from-air-travel-insiders/.

Vega, Robert, and Ruth S. Connell. 2007. "Librarians' Attitudes toward Conferences: A Study." *College and Research Libraries* 68:503–516.

CONTRIBUTORS

CAROL SMALLWOOD received her MLS from Western Michigan University and her MA in history from Eastern Michigan University. She edited *Writing and Publishing: The Librarian's Handbook* and *Librarians as Community Partners: An Outreach Handbook* (ALA 2010) and recently published the novel *Lily's Odyssey* and *Contemporary American Women: Our Defining Passages*. *The Frugal Librarian* is her twenty-third published book. Her magazine credits include *The Writer's Chronicle, English Journal,* and *Michigan Feminist Studies;* her library experience includes school, public, academic, and special libraries as well as being an administrator and consultant.

EMILY ASCH is currently the head of technical services at St. Catherine University in St. Paul, Minnesota. She is the chair of the Technical Services Section of the Minnesota Library Association (MLA). Emily has presented on topics ranging from digital collections to the effects on patron privacy with Web 2.0 services and most recently on the latest trends in technical services at the latest MLA Annual Conference. She was chosen to participate in the Pacific Northwest Library Association Leadership Institute.

EDGAR C. BAILEY JR. earned his MLS at Rutgers University and MA in English from the University of Chicago. He has worked at the Phillips

Memorial Library at Providence College, where he holds the rank of tenured associate professor, for almost thirty years as both reference librarian and library director. He teaches part-time at the University of Rhode Island library school and has published articles in *RQ* and *Reference Services Review*. He has been actively involved in the Providence Community Library since its founding.

KIM BECNEL, juvenile services coordinator for Union County Public Library in Monroe, North Carolina, holds an MLIS and PhD from the University of South Carolina at Columbia. Her recent publications include a personal essay in *Contemporary American Women: Our Defining Passages* (All Things That Matter Press, 2009), *Bloom's How to Write about Amy Tan* and other volumes in the Bloom's How to Write about Major Authors series (Bloom's Literary Criticism, 2008–2011), and *The Rise of Corporate Publishing and Its Effects on Authorship in Early Twentieth Century America* (Routledge, 2007).

GEORGE BERGSTROM is business reference librarian at the Management and Economics Library, Purdue University, West Lafayette, Indiana. He earned a BS in computer science from Rose Hulman Institute of Technology and an MLS from Indiana University–Bloomington. His publications include articles in *College and Undergraduate Libraries* and *Journal of Business and Finance Librarianship*. George has held positions in both public and academic libraries and is currently serving as a faculty fellow at Purdue in a program that matches faculty with residence halls to act as mentors for undergraduate students.

HEIDI BLACKBURN is a reference and instruction librarian in her second year of teaching information literacy for Kansas State University at Salina. She is a member of the Kansas Library Association College and University Library Systems and serves as the secretary for the Kansas Library Instruction Round Table. Her published works include articles in *Education Libraries, Career Trends,* and *IFLA Publications*. Heidi recently presented at the 2009 IFLA World Library and Information Congress satellite meeting in Bologna, Italy. She is currently working on her PhD at Emporia State University.

MARWIN BRITTO is associate professor, director of Library Media Endorsement Program, and director of the Educational Technology Center at Central Washington University. He received his PhD from the University of Georgia and in 2009 completed the EDUCAUSE Institute Learning Technology Leadership Program. Marwin has published in such journals as *Academic Exchange Quarterly* and *Northwest Passage: Journal of Educational Practices* and contributed to *Course Management Systems for Learning: Beyond Accidental*

Pedagogy (Idea Group, 2005) and *Supporting Learning Flow through Integrative Technologies* (IOS Press, 2007). He is president of the Northwest Association of Teacher Educators and has refereed more than sixty academic presentations at conferences.

VANDELLA BROWN, a librarian and author in Springfield, Illinois, obtained her MLS from the University of Iowa. She is the author of *What Is a Zawadi to We: A Poetic Story of Kwanzaa and Gift Giving* (LumenUs Publications, 2007) and *Celebrating the Family: Steps to Planning a Family Reunion* (Ancestry, 1991) and a contributor to *Writing and Publishing: The Librarian's Handbook* (ALA, 2010); her articles have appeared in *American Libraries* and *ILA Reporter*. Vandella presents workshops about book reviewing, planning family reunions, and celebrating Kwanzaa.

MARY CHIMATO is head of the access and delivery services department at the North Carolina State University Libraries, where she provides leadership for key public services that enable users to access the many resources of the libraries. She has a strong background of leadership and management from her previous position as head of access services for the Health Sciences Center Library at Stony Brook University. Her writings on management and daily life in access services can be found at her blog, Circ and Serve.

TOM COOPER is director of Webster Groves Public Library in Webster Groves, Missouri. He has worked in libraries since 1986, previously at St. Louis County Library, St. Louis Public Library, and Richmond Heights Memorial Library. He holds a BA in writing and rhetoric from Webster University and an MLS from University of Missouri–Columbia. Tom has been a book reviewer for the *St. Louis Post-Dispatch* and *Library Journal* and contributed to *Writing and Publishing: The Librarian's Handbook* (ALA, 2010).

LISA L. CRANE is Western Americana librarian at the Claremont Colleges Library, Claremont, California. She obtained an MLIS from San José State University and is a member of ALA, ACRL, the Society of American Archivists, and the Society of California Archivists. Lisa draws from an extensive background in accounting and finance for a medical device manufacturer for nearly seventeen years, her previous career.

ERIN DAVIS is an assistant librarian at Utah State University and current web editor of ACRL's STS section and chair of the Utah Library Association's Academic Libraries section. She earned her MLS from Simmons College. Her recent publications include articles in *RUSQ* and the IFLA Publications series and a contribution to *Library Data: Empowering Practice and Persuasion* (Libraries Unlimited, 2009).

EMILY DILL is an associate librarian at the University Library of Columbus in Columbus, Indiana. She received her MLS from Indiana University–Purdue University Indianapolis and is a member of ALA, ACRL, and Indiana Online Users Group. Emily has a diverse set of research interests including scholarly communication, information behavior, instructional technology, and joint-use libraries. Her recent publications include articles in *College and Research Libraries* and *Journal of Popular Culture*.

COLLEEN DRISCOLL is a library/media specialist and teacher at Breitung Township Schools in Kingsford, Michigan. She received her bachelor's and master's (media and technology) degrees from Central Michigan University. Colleen is a member of the Michigan Association for Media in Education. Her work has appeared in *The Tale of Titletown* and in several newspapers. She has received two Ecolab Awards for Excellence in Education, and her library has received We the People Bookshelf and Picturing America grants.

MARY DUGAN is resource development librarian at the Management and Economics Library, Purdue University, West Lafayette, Indiana. She earned a BS in education from the University of Illinois, Urbana-Champaign, and an MLS from the University of Illinois. She has published in *Reference Librarian, Journal of Agricultural and Food Information, College and Undergraduate Libraries,* and *Journal of Business and Finance Librarianship.* Mary has held positions in public, academic, and special libraries and for eleven years was the information specialist for the Technical Information Service, the fee-based service of Purdue Libraries.

GWEN EVANS is coordinator of library information and emerging technologies, University Libraries, Bowling Green State University. She has an MSLIS from the University of Illinois and an MA in cultural anthropology from the University of Chicago. Gwen coauthored "Moody Blues: The Social Web, Tagging, and Non-textual Discovery Tools for Music," which won the Best Paper Award from *Music Reference Services Quarterly,* and contributed to *Graphic Novels and Comics in Libraries and Archives* (McFarland, 2010).

LESLIE FARISON is a business librarian and assistant professor at Appalachian State University, Boone, North Carolina. She received her MLIS from the University of Kentucky and her MBA from Indiana University. Prior to becoming a librarian, Leslie spent many years in the corporate world. She has published in the *Journal of Education for Library and Information Science* and presented at the Charleston Conference and the University of Louisville. Her research interests include economics in collection development, business information literacy, and international librarianship.

WAYNE FINLEY is assistant professor/business librarian at Northern Illinois University Libraries, DeKalb, Illinois. He earned his MLIS from the University of Illinois and his MBA from Western Illinois University. Wayne copresented "The Baby Manages the Boomers and Beyond: New Library Administrators Managing Older Workers in Small Library Settings" at the 75th Annual International Federation of Library Associations General Conference and Assembly and has contributed to *Behavioral and Social Sciences Librarian.*

LISA A. FORREST is a senior assistant librarian for SUNY College at Buffalo and the founding member of the school's Rooftop Poetry Club. She is the recipient of the 2008 Excellence in Library Service Award from the Western New York Library Resources Council. Lisa's scholarly writings have appeared in a variety of publications, including *A Leadership Primer for New Librarians* (Neal-Schuman, 2009), *Thinking Outside the Book* (McFarland, 2008), *Writing and Publishing: The Librarians Handbook* (ALA, 2010), *Urban Library Journal,* and *American Libraries.* Her first collection of poems, *To the Eaves,* is available from BlazeVox (2008).

LISA FRASER is an adult services librarian at the Bellevue Library in Bellevue, Washington, the largest of forty-four libraries in the King County Library System. She received an MLIS from the University of Washington and a master's in international administration from the School for International Training in Vermont. Lisa has administered library partnerships with human services organizations, colleges, and associations in addition to museums. She teaches courses in marketing and advocacy for libraries at the Information School of the University of Washington.

FANG HUANG GAO, manager of serials services, University of Illinois at Urbana-Champaign, obtained her MSLIS and MA in teaching English as a second language from the University of Illinois at Urbana-Champaign. Fang is also an adjunct faculty member of the Graduate School of Library and Information Science at the University of Illinois. She is a trainer for the National Serials Cooperative Cataloging Training Program (SCCTP), trainer for Fundamentals of Series Authorities, and trainer for the Cataloging for the 21st Century Program: Rules and Tools for Cataloging Internet Resources.

MICHAEL A. GERMANO, library faculty member at California State University, Los Angeles, dedicated to the College of Business and Economics, is primarily focused on teaching courses in financial information literacy as well as business information for decision making. He holds a law degree from Temple University and a master's in information science from Simmons College as well as a master's in English from New York University. Prior to joining California State's faculty he worked at LexisNexis in a variety of sales and marketing positions for fifteen years.

COLLEEN S. HARRIS is the associate head of access and delivery services at the North Carolina State University Libraries. Formerly a reference and instruction librarian, she holds an MLIS from the University of Kentucky and an MFA in creative writing from Spalding University. Her library work has appeared in *Library Journal, Journal of Access Services, LISCareer, Info CareerTrends,* and various book chapters, and her creative writing appears in *Wisconsin Review, Louisville Review,* and others. An avid writer, Colleen works on her creative writing when not contributing to the library world.

JOHN HELLING is the director of the Bloomfield–Eastern Greene County Public Library in Bloomfield, Indiana, and is president of the board of directors of the Greene County Literacy Coalition. He has been a senior librarian at the Aguilar branch of the New York Public Library. John obtained an MLS from Indiana University in 2006, where he currently teaches a course in public library management. He has published an article and numerous book reviews in *Library Journal.*

SUE HISLE is a library specialist and information services desk manager in the Belk Library and Information Commons at Appalachian State University in Boone, North Carolina. Sue holds an AAS degree in library media technology from Lenoir Community College. Sue has twelve years' experience in academic libraries in roles as diverse as instructional materials center specialist, desk services manager, and student training leader. She won a 2009 Appalachian State Staff Award for her library accomplishments and presented on cross-training at the 2009 Tennessee Library Association conference.

ROBERT HOLLEY, professor of library and information science at Wayne State University, Detroit, Michigan, obtained his doctorate from Yale University and his MLIS from Columbia University. He has ninety-seven publications listed in Wilson's *Library Literature and Information Science.* Robert began his study of the out-of-print book market with a research award (2003) from *Library Collections, Acquisitions, and Technical Services.* Since 2005 he has integrated his experiences as a small Internet book vendor into his research and has several presentations and publications on various aspects of buying and selling books on the Internet.

KEN JOHNSON is an assistant professor and coordinator of the Learning and Research Services team in the Belk Library and Information Commons at Appalachian State University in Boone, North Carolina. Ken holds an MLIS degree from the University of North Carolina, Greensboro, and an MBA from Appalachian State University. He has ten years' experience as a business librarian at Drexel University and Appalachian State and has published articles and book reviews in the *Journal of Business and Finance Librarianship*.

JOANNA KLUEVER, director of Julia Hull District Library, Stillman Valley, Illinois, earned her MLIS from the University of Illinois and her MA from Western Illinois University. Joanna recently copresented "The Baby Manages the Boomers and Beyond: New Library Administrators Managing Older Workers in Small Library Settings" at the 75th Annual International Federation of Library Associations General Conference and Assembly, and she has written several successful grants, including a Library Services and Technology Act Grant for $21,700.

REGINA KOURY is an electronic resources and reference librarian at Idaho State University, Pocatello. She has also worked at the University of Southern California with experience in electronic resources, serials, interlibrary loan, and public desk services. Regina received an MSLIS from University of Pittsburgh and is currently taking graduate course work in instructional technology at Idaho State University. She is a member of ALA, the Idaho Library Association, and the ACRL Professional Development Coordinating Committee.

JASON KUHL is manager of information services at the Arlington Heights Memorial Library in Arlington Heights, Illinois. He received his MSLIS from the University of Illinois and is a member of ALA and the Illinois Library Association. From 2000 to 2008, he held various branch management positions with St. Louis County (Missouri) Library.

MARY S. LASKOWSKI is head of information processing and management at the University of Illinois, Urbana-Champaign. She obtained her MSLIS and BA in English from the University of Illinois, Urbana-Champaign. Mary is a member of ALA and the Consortium of College and University Media Centers, where she edits the research publication *College and University Media Review*. Her recent publications have appeared in *Library Trends, Journal of Academic Librarianship,* and *Library Collections, Acquisitions, and Technical Services*.

MARGARET LINCOLN, library media specialist at Lakeview High School in Battle Creek, Michigan, is a database trainer for the Library of Michigan and 2008 recipient of the Carnegie Corporation of New York/New York Times I Love My Librarian Award. A part-time instructor in the School of Library and Information Science at San José State University, she was named an American Memory Fellow with the Library of Congress and a United States Holocaust

Memorial Museum Teacher Fellow. Margaret earned her PhD in library and information sciences from the University of North Texas.

JAMES LUND is director of the Red Wing Public Library in Red Wing, Minnesota. He obtained an MLIS from the University of Wisconsin–Milwaukee and MA in theology from Westminster Seminary California. James has provided and managed library services in academic, graduate, and public libraries. He is an active member of the Minnesota Library Association, serving on the Public Library Division's Executive Committee and presenting at annual conferences. James is also president of JRL Library Services, a library consulting company that specializes in assisting small academic libraries.

J. JAMES MANCUSO is currently the assistant director for library services at Mid-America Baptist Theological Seminary, Northeast Campus, in Schenectady, New York, as well as being employed by Rockbridge Seminary, Nylink, and the Guilderland Public Library. He obtained an MLS and BA in linguistics from Syracuse University. Jim has served in many leadership positions in the New York Library Association, the Hudson-Mohawk Library Association, and Libraries Interested in Theology Across New York. His work has appeared in *Serials Librarian, Collection Management,* and *Publishing Research Quarterly.*

LISA NICKEL is the distance education librarian at the University of North Carolina–Charlotte. She received her BA in history from Rutgers University and MLIS from the University of South Florida. Lisa has published book chapters and journal articles about distance education, information literacy, library leadership, assessment, and electronic resources reviews. She is a member of ALA and ACRL Distance Learning Section and teaches information literacy and research methods at University of Maryland University College.

SARAH NIELSEN, assistant professor of English and coordinator of TESOL at California State University, East Bay, has a PhD in education and an MA in linguistics. Before becoming a teacher trainer, she taught ESL at two- and four-year colleges in both the United States and China. She has published articles in scholarly volumes including conference proceedings and *The Handbook of Second Language Acquisition* (Blackwell, 2005). In 2008 she coauthored *A Book of Firsts in the Voices of ESL Students* (Las Positas College, Livermore, California).

VICTORIA LYNN PACKARD is an associate professor and government information, maps, reference, and instruction librarian and Foundation Center Cooperating Collection supervisor at Texas A&M University–Kingsville. She obtained her MLIS from University of Tennessee–Knoxville. Victoria is a member of ALA, the Texas Library Association, WAML (Western Association of

Map Libraries), and MERLOT (Multimedia Educational Resource for Learning and Online Teaching). She has published and presented at state, national, and international conferences in the areas of government information, geography and GIS, grant research, and distance learning.

SARAH PASSONNEAU is assistant professor at Iowa State University and assistant to the dean at the university library. She works in the areas of instruction, assessment, and outreach. Previously she worked as a reference and media librarian at Normandale Community College, a school librarian in Minnesota, and a county librarian in California. Sarah received an award for cyber-safety curriculum, writes book reviews, and has a chapter in *Greening Libraries* (Library Juice Press–Litwin Books, 2011).

LORIENE ROY, professor in the School of Information, University of Texas at Austin, teaches graduate courses in public librarianship and in reference, including readers' advisory and library instruction. She is Anishinabe, enrolled on the White Earth Reservation, a member of the Minnesota Chippewa Tribe. She was the 2007/8 president of the American Library Association. She is director and founder of "If I Can Read, I Can Do Anything," a reading club for Native American children, and advisory editor for Greenwood/ABC-CLIO's *American Indian Experience,* where you will find her blog "From All Directions."

ALINE SOULES, a library faculty member at California State University, East Bay, has MSLS, MA, and MFA degrees. In her library career, she has worked in a variety of academic libraries, public and private, in the United States and Canada. She has been published in journals, in books, and on the Web, in both librarianship and creative writing; recent examples include publications in *Against the Grain, New Library World, Handbook of Research on Electronic Resource Management, Kenyon Review,* and *Houston Literary Review.*

LOIS STICKELL is the government documents and history librarian at the University of North Carolina–Charlotte. She received her MLIS from Indiana University. She teaches a class in government publications for UNC Greensboro's Department of Library and Information Science. Lois has published journal articles on merit pay, student assistants, and controversial library exhibits and given presentations at the Federal Depository Library Conference and the annual meeting of the National Council of Public History.

TOM TAYLOR is the continuing education coordinator for the South Central Kansas Library System, located in South Hutchinson, Kansas. His previous library experience includes the University of South Florida Tampa Library,

Seminole (Florida) Community Library at St. Petersburg College Seminole Campus, and the Newton (Kansas) Public Library. He earned his MLIS from the University of South Florida. Tom is a member of the Wichita Area Library Association, the Kansas Library Association, the Mountain Plains Library Association, and ALA.

REBECCA TUCK is managing librarian at the Bellevue Library in Bellevue, Washington, part of the King County Library System. She has also worked at the Federal Way and Kirkland libraries, also in the King County Library System. Rebecca received her undergraduate degree at the University of Michigan and her MLIS at the University of Washington. She is a member of ALA and the Washington Library Association. Rebecca has taught classes in business reference at the Information School of the University of Washington.

KACY VEGA holds a master's in education from Grand Valley State University, Allendale, Michigan. As family literacy coordinator for Union County Public Library in Monroe, North Carolina, a position supported by Union Smart Start, Kacy designs, promotes, and conducts early literacy workshops for parents in English and Spanish. She also aids in the development of the library's Spanish collection for children, reviews Spanish and bilingual books for *Reforma,* and is pursuing a certificate in family literacy from Penn State.

INDEX

Page numbers in italic refer to information in sidebars.

You may also be interested in

LIBRARIANS AS COMMUNITY PARTNERS: AN OUTREACH HANDBOOK
Edited by Carol Smallwood

Including 66 focused snapshots of outreach in action, this resource reflects the creative solutions of librarians searching for new and innovative ways to build programs that meet customer needs while expanding the library's scope into the community.

ISBN: 978-0-8389-1006-1
216 PGS / 6" × 9"

MORE ADMINISTRATION, MANAGEMENT, AND FINANCE TITLES

WRITING AND PUBLISHING
EDITED BY CAROL SMALLWOOD
ISBN: 978-0-8389-0996-6

WINNING LIBRARY GRANTS
HERBERT B. LANDAU
ISBN: 978-0-8389-1047-4

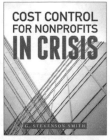

COST CONTROL FOR NONPROFITS IN CRISIS
G. STEVENSON SMITH
ISBN: 978-0-8389-1098-6

THE ALA BIG BOOK OF LIBRARY GRANT MONEY, 8E
EDITED BY ANN KEPLER
ISBN: 978-0-8389-1058-0

INTERLIBRARY LOAN PRACTICES HANDBOOK, 3E
EDITED BY CHERIÉ L. WEIBLE AND KAREN L. JANKE
ISBN: 978-0-8389-1081-8

MANAGING LIBRARY VOLUNTEERS, 2E
PRESTON DRIGGERS AND EILEEN DUMAS
ISBN: 978-0-8389-1064-1

Order today at **alastore.ala.org** or **866-746-7252!**
ALA Store purchases fund advocacy, awareness, and accreditation programs for library professionals worldwide.

DEC 3 0 2011l

₦ 38.00